Rise, Decline and Renewal

The Democratic Party in Maine

Douglas Rooks

Hamilton Books

A member of
Rowman & Littlefield
Lanham • Boulder • New York • Toronto • London

Copyright © 2018 by Hamilton Books
4501 Forbes Boulevard, Suite 200, Lanham, Maryland 20706
Hamilton Books Acquisitions Department (301) 459-3366

Unit A, Whitacre Mews, 26-34 Stannary Street, London SE11 4AB

Library of Congress Control Number: 2017964467
ISBN: 978-0-7618-7018-0 (pbk.) — ISBN: 978-0-7618-7019-7 (electronic)

To Don Nicoll,
who knows more, and remembers more,
about the Maine Democratic Party
than anyone else.

Contents

Acknowledgments

This book emerged from the research conducted for my first one, *Statesman: George Mitchell and the Art of the Possible.* I was fascinated by glimpses of the early days of the Maine Democratic Party, and curious to know what happened to it; by the time I returned to Maine in the 1980s, it seemed that the party's best days were behind it.

This new book has led its author on a circuitous journey, with lots of cul de sacs and mysterious incidents to understand and interpret. I cannot claim to have done so flawlessly, but what I have done is dependent on the help of many individuals and institutions, only some of whom are formally mentioned here.

The archives of Bates College, Bowdoin College, and the University of Southern Maine are important sources in tracing the careers of Ed Muskie, George Mitchell, Frank Coffin, and Ken Curtis; and the newly available oral history interviews at the Joseph Brennan Archives—document availability to follow—were also helpful. The Coffin archives are unexpectedly rich and revealing, especially the unpublished memoirs. Those interested in reading more about George Mitchell and Ed Muskie, in particular, can consult *Statesman.*

Prompt and courteous assistance was always available at the Maine State Law and Legislative Reference Library, and at the Vermont State Archives, amid countless requests.

The photographs are from the private collections of Don Nicoll and the Coffin family, with Nancy Coffin Kurtz generously making them available. The graphs depicting state spending and Maine's bonded indebtedness are the work of Sarah Austin, policy analyst at the Maine Center for Economic Policy.

My mentor, poet Wesley McNair, once again guided me, gently pointing out deficiencies, about which he was almost always right. Don Nicoll, an invaluable source, played a comparable role as reader, correcting many errors of fact and interpretation. Others who offered valuable suggestions include John Allard, John Buell, Frank O'Hara, Earle Shettleworth, and Vermont state Senator Chris Pearson.

This book would probably not have been started, and certainly would not have been finished, without the help of my wife, Janine Bonk. She has been, throughout, my irreplaceable partner.

Because of the unusual nature of this book, for which I could find no precedents, I am, more than anyone, aware of its remaining flaws. It is my hope that others will take up this important work of analyzing, and helping to restore, our political system to health.

Preface

The premise of this book is that the decline of our elective governments, at both state and federal levels, is strongly correlated to the decline of the two major political parties. Americans have always viewed the parties with suspicion—a "necessary evil"—and today, "partisanship" is used only as an epithet, not as describing a basic function of our political system.

The much lamented "polarization" of American politics, often treated as inevitable and immutable, is a direct consequence of the decline of the Democratic and Republican parties in their ability to select candidates through competitive primary elections, and maintain a diversity of viewpoints within parties themselves. The assumption that we now have "red states" and "blue states" is matched by the creation of litmus tests of "correct" belief within each party. When the partisan system was functioning effectively, each party had two "wings," and even within those categories there was often a surprising diversity of views, rarely with any sense that dissent had to be suppressed or denied.

The role of political parties is often misunderstood. One veteran New England scholar recently opined that the Electoral College is more essential to democratic institutions than political parties, simply because it was included in the Constitution. The opposite is nearer the truth. The Electoral College is an outmoded relic of the pro-slavery provisions of the Constitution's original text, while the two major parties sprang up even before George Washington left office, and have continued to organize Congress and the state legislatures for more than two centuries since then. They still retain the characteristics evident at their founding, though the Federalist Party had to be twice reborn, first as the Whigs, then as the Republican Party. For good measure, today's Democratic Party, which can trace an unbroken line back to Thomas Jefferson, was originally known as Republican.

In a parliamentary system, where the executive and legislative are united, a multitude of political parties, each representing a distinct viewpoint or ideology, is possible and perhaps desirable. In America's uniquely divided system of governance—replicated in every state, as well as in Washington—the two-party system is indispensable to enacting legislation and implementing a president's or a governor's program. It isn't going away. Providing more choices on the ballot—or expecting that new parties will arrive out of nowhere—will not redeem our faltering democracy. Reforming and reinvigorating the Republican and Democratic parties will.

Books about politics are more numerous than ever. Books about political parties are rare, and those about state parties almost non-existent. It is my hope that, in tracing the largely forgotten history of the Maine Democratic Party since its re-founding in 1954, including its long decline since the traumatic events of the 1990s, we can more clearly see a prospect for the return of what Frank Coffin called "positive government." We must reclaim the belief that a political coalition can design and implement programs to improve our public life, not just stave off disaster.

Both Maine parties have large tasks ahead of them. Democrats will have to give up their vague and insubstantial political platforms that express a hope for change but offer no specific or credible means for bringing it about. Republicans need to move away from an exclusive focus on restricting government, privatizing its functions, and lowering taxes in the vain hope that doing so will somehow create prosperity in what is, once again—more than sixty years after a competitive two-party system began taking form—New England's poorest state.

The program as outlined in the final chapters includes aspects that will appeal more strongly to Republicans, and others that Democrats are more likely to embrace. Partisanship has its place, but a good idea is a good idea, no matter where it comes from. This new vision, inspired by the best of party platforms of the past, is an attempt to help Maine retrieve its lost reputation as a well-governed state. This happy condition was last seen in the 1970s and 1980s, when Maine achieved national prominence with innovative legislation, and both parties materially contributed to its growth and prosperity. In those two decades, Maine seemed prepared to shed its long isolation and become more than a charming place to visit. We must renew this quest.

While I chronicle the story of only one of the two major parties in this book, it is my belief that a well-functioning two-party system is essential not only to democracy, but to the "pursuit of happiness" envisioned in the Declaration of Independence, as well as the command to "promote the general welfare" in the preamble to the U.S. Constitution. In dark times, we can create the conditions for the sun to rise.

RISE

ONE

Beginning

1954

"When you win a big one you didn't expect to win, the first time, oh, that's something."

— Dick McMahon

On Election Night 1954, the Democratic faithful gathered at the Elmwood Hotel in downtown Waterville, once the city's finest hotel, but whose best days were now behind it. There was a different mood at the gathering, organized by Dick McMahon, Ed Muskie's campaign manager, held in two rooms rented for $6 apiece, at first with a single local reporter on hand. As Don Nicoll recalls, there was "a growing sense that there might be an upset in the gubernatorial race," quite unlike "the frequently false optimism that accompanies increased enthusiasm at party rallies."

Muskie had been campaigning for just five months before the September 13 state election—a vestige from the distant past. Maine was the only state to vote for its elected officials two months before the November presidential election—prompting the venerable saying, "As Maine goes, so goes the nation." That would soon change, along with a lot of other things about Maine politics.

Nicoll, the Maine Democratic Party's executive secretary, and first-ever full-time staff member, kept a professional distance. He had begun the evening in Lewiston, the party's home base, following the returns in Frank Coffin's dining room. Coffin, who had become party chairman just as Muskie decided to run for governor, had been up until 4 a.m. that morning, the last day of campaigning. He'd spent the day in the tiny party office on Lisbon Street, mostly alone. "Feeling as useful as a fifth wheel, I went home," he recalled in his unpublished memoirs. Around the table, there was "mounting excitement as we heard how Muskie was

3

getting far more votes in tiny towns than there were Democrats. Some traditionally Republican towns were even giving Muskie a majority."

The town of Wade, in Aroostook County, enrolled ninety Republicans and two Democrats, but went for Muskie, 17-16. Hancock County, which then had 13,000 Republicans and 1,000 Democrats, nonetheless gave Muskie 3,000 votes.

The candidate was watching, too. "In those days the first precincts to report were the tiny little towns that were mostly Republican, out in the boondocks, and way up north in Aroostook County," Muskie told an interviewer. "Where there weren't any Democratic votes the previous time, there were four or five. Democratic votes doubled."

Dick McMahon called Coffin and suggested he and Nicoll might want to come to Waterville, and they set out, a two-hour drive in the days before the interstates. With "our ears glued to the radio," Coffin said, they followed returns, and, Nicoll said, "wondered, as each town came in, if we were really getting close to victory." Then, at 10 p.m., the Associated Press projected Muskie the winner. Said Coffin, "When we arrived, the Muskie suite was jammed with jubilant and incredulous Democrats. As we entered, I caught Ed's eye from across the room and, reflecting the language of so many of my fellow townsmen, shouted, '*Incroyable*'!"

The hotel provided more space, as well-wishers and reporters kept coming. The rooms "immediately filled with happy Democrats laughing, shouting, drinking whiskey, beating each other's backs and cheering each new figure and each new phone call of congratulations," Muskie biographer David Nevin recorded. McMahon, in politics since boyhood, had never had a candidate like Muskie. "When you win a big one you didn't expect to win, the first time, oh, that's something," he said. "You never forget it, and it never stops feeling good."

Muskie told a Texas crowd in 1968, while running for vice president, "I never had an experience like that. If I win elections from now until the year 2000—this election, if we win it, wouldn't be nearly the exhilarating experience of that one. We won against hopeless odds. We had no resources . . . We had to talk to Republicans who had never even seen a live Democrat in their lives . . . We had to do it against an establishment, a machine . . . which had had a century to entrench itself, and we did it."

Muskie defeated Governor Burton Cross, who was running for a second two-year term—rare for an incumbent seeking re-election. It wasn't close. Muskie took 135,673 votes to 113,298 for Cross, or 54.5 percent. He carried thirteen of Maine's sixteen counties, all but Hancock, Waldo and Lincoln. At the time, Maine had 262,000 registered Republicans, 119,000 unenrolled—and just 99,000 Democrats. Democrats also made modest gains in the Legislature. They won thirty-four seats in the 151-member House of Representatives, up from twenty-four, and six seats in the thirty-three-member Senate, up from two. Muskie was the first Democrat elected governor in twenty years, and just the fourth in a century.

Instantly, Muskie became a national figure. His wife, Jane, remembers a reporter beating on their door at 6 a.m., and there was speculation about November, when Democrats did win back the congressional majorities they'd lost in 1952 with the Eisenhower landslide. *Life, Time* and *Newsweek* profiled Muskie, and he campaigned in seventeen states that fall. The next morning, interview requests poured in, and Muskie appeared on NBC's *Today* show. The Democratic National Committee (DNC) soon dispatched Coffin and Muskie to a regional conference in Indianapolis.

Nicoll remembers flying to New York with Muskie and his wife in the Guy Gannett Co. plane, a favor from new owner Jean Gannett Hawley, who kept the Portland newspapers' Republican alignment but had a soft spot for Muskie. Flying south from Waterville, looking over the landscape, Nicoll remembers thinking, "My God, now we're responsible for that."

RUMFORD AND WATERVILLE

The story of Ed Muskie's upset win in 1954 has been told many times. The story of how it became possible is much less well-known.

Born in 1914, Muskie grew up in Rumford, then a thriving paper mill town of 10,000 people. The key influence of his early years was his father, Stefan Marciszewski, who fled Tsarist conscription in his native Poland to arrive in America in 1903—and lived just long enough to see his first-born son become governor. As Stephen Muskie, he became a tailor, catering to Republican mill managers while expounding his own views, strongly Democratic, during fittings. His son learned similar, though subtler techniques while dealing with a solidly Republican legislature during two terms as governor. Muskie had become a standout in high school, was valedictorian of his class, student council president, and star of the Stephens High debating team. He was shy with girls, and spent much time alone, a lifelong habit that suited his deliberative style in politics.

At Bates College in Lewiston, Muskie began to show the traits that blossomed after his U.S. Senate victory in 1958. Professor Brooks Quimby ran the debate team, and was, wrote David Nevin, "a vigorous, opinionated, articulate, fiery sort of man," who "delighted in a good fight," yet "had a punctilious sense of form, propriety; the standards of a gentleman." As Don Nicoll recently put it, Quimby taught Muskie that "the purpose of a debate was not to defeat your opponent, but to persuade others to agree with your position."

Stephen Muskie had created a unique surname for his son, and nurtured the quiet ambition that carried him on to Cornell Law School.

When Muskie returned to Maine, he purchased a law practice in Waterville from the widow of Carl Blackington for $3,000, cash. He put his practice on hold when he enlisted in the Navy, served during World War II, then returned to Waterville.

Muskie's original office clerk, he said, "made me promise not to run for public office," but she left during his wartime hiatus. When he returned, at age thirty-two, he was befriended by Harold Dubord, one of just six Democrats among thirty lawyers practicing in Waterville, despite the city's numerous immigrant millworkers, almost all Democrats. Dubord had run for the U.S. Senate in 1934, falling just 1,200 votes short of Republican incumbent Frederick Hale, one of the first senators directly elected, in 1916, after passage of the 17th Amendment. Dubord encouraged Muskie to run for the Legislature, and he was elected in 1946 as part of a two-candidate House ticket, ending ten years of Republican success.

Muskie suffered his one Maine electoral defeat in 1947, when he lost a bid to unseat the Republican mayor, Russell Squier. Muskie's campaign was hampered by feuding among ethnic Democratic leaders. Dick McMahon, already his campaign manager, told him he should cut ties with an unpopular Franco boss Muskie considered a friend, a suggestion Muskie received in frosty silence. But it was an object lesson he later applied to the fledgling state party organization.

Re-elected to the Legislature in 1948, Muskie was chosen minority leader by his band of two dozen Democrats, and found his prospects blocked by Republicans who kept key committee assignments to themselves. Some 80 percent of bills "went to committees where there were no Democrats," Muskie said. "They just ignored us. And that's what I used as the first issue. You can make a lot of issues out of one-party government." At one point, Republican leaders sent a State House reporter, Peter Damborg, as an emissary to convert him. Muskie's response was, "You fellows just don't understand—I'm a Democrat because I believe in the Democratic Party. I just don't like the way the Republicans run this state."

The Truman administration was battling a severe bout of Korean War-induced inflation in 1951, and Muskie was offered a post as Maine director of the Office of Price Stabilization (OPS). With the nation weary from World War II rationing, the job was more jaw-boning than lawsuits and regulations, an ideal match for Muskie's budding talents. He had to resign from the Legislature, but he'd already learned all he needed to know about gaining political power incrementally. Muskie traveled the state, meeting with business owners one-on-one and in groups, enlisting them in the patriotic fight against inflation. He resigned in July 1952, however, discontented with congressional efforts to rein in Truman's initiative. He served just a year, but nonetheless convinced an influential group of businessmen he was a Democrat they could take seriously. Though the Legislature held no further interest, Muskie sought and won a seat on the

DNC in 1952, joining Lucia Cormier, later the first Democratic woman nominated for the U.S. Senate.

OUT OF LEWISTON

Frank Coffin's path to politics was different from Muskie's. His father, Herbert Coffin, came from Yankee stock in Providence, R.I., while his mother, Ruth Morey, came from a prominent Lewiston family; her father and Coffin's namesake, Frank Morey, was a legendary Democratic politician, a long-time mayor elected Maine House speaker in 1911—one of only two twentieth-century Democrats to serve there before John Martin was elected in 1974.

Coffin's parents divorced when he was twelve, and he grew up with his mother and grandmother, not reconnecting with his father until after college. His father, Coffin said, was "a cafeteria operator in a shoe shop, and he also did some catering, and for a short time he had his own restaurant." The Coffin family was "strongly Republican," but with his father absent, the Democratic Morey side prevailed. Coffin emphasized the ethnic diversity of Lewiston as greater than most Maine cities, saying he had "Greek friends, Irish friends, French Canadian, Lithuanians, Poles . . . you have a tradition of Franco-Irish rivalry but that doesn't cut as deep as sometimes people make it sound."

Though money was tight, his mother told Coffin to look at several colleges after he graduated from Lewiston High School. He considered Dartmouth, but chose Bates, where his mother and grandfather had gone, enrolling five years after Ed Muskie and, like Muskie, joining the debate team.

His deferments over, Coffin joined the Navy in 1944, assigned to a supply ship he described as "a down-at-the-keel cargo ship, converted at Pearl Harbor for use as a mobile aviation supply depot, or floating department store," and said, "We were always behind the bombings, landings and fighting." Coffin had started at Harvard Law School before the war, and graduated after returning.

Determined to return home, Coffin turned down an offer from a Boston firm, and became a law clerk for John D. Clifford, Maine's sole federal District Court judge. He went into solo practice in Lewiston, served on the school board, then became corporation counsel for the city, a part-time post paying $6,000.

From the beginning, Coffin displayed the high-minded idealism that served him well during forty-one years as a federal judge. In a journal entry, he wrote, "I am to study law with the intention of using it as a tool for social progress. I shall aim at the very top; I pray God that I shall never be blinded from seeing this social goal by any personal considerations." Coffin's idealism, argues Richard Maiman, author of a forthcoming biography, was blended with a pragmatic streak that made Coffin unique among Maine politicians—and judges. In his political phase, he could talk to union members and ethnic voters without condescension, while cultivating friendships with national Democratic leaders such as Adlai Stevenson, who ran twice against Dwight Eisenhower.

Coffin's first political involvement came when, "out of the blue," an invitation to deliver a keynote address at the 1950 Maine Democratic convention in Lewiston arrived. His remarks show that Coffin had the comfortable political base Muskie lacked in Rumford. His Republican friends asked "why on earth I was a Democrat in Maine," and he answered, "Although a Democrat by birth, I find myself in the fortunate position of being able to congratulate my ancestors on the happy choice they made . . . I lack the stuff of which heroes are made . . . The last thing I have in mind is to sacrifice myself on the altar of a lost cause." But he faulted Democrats for huddling in urban enclaves, and said a statewide plan was needed "extending into every last hamlet and crossroads," and reaching "the lumberjack, potato-digger, farmer, shoeworker, loom operator, shopkeeper, fisherman, school teacher and housewife."

He later spoke at the Bates College chapel, "trying to rub a bit of glamor off the independent voter," who, he said, "stood back, content to vote for someone picked out for him by the organized parties." Only hard work at the precinct level, to "ring doorbells, make phone calls, address cards, make checklists, enlist workers . . . get babysitters, plan rallies" would produce success. The speeches were enthusiastically received: "I had become, through speeches alone, a Democratic personage."

After these speechmaking forays, Coffin devoted himself to his law practice, and began attracting clients. One was incumbent Republican Governor Frederick Payne, who asked Coffin to defend him against charges he'd received kickbacks to steer business to a liquor distributor. Twenty years after Prohibition—and nearly a century after Maine became the nation's first "dry" state—liquor was still faintly disreputable, but a major source of state revenue. Charges of favoritism by disgruntled Gardiner wine merchant Herman Sahagian seemed at least plausible; the legislative hearings got New England-wide coverage. Coffin remembers "many tedious hours," including recital by a New England Telephone official of all calls logged by the governor's office. Ultimately, Coffin showed that liquor proceeds for the suspected beneficiary actually declined under Payne, and the governor was exonerated.

Payne then defeated Owen Brewster, the incumbent Republican, in the 1952 U.S. Senate primary; Brewster was an ally of Senator Joseph McCarthy. Though McCarthy was the primary object of the "Declaration of Conscience" speech by Maine's other Republican senator, Margaret Chase Smith, in 1950, Brewster was implicitly condemned. The resulting Republican divisions, with a lingering taint from the liquor scandal, helped Coffin, Muskie and Nicoll in planning the 1954 campaign.

In late 1952, Coffin decided he could provide more security for his growing family—he and his wife, Ruth, had four children—if he joined a law firm. He assisted, then replaced, an ailing partner at Verrill Dana in Portland, which catered to Republican clients, but was willing to give Coffin, a Democrat but also Protestant, a chance. By contrast, George Mitchell, a young Democrat, and Catholic, who'd just returned to Maine in 1965 after serving as Ed Muskie's executive assistant, left an interview when a partner asked about his religion.

The Verrill Dana partner who recruited Coffin was Edward Gignoux, soon to become a U.S. District Court judge, succeeding John Clifford. Gignoux was an impressive lawyer, "agreeable as he was brilliant, well endowed in all respects," Coffin wrote, adding, "Neither of us would have imagined that in another 13 years we would have chambers abutting each other." Coffin was nominated by President Lyndon Johnson to the U.S. 1st Circuit Court of Appeals in 1965.

CROSSING THE RUBICON

Don Nicoll was among those urging Frank Coffin to go beyond speech-making and run for office. The two met after Nicoll was hired as a reporter for WLAM, Lewiston's leading radio station. The job Nicoll had in mind was 2nd District congressman, then the middle of Maine's three districts, where he thought incumbent Republican Charles Nelson was ripe for a challenge.

The political pace quickened in 1953. Coffin gave a rousing speech at the Jefferson-Jackson Day Dinner in Westbrook on April 22, where, Don Nicoll recalled, "He called on the party to mount the ramparts and change the state of Maine." Coffin's own recollection is more reserved. He said that the occasion "was usually a moribund gathering of aging activists who remembered the glory days of FDR." And he again chided his audience, saying the Democratic Party "in the 42 years since it had captured the Legislature," had "wandered off without telling the people where it was going or when it was coming back." The Lewiston *Daily Sun*, he said, ran "virtually the entire speech," and editorialized that it was "the best Democratic Party speech made in this state in many, many years." It noted Coffin's call for Democrats to expand beyond their ethnic, urban base and concluded, "We hope the Democratic Party can soundly grow into a formidable minority, even if it is too much to hope for occasional majority status."

Afterward, Coffin wrote to Muskie, saying, "I am really dead serious about the necessity for a planned series of meetings throughout the state between now and the next convention and wish that you and the State Committee might be able to start the ball rolling . . . something should be done now, or else we should fold our hands for another four years."

Before Muskie could even receive the letter though, he suffered a nearly catastrophic fall that could have stopped the incipient Democratic revival in its tracks. He was renovating an upstairs hallway at home in Waterville, and leaned against a temporary railing, which collapsed, sending him down the entire flight of stairs. Muskie broke his back and was in a coma for two days. His recovery was slow and painful, but by summer, he was well enough to invite the Coffins, on July 18, to visit his China Lake camp, saying he'd read the Westbrook speech, wanted to "talk about political matters," but couldn't travel. Ruth and Frank joined Jane and Ed for barbecued steak, and a pleasant and serious day. "This was our first private time together, and really the beginning of our life-long personal and political friendship," Coffin wrote.

Coffin had "crossed the Rubicon" to enter politics, though adding, "I did not know this at the time." He'd spoken to the Kennebec County Democratic Women's Club, where he laid out ideas later incorporated into the 1954 party platform, "the conservation of natural resources, the development and promotion of industry, an examination of state services, especially the compensation of teachers and services for the aged, and the need for constitutional revision—abolition of the ancient colonial device of the Governor's [Executive] Council." The *Kennebec Journal* provided front-page coverage, but editorialized that "Republicans have done pretty well for years with slipslop platforms hacked together on the eve of a biennial convention," and concluding, "Platforms mean little or nothing in a campaign, candidates everything." Coffin was about to disprove that contention.

As 1954 began, Coffin received a letter from Margaret Murray, representing the very Republican Hancock County on the Democratic State Committee. She told of "a recent stormy state committee meeting in which Irving Fogg had resigned as both [House] Minority Leader and platform chairman." She urged Coffin to write to the party chairman, Jim Sawyer—also thinking of stepping down—and offer his help on the platform committee. "I had no intention of taking her advice," he added.

On January 12, the Lewiston *Daily Sun* carried Coffin's photo with a caption saying he'd been "Chosen by Democrats" to chair an "interim platform committee," joined by Dick Dubord, mayor of Waterville—Harold Dubord's son—and Jim Oliver, a former Republican congressman who'd run for governor as a Democrat in 1952, losing to Burton Cross; Oliver was aiming for the 1st District congressional seat. Coffin said "I was furious." He immediately called Don Nicoll, who recently confirmed that Coffin was "as angry as I ever saw him." Nicoll said Coffin was especially bothered "at the discourtesy of treating him as if he could be used." Nicoll, as Coffin said, then "sagely advised that I batten down my feelings and accept." After mulling awhile, he did.

Muskie later conceded he might have initiated Sawyer's invitation via newspaper, working through his political confidant, Dick McMahon.

Given the upheaval at the state committee, Coffin might have been not only the best, but perhaps the sole available candidate. "We had just about two months," Coffin wrote, "more than enough to do the job in the old way, but not too much if we were to try for a fresh, democratically arrived at, 'grass roots' document."

Coffin tried an idea he'd encountered earlier—an issues question-naire, mailed to voters, who were invited to weigh in on the platform. The idea came from Mike Harder, a Kansas Democrat, and Coffin recog-nized it had never been tried before, helping create the impression Demo-crats were up to something new.

In February, Coffin had hosted an "issues conference," producing an unexpectedly strong turnout of 250 Democrats, but the questionnaire was even more influential in creating a new atmosphere. It reflected Coffin's serious approach, with six pages devoted to "opinions concerning changes to the state Constitution, conservation, labor, welfare, education, public utilities, highways, the administration of justice, and taxation." Coffin and Nicoll "collated and tabulated the returns, and somehow boiled everything down to a four-page brochure," Coffin wrote.

The questionnaire proved useful even among adversaries. Nicoll was in the WLAM TV studio, preparing to interview Governor Cross, accom-panied by his commissioner of Human Services, Dean Fisher. Nicoll re-called Fisher coming in "waving this questionnaire he had received and making very loud and scatological jokes about the Democrats, and what did they think they were doing." Nicoll later concluded, "It was the be-ginning of the downfall of that administration."

The platform presented to the convention relied heavily on the voter responses, and the framework Coffin had created. It "called for certain changes in the Constitution"—abolishing the Governor's Council, mov-ing the state election to November, a four-year term for governor—"uni-fying forestry, inland fish and game, and sea and shore fisheries into one Department of Conservation; laws reducing pollution, increasing fish-ways, and regulating tree cutting; more emphasis on industrial develop-ment; a six-year program of step increases in teachers' salaries; and the disclosure of lobbyists' compensation and expenses." A late addition was an eighteen-year-old voting age. Young Republicans issued a statement opposing votes for eighteen-year olds, a four-year term for governor, or the election change. "The juniors have acquired hardening of the arteries at an early age," responded the *Portland Sunday Telegram*. Press treatment, Coffin said, "was uniformly favorable, no mean achievement in those days." Ed Muskie, in his 1972 campaign book *Journeys*, said the platform "was regarded as an outstanding example of its kind at the time. My preoccupation with ideas as the center of the political process is as old as my involvement in politics."

The genius of the 1954 platform was that, while it suited Coffin's aim of establishing Democrats as the "party of ideas," the ideas weren't obviously ideological. It emphasized points Republicans liked—such as better highways—as well as land conservation associated with prominent Republicans such as Percival Baxter, donor of Baxter State Park. By presenting an energetic vision for state government, it attracted new supporters without alienating those who traditionally voted Democratic.

The convention featured Dick Dubord's keynote address, and a lengthy oration by Averell Harriman, the patrician nominee for governor of New York. Coffin pronounced the event, with seven hundred delegates, "a smashing success, compared with earlier mournful exercises," and applauded the decision to add a denunciation of McCarthyism, "which by that time was hanging like a deadweight on the neck of the GOP."

Three days before the convention, the Androscoggin County committee met and decided Coffin should join the state committee. A Lewiston legislator and high school classmate of Coffin's, Albert "Fat" Cote, was next in line, but happy to step aside. In announcing Coffin's appointment, the party said it was "looked upon as a step toward the state chairman's post." Jim Sawyer stepped down and, as Dick McMahon pointed out, the "path to state chairman is clearly open."

Since his 1950 convention speech, Coffin had talked about what could be done "if we could afford the services of a loyal, capable, full-time worker in this task of building an organization." Four years later, Don Nicoll was hired. He'd volunteered for specific tasks, such as the questionnaire, and Coffin noted his abilities. After Coffin raised $1,000 in pledges, he offered Nicoll the job. He resigned as radio news editor to start on June 4, a decision his mother couldn't understand, though it represented a pay raise—$100 a week, $25 more than WLAM paid. After growing up near Boston, graduating from Colby College and studying for a master's degree in government, Nicoll was ready to help create a two-party future. After the convention, though, there was still one problem, Coffin said: "We had no candidates."

HUNTING FOR A TICKET

The April filing deadline loomed, and though there'd been interest in the congressional seats, Coffin and Muskie couldn't find anyone to run for governor, the position they valued above all others. Worse, the candidate they thought would run against Margaret Chase Smith for Senate, Paul Fullam, a Colby College professor who'd inspired Nicoll and many others, had been advised by his doctor not to run because of a serious heart ailment.

Coffin saw 1954 as "a building year." As of early April, "We were not counting on victory . . . We knew we had nowhere to go but up. That in itself was exhilarating. But we had no effective central organization and only a few committees in the towns and cities, outside of the traditionally Democratic strongholds . . . We had no pool of seasoned and attractive candidates and a pitiable lack of any kind of candidate in most of the sixteen counties. We had no money."

Coffin himself considered running for governor, but not until 1956. Warring Republicans created an earlier opportunity. In 1952, Burton Cross had defeated two more moderate Republicans, Leon Hussey, an Augusta hardware store owner, and Neil Bishop, a casual farmer and gadfly. Bishop was so incensed he got on the ballot as an "independent Republican," as was then possible. Another factor was the Democrats' slogan, "Maine Needs a Change." Coffin said of voters, "Many of them had never known what it was to have a real choice of candidates and programs. We had underestimated how open citizens were."

The opening could quickly disappear. A name from the past seemed the best idea. Muskie spoke with his mentor, Harold Dubord, whose 1936 bid for governor was less successful than his 1934 U.S. Senate campaign. He had no interest in a comeback. Carl Moran, a congressman from the 1930s, was equally emphatic. Henri Benoit, department store owner, was flattered, but declined. Paul Thurston of Bethel, a respected banker, was another "no." They kept asking why Muskie didn't run himself. He'd earlier been penciled in as a 2nd District candidate, but Coffin always saw Muskie running for governor: "I think he had no desire to leave Maine at that point."

Muskie was coy about when he decided, but Dick McMahon said, "No one wanted to be the sacrificial goat, and they kept telling him, 'Listen, if you're so goddam hot for someone to run, why don't you run yourself,' and when that got hard to take, he did."

With Muskie on board, the ticket filled out. Jim Oliver, described by Coffin as "a feisty, former Republican" was "raring to go" in the 1st District. Elected to Congress in 1936, Oliver served three terms. But he supported the "Townsend Plan," an early version of Social Security, and was spurned by the Republican establishment, defeated in a primary, and became a Democrat. Tom Delahanty, Lewiston lawyer and Coffin friend, was more reluctant, but tried the 2nd District. Son-in-law of Judge Clifford, Delahanty served on the Lewiston City Council and succeeded Muskie as House minority leader. The northern, 3rd District candidate was Ken Colbath, a music store owner in Presque Isle. The Senate nomination remained open.

Coffin had a long list, and while conversations were pleasant, no one said yes. He called Muskie four times on April 15, just before filings were due, and said, "Our criteria had dwindled to one: the candidate must be honest. Experience, ability, personality would be bonuses." He finally tried Edgar Carswell, a Gorham drug store owner, though "just how I got Edgar's name I do not recall." After some "bland pleasantries," Coffin said, "We'd very much like you to run for the Senate—no, not in Augus-

Frank Coffin (left) and Ed Muskie head off in Coffin's Oldsmobile 88 for a summer day of campaigning in the 1954 governor's race.

ta. The United States Senate . . . That would be against Senator Smith . . . We have a terrific ticket and you would be of great help to it and Ed Muskie in particular." Carswell said he'd think about it, but needed "a walk around the block" first. Before he returned, Muskie called to say Paul Fullam had decided to run. Over the weekend, Democratic petition circulators produced not only the required 4,000 signatures, but 2,000 more than the statutory maximum.

Fullam later told them what happened. Walking with his son near his home in Sidney, north of Augusta, they'd seen "Way up high, overhead, a transatlantic plane flying to Boston," Coffin recalled. The boy asked, "Is that the plane that carries the bomb?" and Fullam decided to run; he "was deeply disturbed by what he considered unduly belligerent policies of the Eisenhower-Dulles administration."

The five Democratic headliners for the September election appeared together unusually often, partly by Coffin's design. In addition to abundant newspaper coverage, he and Nicoll used plenty of radio time and, the first year it was available, television appearances. Togetherness was dictated by the grand total of $18,000 raised by the party to support the five. No one except Muskie had "anything resembling a campaign staff," Coffin said. The combined schedule was kept "on one 8½ by 11-inch piece of graph paper, blocked out in squares and rows," and carried in

Don Nicoll's pocket. "As time went on, with changes of schedule and TV and radio times added, the paper became almost indecipherable," Coffin said. "But it was our indispensable navigation chart."

There were tensions between Fullam and Muskie. Fullam got credit as the better speaker; Muskie had yet to find his voice. Muskie retrospectively praised Fullam, saying, "You couldn't conceivably think of him as someone who was running for selfish reasons. Nobody had any idea he'd win. Yet he campaigned as though he would . . . he just added class to the ticket." Don Nicoll thought Fullam was "a superb candidate," who "could talk about Aristotle to a Democratic rank-and-file rally, and people would lap it up." Fullam saw his campaign against Smith as "a crusade against the warmonger," and was miffed, Nicoll said, that Muskie "was giving dull speeches about two-party government, and getting all the attention."

CIRCUIT RIDING

Frank Coffin knew the campaign couldn't proceed along familiar lines, or no Democrats would win. At the start, there were only 123 Democratic municipal committees, even on paper, in a state of nearly five hundred cities, towns and plantations. By the end, there were three hundred. Organizing was directed at future campaigns; since so few municipal and county candidates had filed, the only way to promote Democrats for September was a cumbersome write-in routine. "Above all, we needed voters," Coffin said. "We learned that many towns lacked voter enrollment books. All too often, the clerks were elderly folk who knew no other party than the GOP and automatically enrolled every new voter as a Republican."

In a state where Democrats were invisible outside mill towns, Coffin worked hard to expand the party's reach. In May, he persuaded the DNC chairman, Stephen Mitchell, to visit Maine; Muskie's position on the DNC helped. In Portland, "eighteen party notables" gathered at the Lafayette Hotel—owned by Helen C. Donahue, former DNC member, Portland postmistress and friend of Eleanor Roosevelt—which produced a "priceless" photo that ran on the *Press Herald*'s front page. It depicted Mitchell with Henri Benoit and Kenneth "Casey" Sills, the "beloved president of Bowdoin College," who had been the Democratic candidate for U.S. Senate back in 1916, was later named president of Bowdoin, and, now seventy-five, agreed to chair the Democrats' Maine Advisory Council. Sills, said a biographer, had "a deep conviction that scholars and political activity were not mutually exclusive terms," and "had always stressed to his students the responsibilities of citizenship."

Stephen Mitchell's visit, which included a stop in Bangor, was paid for partly out of Coffin's own pocket, but he called it "the best investment

DNC Chairman Stephen Mitchell (seated right, with Lucia Cormier) on his 1954 visit to Maine. Standing are Alton Lessard, Eddie Beauchamp, Frank Coffin, and Tom Delahanty.

we ever made." Coffin said, "the trip was a coup." Further, "As I look back, I realize that our zeal in having him visit Maine stemmed from his clean-cut, almost boyish appearance—hardly that of a Tammany boss—and his known close friendship with Adlai Stevenson."

It was the beginning of a productive relationship between Maine and the national party. Under Mitchell and his successor, Paul Butler, who served from 1956-61, the DNC focused for the first time on building and coordinating state parties. It was a rare moment of cooperation among Democrats at all levels, and led to forty years of dominance in congressional elections and many state legislatures.

Coffin's conviction that the candidates needed statewide exposure was put into practice: "We did not ignore the cities, but we went into the countryside and went to groups that hadn't seen a Democrat since long before the Civil War." He noticed that the seven most Republican counties had lost population since 1900, and decided they might be open to a different message. Burton Cross suggested the problem was attitude.

Coffin said Cross "told the inhabitants of Washington County to pull themselves up by their own bootstraps, but by that time their own bootstraps had eroded pretty heavily." In Washington and Aroostook counties, Muskie was particularly effective.

In Fort Fairfield, a columnist wrote that enthusiasm for Democrats "is really on the up from men who have voted Republican most or all of their lives." A Grange hall supper in solidly Republican Kenduskeag was so popular sponsors needed two sittings. On the stump, Muskie strongly criticized Cross's plan to have dairy farmers convert to bulk tanks to make transportation more efficient, "subjecting the small dairyman to enormous expense." He also faulted Cross's plan to turn over maintenance of 2,000 miles of rural state roads to towns, and close a state sanatorium.

Muskie used a bullhorn while making unannounced visits to small towns. According to David Nevin, "Dick MacMahon would stop at the square, Muskie would hop out, raise a crowd with his bullhorn and start talking sense; it was a novel experience for most of the listeners and they paid attention."

On July 13, the party headquarters officially opened at 118 Lisbon Street in Lewiston, a few doors from Coffin's office, with the *Lewiston Journal*, Coffin said, running "a picture of me, standing and perusing a sheaf of papers, and Don [Nicoll], sitting at a typewriter. This had to be our positions, because we had only one chair." It was the first permanent party office in Maine.

FINDING ED MUSKIE

Ed Muskie brought assets to the campaign no Maine Democrat had possessed. His business background with OPS gave him a foot in the door. His craggy face and six-foot, four-inch stature would stand out anywhere, and his speaking style, once he developed it, was unique in his listeners' experience. It was a speech in Rangeley in July, and then a visit to Castine, that marked the turning point. Muskie had stopped to visit his father in Rumford, who was then seventy-two, and ailing, and on the road north to Rangeley he pointed out to Dick McMahon fishing spots where they'd camped. "That was the only time I saw him get emotional that way," McMahon told a biographer. "He's gone back to the days when he was eleven or twelve." They stopped at the height of land overlooking Mooselookmeguntic, one of Maine's most beautiful lakes, then drove on. That night, Muskie discarded his prepared remarks about new fishing rules and talked about his father. McMahon said, "You could hear a pin drop. They came there expecting to hear him talk about why he ought to be governor and instead he's telling them about fishing with his father." Muskie knew what he'd found, saying later, "I acquired the beginnings of a campaign style that night that I embellished as the campaign went along."

In Castine, before an audience of elderly women, he reduced them to tears as he spoke about their sons leaving Maine to find work, and the need for industrial jobs "that would make it possible for the young to drop their welding torches in Bridgeport, Hartford and Worcester and return to the good life of Maine," McMahon said. "I had to leave, I couldn't stand it. The guy was hot." In September, Muskie carried Castine, where Republicans outnumbered Democrats 4-1.

One can sense Muskie's mood shifting in his letters. In April, he wrote a supporter, "On form, the possibilities are not strong. However, there are factors involved in this election which make victory a distinct possibility." On April 27, he told Ken Colbath, the 3rd District candidate, "The Secretary of State's office was quite surprised all Democratic candidates filed the maximum number of signatures." To John Donovan, later his Senate chief of staff, he wrote in June, "The reaction through the state is certainly much more favorable than I ever expected." To Mose Byer of Orono, he offered, "As one who has gone through some of the blackest days in the history of the Democratic Party in Maine, I find it difficult to believe what appears to be happening." And in July, he reported to Rumford attorney William E. McCarthy, "The campaign is coming along better than I ever dreamed it would. The encouragement I receive from Republicans all over the state is nothing short of amazing."

The party made good use of its assets. One was Dick McMahon. With a well-paid, part-time position as Waterville treasurer, McMahon could travel the state with Muskie at a time campaign managers were almost unheard of in Maine. Frank Coffin affectionately called him "a fat Irishman with a big fat cigar," and Don Nicoll said his nickname was "Friar Tuck." Nicoll also called McMahon "perhaps the savviest political mind that we had."

Another asset was Frank Coffin, an expert at stretching a dollar, even when they were his own. Lack of money forced the campaign to innovate. "I remember George Mitchell's brother-in-law, Eddie Atkins, a printer, giving us credit so we could run up quite a bill but eventually pay it," said Coffin. Early, the party sponsored a "reverse press conference"—an idea Louis Jalbert, a legislator from Lewiston thought up—where Democrats asked reporters for ideas. Reporters became "intrigued with the Democrats," Nicoll said. Along with Portland's Peter Damborg, Lewiston writers Edward Penley and Lionel Lemieux "were all paying attention." Doc Arnold of the *Bangor Daily News*, Nicoll said, "was a very good reporter and a good guy," even though he wrote for the most rock-ribbed of the Republican dailies. Coffin had occasional complaints, but said of reporters, "They felt that politics was getting more interesting. And they were fair . . . they covered everything we did."

The DNC began by requesting donations from the Maine party, but eventually came through with essential cash and loans that funded Nicoll's salary, and launched, Coffin said, "a singularly effective and enduring" political career. The DNC matched contributions raised from other sources, eventually contributing "$9,440, or about half our grand total."

Frank Coffin said he was not joking in calling Republicans "our biggest asset," and Burton Cross "our best campaigner." By early September, Cross scuttled some cost-cutting proposals, allowing Coffin to accuse him of "reaching for some Utopia to offer the voters in areas where he thinks he needs it."

Though Maine Republicans still looked invincible, 1952 had taken a toll—even, ironically, Dwight Eisenhower's breaking the twenty-year Democratic grip on the White House. The disappearance of federal patronage, which in Maine included presidential appointments of hundreds of postmasters, created the space Coffin and Muskie enjoyed on the Democratic side, as old-time party leaders left. For Republicans, the sudden windfall invited squabbling. As Muskie realized, after joining the Senate, choosing party loyalists for postmaster "created one friend and nine enemies."

Burton Cross did nothing to placate backers of his 1952 primary opponents, ensuring lukewarm party support. Ed Pert, a Nicoll successor as party executive secretary and later House Clerk, said Cross "didn't try to patch things up . . . he was not going to forget that primary and this irritated many Republicans, and they were white hot angry by the time 1954 came along." The Senate race had been divisive. Frederick Payne, in ousting Owen Brewster, completed Margaret Chase Smith's victory over the McCarthyites, but also roused resentment.

Coffin found Democrats united as he'd never seen them before. Far from resenting his "upstart" chairmanship, "Our oldsters on the committee and all over the state welcomed us with open arms . . . There was room enough for anyone who wanted to participate."

Governor Cross, meanwhile, seemed to believe he had nothing to worry about from Muskie. To a correspondent, Muskie described a Cross speech with satisfaction: "My opponent even hurled the label New Dealer at me. I suppose he thought it was a bad word, but I don't think his tactic helped him." In July, Cross predicted an even bigger victory than in 1952. It wasn't until far too late he realized he needed to change course.

CONTRASTS AND SUCCESSORS

The partnership between Ed Muskie and Frank Coffin produced enduring benefits for the Maine Democratic Party, though political ambition soon set them on different courses. Physically, they were an odd couple. Coffin, almost a foot shorter than Muskie, said when they appeared to-

gether, "I just about came up to his belly button." When they spoke,
Coffin was effective in small groups; Muskie was adept at the pointed,
plain talk Maine voters preferred.

After Muskie went to Washington in 1959, his vocal range commanded attention. "The first time people see Muskie's temper they are
usually startled by the change . . . He gets bigger, he seems literally to
swell up, his face reddens," one biographer wrote. "It *is* startling; suddenly this remote, quiet man is raw and vibrant, his eyes are bright, the
very features of his face seem intensified and force pours out of him."

No one recorded Frank Coffin's getting angry in public, and his judg-
ments of political adversaries are notably mild. Coffin had a judicial temperament long before he became a judge.

There were other contrasts. For Muskie, his father was the dominant
force. Coffin's father was absent; it was his mother he looked to. Coffin
was serious about his legal practice, known for meticulous preparation.
Muskie saw the law primarily as a backdrop for politics. Though he
joined a Washington law firm after leaving the Senate in 1980, he found it
a letdown.

There are parallels in the next generation of Maine Democratic talent.
Muskie communicated best orally, in speeches, debates and daily exchanges of lawmaking. His only book, *Journeys*, seems almost wooden.
The governor who most resembled him, Ken Curtis, had a sunnier dispo-
sition, but was also disinclined to write out his thoughts, and — like Muskie — found talented writers to set down his words and actions.

Coffin was always an effective writer, and often an artful one. On
being a judge, he said, "A remarkably effective device for detecting fis-
sures in accuracy and logic is the reduction to writing of the results of
one's thought processes." Coffin found writing an essential part of decision-making. In this, he resembles George Mitchell, who, like Coffin,
served only in Congress; both lost bids for governor, Coffin in 1960 and
Mitchell in 1974. Mitchell, a brilliant lawyer, was an inveterate editor of
staff memos, and spotted flaws in an opponent's arguments with unnerv-
ing precision. Coffin published four books and wrote a three-volume
memoir. Mitchell, to date, has six books.

The Coffin-Muskie partnership worked in part through complementary skills. Don Nicoll said, "They agreed on broad principles, but Ed had
almost no interest in working on details of campaigns, where Frank excelled. Where Ed did pay attention to details was on legislation, where he
almost drove his staff members batty. He operated by knowing more
about the subject than anyone, and using that knowledge." In the early
campaigns, "Frank was insistent about performance, about getting things
done." Looking back at the 1954-60 races, when they worked together,
Nicoll is struck by a transformation: "It was a party of extraordinary
diversity, and had a solid and growing base."

Coffin's last impressions of the 1954 campaign are in his memoirs, dating from 2004. "The ensuing five months launched the major political career of one of the nation's most constructive and sane statesmen of the last half of the twentieth century. It also ushered in a fresh, open, and competitive approach to political life for Maine people that has endured for nearly half a century."

A few years earlier, he said Democrats' greatest achievement was re-establishing Maine as a two-party state. "It's been a very refreshing thing and to me it has changed the whole cast of Maine politics and improved both the Democrats and the Republicans. You have people like Senator Cohen and Senator Collins and Senator Snowe . . . brought out of the woodwork by this feeling that Muskie started, by saying that you talk the issues, and you campaign hard and clean, and show you care about people. We've had a George Mitchell because of Muskie. It's a very deep thing that he brought about."

TWO

Building

1955-1965

"The success of a political party is not an end in itself. It is merely a means of service to our state and our country."
— Ed Muskie, 1954 State Convention Speech

The first order of business for Maine Democrats following Ed Muskie's election as governor in 1954 was to prove it represented a genuine revival in the party's fortunes, not just an interruption of Republican rule. Twice earlier in the twentieth century the party seemed on the mend, only to fall back even more deeply into minority status.

In the Progressive era, which began during Theodore Roosevelt's presidency and ended, decisively, with America's entry into World War I in 1917, Maine Democrats showed signs of life, aided by fractures among Republicans. Democrat Frederick Plaisted of Augusta ousted an incumbent Republican, Bert Fernald, in 1910—the same year Democrats gained the majority in the House of Representatives and chose Frank Morey, Frank Coffin's grandfather, as speaker, while Nathan Clifford, a Democrat and former Portland mayor, became Senate president. An Irish Catholic who was also Frank Morey's law partner, Daniel McGillicuddy, entered Congress from the 2nd District, serving three terms and breaking the Republican monopoly on the four House seats Maine held until 1932. But Governor Plaisted was defeated in 1912 by Republican William Haines, though Haines then lost to Democrat Oakley Curtis of Portland in 1914, reflecting the period's political turbulence. With Curtis's defeat in 1916, as well as McGillicuddy's loss to Wallace White—many years later U.S. Senate majority leader—the Democratic boomlet came to an end.

Democrats collectively held the governorship and Legislature for only two years, 1911-12, but they had some notable achievements. Perhaps the most important was electoral reform: direct primary elections for state offices, replacing party caucuses, and a constitutional amendment for the initiative and referendum system that allows citizens to directly enact legislation; in New England, only Massachusetts followed suit. While the initiative alternative lay largely dormant until the 1970s, it's since become a major part of Maine's political life. The 1911-12 session also increased property taxes on "wildlands," enacted a Corrupt Practices Act, and ratified federal constitutional amendments for a progressive income tax and popular election of U.S. senators.

The next uptick came with Franklin Roosevelt's 1932 landslide win over Herbert Hoover and the beginning of the New Deal. Louis Brann, Lewiston's mayor, was elected governor, and re-elected in 1934—the first Democrat to serve two terms since the Civil War. Two Democrats won Congressional seats: Edward "Carl" Moran in the 2nd District—among those approached by Muskie and Coffin in 1954—and John Utterback in the 3rd. Utterback lost in 1934, and Moran didn't seek re-election in 1936. Though Brann ran a close race for U.S. Senate in 1936, he fared poorly in subsequent tries for governor and Congress, as Democrats returned to the minority. Republicans kept their legislative majorities throughout.

Nearly 20 years later, Frank Coffin struck a firm note of optimism: "When we started to build the party, this was a very unique time. We owed nothing to anybody. At least at the start, there was very little prospect of anybody getting elected that year. We were setting out to build. And we were talking about issues. And it was about as pure a time for politics as I suspect has existed."

Elsewhere, Coffin implies the decks were cleared, new leaders were welcomed with open arms, and there was rarely a note of dissent. That wasn't entirely true.

No one personified the old-line Democratic Party, and its urban ethnic base, better than Louis Jalbert of Lewiston, Maine's second largest city and the party's base. Jalbert, who considered himself a protégé of Louis Brann, emerged from the collapse of the city's old guard amid corruption scandals and adoption of a new city charter in 1939. After Brann exited to become governor, the Board of Aldermen became increasingly corrupt, with open buying and selling of city jobs. The "Big Four" aldermen were indicted, with three convicted and the fourth fleeing to Canada.

Jalbert was elected to the Maine House in 1944, eventually serving 19 terms, a record until it was surpassed by long-time House Speaker John Martin, elected to his 20th House term in 2014. Jalbert had brushes with the law, from shoplifting and numbers running in his youth, to domestic violence charges involving his second wife—they divorced but later reconciled—and, while in city government, conviction on bribery charges. He was a polarizing figure, initially rarely scoring high on the legislative ballot, a combined list of candidates for Lewiston's five-member House delegation.

Jalbert was elected minority leader in 1946 during his second term—and Ed Muskie's first—but stepped aside when Muskie assumed the role in 1948. Instead, Jalbert gained a seat on the Appropriations Committee, the most powerful in the Legislature, and chaired the Androscoggin County delegation. In those roles, he exerted considerable and—to detractors—malign influence over legislative affairs until his death in 1984.

His tenure in the House was interrupted only once, when he unwisely decided to run for Lewiston mayor in 1954, taking a beating from archrival Ernest Malenfant. While Jalbert was clever and unscrupulous, Malenfant was called "Dummy" by critics—mostly due to his uncertain command of English, his second language, as it was for most Francos. When Malenfant was sworn in, his wife was presented a bouquet and, as applause receded, he thanked supporters for the flowers, "and for giving me the clap."

During nearly four decades in the Legislature, Jalbert billed himself as "Mr. Democrat," and insisted to an interviewer, "The words 'boss' and 'machine' are not in my vocabulary." A characteristic self-assessment came during a talk to the Lewiston Senior Citizens, when he said, "If I can't do it, it can't be done."

Jalbert reminded people of everything they didn't like about the Democratic Party. Lewiston attorney John Beliveau paid grudging tribute, saying "He had to dominate meetings, he had to dominate people, and was very successful at it." Tom Delahanty, Jr., a U.S. attorney—son of Coffin's friend and 1954 congressional candidate, Tom Sr.—said of Jalbert, "You didn't want him with you but you didn't want him against you, either." Coffin and Muskie usually employed that strategy, and since Jalbert never left his legislative perch, he could be avoided or eluded. Don Nicoll remembers Jalbert confronting Muskie outside the Lewiston convention hall in 1954, jabbing at him and saying, "You're all through, Muskie. You're all through." Instead, it was just the beginning.

LABOR ALLIES

Fortunately for Coffin, there were allies in Lewiston, notably in the labor unions that then dominated the workforce, with 8,000 members in textile mills and thousands more in shoe shops. The most engaging and effective was Denis Blais, who rose to prominence in the national textile union. Born in Quebec, the youngest of twelve children, Blais moved to Providence, R.I, and then, after the death of his father, to Lewiston, becoming a union organizer at age fourteen.

Blais knew how to be persuasive. When first hired as a stock clerk, he was told to win over the "loom fixers," some of the higher paid hands, who were reluctant to join the union. "We didn't do any arm-twisting," he said, "but if they wouldn't sign a union card somehow I was out of parts." He called himself a "real radical," and said unions aren't just about pay rates: "More important than wages, because the economy's going to take care of that, but people having a say in how they're going to work and how they're going to be treated . . . a kind of independence, not being under a whip all the time."

For Don Nicoll, who initially dealt mostly with older labor leaders, Blais was "young, bright and modern" and a welcome balance to Ben Dorsky, who in 1955 headed Maine operations for the newly merged American Federation of Labor and Congress of Industrial Organizations—today's AFL-CIO. Dorsky was a Republican, from a time when only Maine Republicans were worth dealing with. Blais saw it differently. He got the textile workers behind John Maloney, a Democrat running in 1950 against Charlie Nelson in the 2nd Congressional District—a campaign including a sound truck and street-corner rallies, techniques new to Maine. His initial impression of Muskie was far from the self-confident, imposing candidate most remember. Out campaigning, Blais said Muskie "was always very friendly with me but we'd go to some place and he kind of hung back," appearing in photos "as though he doesn't want the limelight." Still, Blais was eager to support Muskie, and recalls a meeting with Coffin, Muskie and Victor Reuther, brother of the legendary Walter Reuther, CIO founder. One result was "signing a check for five hundred bucks, I think the first contribution over two dollars Muskie got." More important than money was union member voting as, Blais said, "We went to work and to everyone's surprise, including me, Muskie was elected."

After the AFL-CIO merger, Blais became Maine secretary-treasurer while Dorsky was president. There were many pitched battles over political contributions and endorsements, and the textile union's withdrawal, for a time. It wasn't until Muskie ran for U.S. Senate that Blais prevailed. Before Dorsky retired, he "started coming around," Blais said, but it took years.

Blais was a man ahead of his time. In 1955, he led the union during the Bates strike in Lewiston, after Bates Manufacturing tried to lower wages 10 percent, to the level in the company's southern mills. The strike succeeded because strikers had the support of the community, churches and even local government. When the company began hiring workers from the Dominican Republic and "there was quite a bit of resentment," Blais not only welcomed them, but helped them rent a hall for parties and invited them to his house. "The resentment gradually died down among some of our white people," he said. "This was evolution, it just took time." In the end, few of the Dominicans had obtained green cards, and most were deported.

By the mid-1970s, most mills were gone, but Blais disagrees they "moved south" before moving overseas. The Maine mills, he said, had been run beyond capacity during World War II, and afterwards owners didn't reinvest, a development later echoed in Maine's declining paper mills. Said Blais, "They just let them run down, and shut them down."

TOOLS OF THE TRADE

For the most part, Muskie and Coffin—who were neither Irish nor Franco—managed to avoid this perennial ethnic conflict. At least until the turmoil of the 1960s, the emphasis was on economic, lunch-bucket issues that united Democrats, rather than the social issues that proved so divisive. Coffin said "I had much going for me. My grandfather's reputation as an extraordinarily able trial lawyer and intensely loyal friend and fighter for his largely mill worker clientele was an ever-present, almost tangible benefit."

After the 1954 election, he resumed party-building immediately. His priority, following on the success of the first platform, was a "pre-platform issue development campaign" for 1956 "even more ambitious than our first one." Coffin convinced Bowdoin College Professor Herbert Ross Brown, "one of the most likeable, able and witty persons in the state," to chair an issues conference in Waterville that spawned 16 subcommittees, and a newspaper editorial headlined, "Maine Democrats Have the Ideas." Coffin's Republican law school classmate Bill Trafton—Muskie's 1956 opponent—suggested the Maine GOP follow suit, "but was coldly rebuffed."

Don Nicoll was charged with starting a party newspaper; *The Maine Democrat* was the result. Given Nicoll's journalism experience, it was a serious effort, far more than a propaganda sheet. Through print, Democrats scattered around Maine learned what town and county committees were doing, along with state and national developments. The idea the publication would be self-supporting through advertising sales was probably unrealistic, and after two years it went out of circulation. A publication with the same name returned later, but again went out of print.

There were growing pains. Coffin, party chair, and Muskie, newly elected governor, consulted about Muskie's replacement on the DNC. They decided Ken Colbath, who'd run in the staunchly Republican 3rd District, deserved a reward. Unbeknownst to them, another group was boosting Dick Dubord, "also our friend," as Coffin put it. Dubord was willing to withdraw, but "his supporters would not hear of it." The state committee voted, and the Coffin-Muskie forces lost, 18-9. Coffin took it hard, saying, "in part owing to a cold and fever, I succumbed to a fit of despair and self-pity." He wrote, "Had I come to the dead end of the street? There was much evidence that this was so."

The mood passed. By convention time in 1956, Coffin and the party were thriving. There were 1,833 delegates, far more than ever before, and 3,000 people attended. Hollywood actress Bette Davis, delegate from Cape Elizabeth, was a celebrity attraction. For his chairman's report, Coffin gave a rousing speech, saying, "There is one big trouble: You people don't know your place; you've forgotten that you were supposed to be the minority party. You weren't supposed to elect a governor two years ago. You're not supposed to have more than one-fifth of the Legislature. You're not allowed any congressmen. You don't know this. But I say to you: Ignorance is bliss."

A parallel effort was underway at the DNC. Under Stephen Mitchell, from 1952-54, and then his successor, Paul Butler, chairs emphasized state party organization in recovering from the Eisenhower sweep that put presidency and Congress back in Republican hands for the first time since Herbert Hoover. Butler created an Advisory Council on Political Organization and named Coffin a subcommittee chair. There were regional meetings, Washington meetings, and work with other state parties. Neil Staebler in Michigan was especially helpful, promoting the innovative platform-building nationally that Coffin had pioneered in Maine.

This era of state and national party cooperation ended after John Kennedy's election in 1960. Butler resigned; his liberal views now clashed with party leadership. Regional organizations withered, and the impact of the 1958 Democratic sweep, which paid dividends when Lyndon Johnson proposed his Great Society programs, receded. Don Nicoll said of Butler's demise, "A great opportunity was lost." Kennedy picked his chief political fixer, Larry O'Brien, as DNC chair, and returned the party to its usual role of supporting the president's re-election.

GOVERNOR MUSKIE

In the public arena, the main event for Democrats during Coffin's two years as chairman was Ed Muskie's first term as governor. With an overwhelmingly Republican Legislature to work with, and an all-Republican Governor's Council vetting appointments and state contracts, he operated under tight constraints. Coffin said of Muskie, "He knew that to survive he had to appear, and be, reasonable to independents or more particularly to Republican leaders . . . He was cautious, always cautious, but he had a good sense of timing."

One key appointee was Maurice Williams as chief of staff, a Republican who'd served in GOP administrations for years. Williams's assessment was recorded in a Muskie biography: "Maine had been run by such conservative people that when Muskie took over it was far behind in all sorts of things . . . And Muskie had that touch, you know, to make people understand. He would tell them about mental hospitals where patients had been sleeping in the kitchens and corridors for years. The teacher's colleges . . . kids were stacked in tiers of three, the light they studied by just a bulb hanging on a cord from the ceiling. But you have to make people see these things to understand them."

Muskie was also the most visible governor Mainers had ever known. Future party executive secretary Ed Pert said, "Muskie from day one as governor was extremely accessible, and not only at the State House on a daily basis for press briefings, but also, as he traveled the state, did all he could to accommodate the press." Floyd Nute, United Press State House correspondent, became press secretary and a trusted advisor.

The new governor knew that Democrats, from New Deal days, had the reputation of "spenders," so he decided to get Republicans interested in spending, too. After hearing from aides that he could balance the budget if the state did nothing new, he said, "Why don't we keep the old budget, and have a new budget, too?" He submitted a current services budget for $68 million. The supplemental budget plan for new services covered everything from state hospital improvements to local school budget assistance, costing $10 million. Though the governor and legislative leaders still clashed over taxes, the device won consideration of many improvements, and became especially useful for Ken Curtis as governor. Today, though the budget still uses this format, the distinction between the two halves has disappeared from public view.

Muskie was tested by Bob Haskell, Republican Senate president and president of Bangor Hydro-Electric, the state's second largest utility. Haskell was as dominant in the Legislature as Muskie was as governor, and the two clashed early. Slowly, though, Haskell evolved from the governor's "chief antagonist" to his "frequent ally" following many end-of-the-day talks. Haskell tried to block Muskie's replacement of an ineffective agency with a new Department of Economic Development, and relented only when Muskie vowed to take his case to the people.

A showdown over the supplemental budget followed Muskie's insistence the Republicans stick to the administration's revenue estimates, rather than their own, higher, figures—painting the Legislature as the big spenders. Political advisor Dick McMahon rejoiced, saying "They had the power to sack him up like a ham, but Muskie whipped them flat and by the end of that first session they knew it." It helped that, in 1956, Muskie was re-elected by a huge margin. But Muskie did his part. Knowing that couldn't sustain a veto, he often negotiated changes before legislation reached his desk.

Muskie's second term was more successful than his first. The Governor's Council became more amenable, and Republicans approved a one-cent sales tax increase, to three cents, to fund new programs. They also authorized major bond issues, $24 million for highways, and $13 million for state hospitals, the University of Maine, and teacher's colleges, which voters approved. Two-thirds of Muskie's legislation was enacted.

Once he confided he wouldn't run again, Muskie won approval in 1957 for two important constitutional amendments—one establishing a four-year term for governor, which Republicans were sure, post-Muskie, they could win; the other, moving state elections to November. Voters ratified both, but the four-year term started in 1958, the November election not until 1960, producing fateful consequences for the growing Democratic Party. Muskie made one concession; he preferred no term limit for the governor, but agreed to a two-term limit, just as Congressional Republicans had initiated the 22nd Amendment, limiting presidential terms, a decade earlier.

CANDIDATE COFFIN

By the end of 1955, Frank Coffin decided he'd finally run himself. It wouldn't be for governor; Muskie was seeking re-election. No Senate seat was available, so it would have to be the Congressional 2nd District. There was tension between Irish and Francos in Lewiston, home to most Democratic candidates. The 1954 nominee, Tom Delahanty, from the Irish clans, was available, but didn't want a divisive primary, and Eddie Beauchamp, a prominent Franco and county attorney, had noticed Democrats' improving prospects. He'd run for the seat in 1944 and 1946. Coffin observed, "Neither one of them wanted to withdraw in favor of the other, but each of them was willing to withdraw in favor of me."

The opportunity became more inviting when, on March 15, the incumbent, Charlie Nelson, bowed out. A college classmate of Coffin's, Jim Reid of Augusta, became the Republicans' favorite, and had the credentials—city attorney, state Senate majority leader, GOP chairman and Eisenhower backer.

Coffin entered to prevent an unpleasant primary, but got an opponent anyway, Roger Dube, the U.S. Senate nominee against Frederick Payne in 1952. Dube, a motel and grocery store owner who did roofing and siding and sold used cars, ignored advice to stay out. Coffin said having a challenger made him a better candidate: "If I had not had to work hard in the primary, I would not have been either so sensitized to people's perceptions and reactions, or so well known in the general election. Roger made me realize that there were other levels to campaigning than the cerebral."

Coffin asked his friend, and eventual successor as chairman, Bates College Professor John Donovan, for a portrait of the 2nd District, which reflects how much the state has changed in the subsequent sixty years. "This was Maine's middle district. It stretched from Lewiston to Quebec, from New Hampshire to the offshore islands of Monhegan and Matinicus. It contained 12,000 small farmers, and 40,000 industrial workers in shoes and textiles mainly." A majority "had less than $3,000 of income a year. There were twice as many enrolled Republicans as Democrats."

Coffin's mailing to prospective constituents included pledges that would be familiar today, including aid to family farms and small businesses, and "to seek sensible aid for our schools, our aged citizens, our ports and highways," as well as some that would not: "To stop the dollar drain on New England, promote our coastal fisheries [and] to increase trade with Canada." The point he emphasized most: "To give Maine two-party government in Washington."

Estimates of Coffin as a candidate vary. His speeches were well-received, but some decided he was less of a natural than Ed Muskie. Peter Mills, a Republican state senator like his namesake father and grandfather, was then a teenager, and remembers in Farmington "the face of Frank Coffin being stapled up on telephone poles all over town," but found "Frank's rather severe facial features . . . made him a less attractive candidate" than the judge he later found "brilliant, wonderful to talk to, and extremely warm." Dube was a frenetic campaigner, and stoked populist resentment of Coffin as "an ineffectual slick city feller."

Coffin began by touring the hinterlands. Guided by Tom Delahanty, his first stop was the International Paper mill in Jay—the old brick one— where the manager supported Muskie "but dreaded the thought of state anti-pollution legislation." On the streets, "If I were with Democrats, we would talk about our chances. If I were with Republicans, I would ask about their business." He headed north through Farmington, then to Rangeley, meeting "a fascinating set of characters—a young Swedish hardware store manager who was for Muskie but also Eisenhower; an enterprising young fellow who ran a grocery store, an appliance business, a filling station, and a bottled gas distributorship; and some unpredictably open-minded woodsmen." He even ran into a woman whose ex-husband retained his opponent, Jim Reid, in a divorce case. Returning home, he and Delahanty were "strangely, exhilarated." In the June 18 primary, Coffin defeated Dube, 2-1. Jim Reid easily bested Neil Bishop, who was becoming a perennial candidate.

The 1956 2nd District campaign was startlingly polite; the candidates respected each other, and Reid seemed out of character when he tried to attack. Reid kept a more leisurely pace than Roger Dube, and Coffin criticized the all-Republican delegation, in place for nearly two decades, as providing "narrow errand-boy congressional representation, too often content with performing the merely routine duties of the office."

The campaign's most notorious moment was provided not by any candidate, but by the pro-Republican newspaper, the *Boston Herald*, which had readers all over New England. On September 2, eight days before the election, it ran a prominent photo of Governor Muskie at his desk, with Denny Blais, the union chief, by his side. Blais's CIO was then considered a "radical" union, and the photo prompted outrage from national Republicans. Muskie's opponent, William Trafton, said "We do not want an extension of Walter Reuther's king-making into Maine." Three days later, Muskie appeared on TV to expose the trick. The *Herald* photo had been taken a year earlier, when Muskie attempted to mediate the Bates Manufacturing strike in Lewiston. The Bates management official in the original photo, Louis Laun, was cropped out. "Needless to say, we were grateful to the *Herald* for this boost to our campaigns," Coffin wrote.

Coffin defeated Reid with 54 percent of the vote, the same as Muskie's 1954 margin over Burton Cross, and Jim Oliver nearly unseated Robert Hale in the 1st District, a margin requiring a recount. The *New York Times* profiled Coffin, calling him "the only bright spot on a rather grey horizon," and only the third Democrat in a century to win the 2nd District.

REVERSAL OF FORTUNE

Frank Coffin, during the four years he represented Maine, became an effective congressman, impressing both House Speaker Sam Rayburn and Majority Leader John McCormack, a fellow New Englander. The only Democrat from New England outside Massachusetts and Rhode Island, on McCormack's recommendation he joined the Foreign Affairs Committee, and in later years speculated he might have become its chairman.

Coffin was impatient with committee work, and the frequent "irrelevant observation or questions that did not advance the dialogue." But he dug into the budget, and was included on European trips that, amid the Marshall plan, were required for ambitious congressmen. He joined Foreign Affairs in time for debate over the Suez crisis, when Israel joined France and Britain in a military action against Egypt blocked by the Eisenhower administration. The experience benefited Coffin's post-political career, when President Kennedy appointed him to the State Department's USAID program, and a later posting in Paris that preceded his federal judgeship. He was involved in early cooperative efforts that led, over many years, to establishment of today's European Union.

The year 1958, however, produced a political crisis for Maine Democrats, and a breach in the Coffin-Muskie relationship never entirely healed, despite nearly four decades of friendship. Muskie had decided he would not run for governor again. While he'd enjoyed successes exceeding what most expected, Muskie, ever the realist, saw little chance that he'd ever work with a Democratic Legislature, and the Governor's Council was an added constraint. Like many of his predecessors, he considered the U.S. Senate the next logical step, and was providing private assurances of his departure to Republicans a year earlier when negotiating the

Don Nicoll (standing) with Frank Coffin in his Longworth Building Congressional office, 1957.

four-year term. Publicly, he made no commitments. As late as March 1958, he was still saying he might run for the Senate, for governor, or for no office at all. Behind the scenes, he was insisting Frank Coffin be his successor.

Coffin and Muskie had returned to the China Lake camp to discuss politics, joined by an "inner circle of loyalists" including Dick McMahon, Tom Delahanty, Dick Dubord, John Donovan and Don Nicoll, who'd joined Coffin in Washington. The governor's race was featured and, Coffin wrote, "Opinion within the party was split, with little outside opinion pushing for my running for governor. I felt that there wasn't enough interest at that point to justify a decision." Though he had once aimed at the governorship, Coffin was now committed to a career in Washington. He wrote to Muskie at the end of 1957, saying "Even after giving the greatest weight to your observations, I am convinced that I should not run for governor. I still cannot see how it is possible for me to plan and execute a campaign. And at bottom, even if it could be done, I do not think it would be right."

Muskie wasn't satisfied and was, Coffin said, "unrelenting." A month later, "He sent me a handwritten letter, pleading with me, for the sake of the party, to leave Congress and run for governor. He stressed the duty we owed to the party and, ironically, observed that of course, unlike him, I might be planning a career as a politician . . . I am bemused by the thought that this governor, future senator, vice presidential and presidential candidate, could fancy me as the career politician."

Coffin and Muskie never came to agreement. It wasn't until May that Coffin formally announced for re-election. Two other candidates sought the Democratic nomination for governor, and Muskie's plan never came to fruition. The 1958 election was the last time the political partners appeared on the same ticket, and Muskie's pressure was something Coffin never forgot.

Don Nicoll said that in conversations even during Coffin's last years, he could display "a level of anger" about 1958 that was rare, adding, "Frank was a very modest person in terms of his behavior, but he had a strong sense of his own worth." Nicoll said that, when Muskie was pursuing the Appeals Court appointment for Coffin in 1965 with a highly reluctant Lyndon Johnson, he went "way beyond the point a politician would normally go, but it didn't quite wipe out the resentment." When Muskie spoke about running for the Senate, he avoided the topic, saying, "I dragged my feet and finally I made the decision to run for the Senate because if I didn't that would largely be the end of the effort to make Maine a two-party state." The conflict was in some ways unique, but foreshadowed infighting over who should represent the party in major elections that extends right down to the present.

While Coffin was still disagreeing with Muskie, he was approached by Clinton "Doc" Clauson, mayor of Waterville, "one of our elders," as Coffin put it. Clauson was a chiropractor, and had also headed the IRS office in Maine, then a prime patronage appointment. "He was clearly interested in running for governor, and wanted to sit down with Ed and me and talk things over," Coffin wrote. Finally, on February 11, Clauson, "who had held off with great restraint, awaiting Ed's and my joint decision—which never materialized—announced his candidacy."

Coffin and Nicoll preferred another candidate—Maynard Dolloff, master of the Maine State Grange. The need to broaden the party's base was urgent, and Dolloff seemed situated to make inroads in rural Maine though, in retrospect, "he wasn't as strong a candidate as we expected him to be," Nicoll said. Muskie stayed neutral. In the June primary, Clauson, with the support of old-line Democrats, defeated Dolloff by 1,400 votes. Republicans convinced former Governor Horace Hildreth, who'd served from 1945-49, to come out of retirement, and he was the frontrunner for the final September election.

The Muskie-Coffin ticket provided a greater boost than expected, and 1958 was a banner year for Democrats nationally. Many leading Senate liberals, who later provided votes for President Lyndon Johnson's Great Society programs, came aboard, giving then-Senate Majority Leader Johnson a nearly two-thirds majority. In Maine, Jim Oliver was elected in the 1st Congressional district, Coffin easily defeated Neil Bishop, Muskie ousted Frederick Payne from the Senate—and Clauson upset Hildreth, winning by 11,000 votes. Perhaps equally impressive, Democrats took twelve seats in the state Senate, and fifty-eight in the House—enough to uphold vetoes by the new governor. Aspirations rose; if even Doc Clauson could beat the best candidate Republicans had, maybe two-party government was more than a slogan.

Clauson's deficiencies as a campaigner were well-known. He was a poor public speaker who would often start a speech by reading his own press release, including the phrase, "Dr. Clinton A. Clauson said today." Out of concern Clauson might be a drag on the ticket, Muskie dispatched Dick McMahon to investigate, and he found things were worse than they thought. But Muskie was so popular that Clauson, who attended as many Muskie events as possible, was carried along.

After the inauguration, Maurice Williams, who wanted to join Muskie in Washington, agreed to stay on with Clauson, after Muskie picked John Donovan and Bob Huse, the party's executive secretary, as his top aides. Williams was from Newport, and he dreaded the new governor's visit to his home town. Clauson insisted on leaving early, and, to Williams' surprise, spent an hour shaking the hand of every person who came into the hall. Clauson gave his usual rambling remarks and then made a beeline for the exit, where he again shook everyone's hand. The next morning, Williams went downtown, expecting the worst, but everyone told him how wonderful the new governor was.

In Augusta, Clauson kept the Muskie staff that was still available, and used his predecessor's budget as a blueprint. With four years ahead, he could afford to relax. But the Clauson administration turned out to be one of the shortest in Maine history.

RIGHTING A WRONG

In November 1959, Maine Democrats packed the Calumet Club in Augusta, center of Franco social life, for an issues conference and dinner with John F. Kennedy, who had recently launched his campaign for president. Organizers expected two hundred people; six hundred showed up. That evening, Kennedy, his aide and biographer Ted Sorensen, and Connecticut Governor Abe Ribicoff joined a late-night Blaine House session, making it clear, according to Frank Coffin, that "our visitors expected to leave the next morning with a ringing endorsement from all of us." Coffin demurred, but by December 28 the endorsement was ready. He called Clauson, urging him to support Lucia Cormier to run against Senator Margaret Chase Smith in 1960, since Coffin had already decided on a third term in the House.

The following evening, December 29, Clauson, who Coffin described as "at age 64, the picture of a hale and hearty man," attended a banquet in Lewiston. At 2:30 a.m., he died in his sleep at the Blaine House. Muskie called Coffin at 4 a.m., who said, "I couldn't immediately absorb the news. Then layer on layer of implications piled up. The best-laid plans are so vulnerable. Needless to say, I slept no more." Republican Senate President John Reed, in that office himself for just a year, was now governor.

Coffin appreciated the irony. "I had, not so long ago, vigorously and painfully fought against running for the office. I was on a rising tide of experience, popularity, and power in the House," he wrote, but added, "The specter of running for governor could no longer be avoided."

It didn't take long to decide. As he said, "My principal feeling during these early days was one of anger that the leadership of the state, which we had won fairly and squarely, had been so unfairly snatched away by Doc's untimely death. Running for governor took on the coloration of righting a wrong."

Coffin announced on February 3 and critically evaluated the TV tape: "I was impressed. I appeared confident, clear, and concise . . . also humorless. I gratefully acknowledged that my party had let me decide, free from any concerted pressure." He vowed to continue the work of his Democratic predecessors, and said, "Service is the only proper goal of public life, not security in office." He concluded, "My faith is that in joining once again the battle which was fairly won in 1958, I am helping the cause of good and forward-looking government in Maine. For this cause I am willing to lay my political career on the line, win or lose, without reservations, reluctance or regrets."

There were skeptics, including the all-Republican Governor's Council, who, Coffin said, "could not believe I would give up my safe seat." A commentator noted that no congressman since Israel Washburn in 1860 had returned from Washington to run for governor "and Congress has usually been seen as a step up from governor." Another pointed out that, with the election shifting to November, another 50,000 to 70,000 voters would cast ballots, "most of them predictably Republican." Coffin said,

Frank Coffin, accompanied by his wife, Ruth, and state party chairman John Donovan, speaks from a flatbed truck made to resemble a "whistlestop" train during his ill-fated 1960 campaign for governor.

"In my enthusiasm in responding to what I saw as a clear call of duty, I completely overlooked the significance of these figures."

Governor Reed, a potato farmer from Fort Fairfield, announced he would run in the special election for the last two years of Clauson's term. Coffin had no primary challengers; Jim Oliver ran for re-election in the 1st District, while John Donovan, the party chair anointed by Coffin, ran for the 2nd District seat Coffin would vacate, and David Roberts, later a state Supreme Court justice, contested the 3rd District—soon to disappear due to Maine's lagging population. Lucia Cormier appeared on the cover of *Time* magazine, along with Margaret Chase Smith, as the first two women to contest a U.S. Senate seat.

Coffin made Shep Lee his campaign manager, who was close to Muskie and later, George Mitchell, while Jean Sampson headed the issues committee. During the campaign, Coffin gave sixty major speeches on seventeen distinct parts of state government. At the April party convention in Portland, delegates adopted the kind of "detailed and powerful platform" Coffin had invented six years earlier. It addition to abolition of the Governor's Council, it called for Senate confirmation of appointments and addition of a lieutenant governor. There was a less pleasant moment. Louis Jalbert, in "an effusion, perhaps induced by alcohol," Coffin wrote, denounced him for choosing Lee "because he was a Jew. I was astounded and devastated to hear such talk," which "was never repeated." Senator Hubert Humphrey, already a close Muskie ally, gave the keynote. In Coffin's speech, "Progress with a Purpose," he challenged the party to find out "why homes break up, why businesses fail, what industries can profit best in our state, where lobsters spawn, why young people don't go to college, what elders need, how the disabled can lead useful lives, how forests should be used."

A welcome addition to the campaign staff was Peter Cox, later co-founder of *Maine Times*, the statewide newsweekly published from 1968-2002. Cox, a Yale graduate, had just finished his Army service, and worked for Coffin unpaid until the campaign could afford it. He was Coffin's advance man, driver and confidant—similar to the role Dick McMahon played for Muskie. Coffin said of Cox, "He was an intelligent and alert conversationalist and companion. He made life on the hustings tolerable."

Money was, as usual, a problem, though Coffin aspired to raise $25,000-$35,000. "Although politics was deep rooted in our people, contributing to politicians was looked on as abnormal," he said. Not every dollar was accepted. Congressman Tip O'Neill, future House speaker, set up a meeting with Boston contractors, who made it clear the price for their contributions was a guarantee of future Maine contracts. Said Coffin, "They could not believe that we were so stupid and naïve. But of course we were."

Coffin sized up his opponent: "John Reed was a year younger than I, 40, somewhat taller, lean of build, equipped with a stentorian voice, and a buttoned-down but not unimpressive presence. His career in the Maine Senate had been modest." David Nichols, the Republican Party chair, said, "If the election were held today, I doubt if we would retain the governorship."

Estimates of the candidates reflect hindsight. Coffin biographer Richard Maiman said Reed "was just the better candidate." Don Nicoll, who interviewed Reed not long before his death, came away impressed by his knowledge of the world—he served as ambassador to Sri Lanka—and by his dissents from party orthodoxy.

Coffin was the front-runner on most lists, however. In a column, Peter Damborg, comparing Muskie and Coffin, called Muskie "the magnetic popular leader and the dominant public figure," while Coffin had "the more brilliant mind," adding, "what he lacks in power as a speaker, he makes up in clarity and incisiveness."

Nearly fifty years later, in 2004, Coffin looked back to describe the difference between those times and ours. "In these times of disillusion with government and skepticism born of many failed efforts, it is hard to imagine a time when there was a general air of confidence that great things could be done, a widespread understanding that it was high time that they should be done, and a heady expectancy that somehow they would be done. The opportunity of making changes for the better in so many aspects of our state government was high octane fuel for us."

Muskie campaigned with Coffin, often standing out more than the candidate: "The workers had a hard time seeing me across the aisles and over the benches," he said. "By October I had already visited 120 towns and more than 100 industrial plants." He toured jointly with the three congressional candidates, as Muskie had in 1954, more out of loyalty than necessity. He raised the full $35,000, and said of the joint tours, "whether this was the wisest course for me I doubt." Denis Blais was terse in opining that Coffin should have spent more time in vote-rich cities than seeking votes on the "chicken farms" of rural counties.

John Kennedy won the presidency in November, but Maine Democrats were routed. Coffin's race was the closest; he ran ahead of Kennedy. Jim Oliver lost his congressional seat, and other Democrats lost 2-1. Legislative seats also disappeared. Whether the 1960 election represented a provincial backlash against the nation's first Catholic president is debatable, but the size of the Republican tide was extraordinary. Coffin polled 17,000 more votes for governor than Muskie had, yet lost to Reed by more than 20,000. The turnout of 417,000 broke the previous record by 100,000 votes.

Coffin concluded, "In two years, with no presidential election, I would have had a better chance." A national columnist, Leonard Cohen, wrote that "The only thing that seems to explain it is the religious issue — the fear of thousands of small-town Protestants against placing a Catholic in the White House." And Coffin recalled, "I was on the street in Lisbon Falls, and the priest came by, and of course my background is Baptist. But the priest was also thinking that I was also an Irish Catholic. And so the priest says, 'Ah, Mr. Coffin, you're doing a fine job. And don't let them know you're a Catholic.'"

What is beyond dispute is that the fledging Maine Democratic Party suffered a serious setback in 1960, just as party-building exercises and organization of municipal and county committees championed by Coffin were taking hold. Ed Muskie was just beginning his career in Washington, and he continued to be the unquestioned leader, especially after Coffin accepted Executive Branch appointments and then left politics for a long career on the federal bench. Coffin never questioned the voters' decision. "I had to confront the fact that I had not persuaded the people of Maine to support me. This was humbling. Up to now, I had moved from success to success, both in law and in politics. Now I knew I had limitations."

He had made an impression, however. Much later, Peter Cox wrote to Coffin about his first experience in politics, and Coffin's last: "This was an issues-oriented campaign unlike few in the past and even fewer in the future. I was so affected by how you presented these issues, particularly relating to the economy and the environment, that they became the backbone of the thinking that launched *Maine Times* eight years later. You made me see Maine as one state, with a common interest that transcended any geographical differences."

LEADING FROM A DISTANCE

Ed Muskie had told Maurice Williams that Washington life would be too rough for his taste, instead taking with him the party's post-Coffin team of John Donovan and Bob Huse. He was unsatisfied with the results, however, and after Coffin's defeat in 1960, told Don Nicoll he wanted him as a legislative and press aide. A year later, Donovan left for the Labor Department, and Nicoll became chief of staff, a position he held until 1971, later returning to Maine.

In Washington, Muskie became what Coffin aspired to be, had he become governor: legislator in chief. Despite the attainments of other Maine senators, including Margaret Chase Smith, Bill Hathaway, Bill Cohen, and Olympia Snowe, no one except Muskie's successor, George Mitchell, has written and passed major legislation that altered the course of the nation's public life. Despite a disastrous start with Lyndon Johnson, who exiled him to three obscure committees, Muskie began building the expertise he deployed strategically during twenty-two years in the Senate.

At first, it was discouraging. Though the Senate was a promotion, given his modest job description as governor, Muskie found it difficult, telling a biographer "You come down here after having run your state and find you don't amount to a damn. It is a very depressing experience for the first few years." Things improved after 1960, when Lyndon Johnson left the Senate to become John Kennedy's vice president. Mike Mansfield of Montana, with whom Muskie forged a close relationship, took his place as majority leader.

Public Works was a potential power base for Muskie, since it controlled a lot of federal grants, but the leaders, Robert Kerr and Dennis Chavez, came from the party's conservative wing. They died in office six weeks apart, and the new chairman, Pat McNamara of Michigan, was a liberal who picked Muskie to chair a new subcommittee on air and water pollution. Its growth under Muskie's leadership was so spectacular the committee was renamed Environment and Public Works.

Muskie's cohort, the class of 1958, disrupted the staid Senate, and, for a time, it became the bulwark of liberalism. Senators like Phil Hart of Michigan, Eugene McCarthy of Minnesota, Frank Moss of Utah, Gale

McGee of Wyoming, and Muskie sat together, entertained together, and soon changed the Senate.

Muskie built an effective staff. He was demanding, and those who didn't measure up soon left, but he was a shrewd judge of talent and built loyalty as well as expertise. Don Nicoll was the anchor, and Nicoll hired George Mitchell to his first job in politics, as Muskie's executive assistant. Muskie was able to harness large personalities such as Leon Billings, his top environmental aide and his last chief of staff. His approach to legislation was as a problem-solver. John McEvoy, another chief of staff, said of Muskie, "He devours alternatives. He rejects an *a priori* argument, rejects things that are not factually based, not founded on data, that one can't explain and defend. Many public men prefer not to have alternatives . . . Muskie is always interested in alternatives, and usually has some of his own."

Muskie's patience was as legendary as his temper. He could spend hours at a committee markup session waiting for the right moment to call a vote and make a deal. The monuments he left behind in the Clean Air Act of 1970 and Clean Water Act of 1972 were preceded by smaller bills that established, incrementally, a federal role in controlling pollution, and spending money to do so. Already competing with the funding drain of the Vietnam War, Muskie skillfully upped budget appropriations, year by year. He confronted Ralph Nader, who issued a stinging report about proposed Clean Air legislation, claiming Muskie's approach was insufficiently radical. In a calm and measured response, Muskie said, "Our way of being tough in our part of the country is to do it without name calling or recrimination, but to develop clear ideas of what we stand for and to press for them as hard and as effectively as we can. We don't think it is necessary to be nasty . . . to really make this society work, we're going to have to move across the lines of confrontation, reach agreements, get results. To do it needs toughness. It needs courage. But it also requires effectiveness."

Muskie became undisputed leader of the Maine Democratic Party, particularly after his national campaigns, for vice president in 1968 and for president in 1972, until he left the Senate in 1980, but he exercised authority with a light hand. Concerning candidates, "he would encourage but not select," Don Nicoll said, starting with neutrality in the 1958 gubernatorial primary.

Jerry Plante was elected to the House in 1956 at age 21—the first Democrat to win in Old Orchard Beach since Reconstruction. He became assistant minority leader in 1958, and was considering running for leader when Muskie telephoned. "He wasn't calling to tell me what to do," Plante said, "but he wanted to give me some background on how they had encouraged a gentleman named Irving Fogg from Madison, a heavy Republican area, to run . . . and would I step aside?" It was part of the Muskie-Coffin base-broadening, and Plante agreed. Fogg served one more term, and Plante learned from him, finding Fogg's deliberative style a complement to his own impetuousness. Two years later, Fogg stepped down and Plante became leader. "Sometimes it pays to be patient," he said.

PROFESSIONAL HELP

Frank Coffin's chairmanship, and selection of Don Nicoll as a professional executive secretary, set a pattern that served the Maine Democratic Party well for a whole generation. Chairs usually served two years, often leaving to run for office, while executive secretaries—later executive directors—often stayed longer, providing continuity and expertise at a time when the Republican Party had no paid staff.

Coffin left the post to run for Congress, and his success in 1956, along with Muskie's Senate election in 1958, created new opportunities. John Donovan, Bates professor and Coffin's close friend and successor as chairman, went to Washington with Muskie, along with Bob Huse, Don Nicoll's successor. Ed Pert of Bath was hired as executive secretary in 1957, and stayed four years. In 1962, Bill Hathaway took over as chairman, followed by Peter Kyros in 1964 and George Mitchell in 1966. In that six-year span, the party was led by two future U.S. senators and a four-term congressman. In 1968, Severin Beliveau took the reins and served five years, to date the longest tenure. While Beliveau later was known as a lobbyist, he was elected to the Maine House and Senate, and ran for governor in 1986.

Ed Pert, whose long tenure as House clerk, from 1974-92, nearly matched John Martin's as speaker, took to politics like a duck to water. He grew up in solidly Republican Bath, where his father was a Republican and his mother a non-voter. Pert said, "I think my father . . . was kind of dumbfounded by the intensity of my political interest at an early age." In high school, he led the outnumbered Harry Truman forces in a debate against followers of Republican Thomas Dewey. And, despite his enthusiasm, he found that "The Maine Democratic Party was weak and factionalized and had little or no money." He recalls corresponding with the 1948 Democratic nominee for governor, Louis Lausier of Biddeford, who "said he was nauseated by the lack of organization or the unwillingness of those people who were Democrats to step forward and to give him a hand."

The post-FDR period was hard. In the Maine House, "they were a small and loyal band, and many of them were from the cities," Pert said. He found that some legislative Democrats in the 1940s decided "to be even more conservative than the Republicans in hopes of gaining public support by keeping taxes down." The economic stagnation, and outflow of young people, produced "the brain drain, and many people who might have voted to make changes in Maine, just left Maine." Things improved by 1950; Pert said Lucia Cormier's impressive run in the 1st Congressional District "got Democrats excited for the first time in years."

Pert joined the city and county Democratic committees, organized a Young Democrats chapter at the University of Maine, published a newsletter called "The Donkey Serenade," then toured the state to try to set up similar groups. Party elders discouraged the effort, however, saying they needed everyone of voting age to join regular party committees. The Bath committee raised $200 for a rally during the 1954 campaign, and Pert's first encounter with Frank Coffin was a request they donate the proceeds for a statewide television effort, which they "gladly did," and held the rally, too.

Pert worked at the *Bath Daily Times*, and was serving on the state committee when he became executive secretary. He ran for the Legislature himself and won a House seat in 1958, splitting time between Augusta and the party office in Lewiston. His attempt to move to the Senate in 1960 failed, as Democrats lost races all the way down the ballot. For the party, Pert was a fundraiser, event planner, editor of the *Maine Democrat*, caucus organizer, and recruiter. During his tenure, he said, the party's fortunes "got better every day."

The 1964 Johnson landslide over Goldwater brought Maine Democrats a brief moment in the sunshine at the Legislature, filling posts they hadn't seen in half a century. Pert became Senate secretary as a protégé of Carlton "Bud" Reed, the new Senate president. That two-year stint became his calling card when, in 1974, Democrats finally won the House again. He hopped in his Volkswagen beetle and toured the state, lining up enough caucus votes to begin his long run as House clerk.

Pert's successor as executive secretary, Ed Schlick, was perhaps a less fortunate choice.

Schlick had worked his way up at the *Lewiston Sun* from obituaries to political writer. He applied for the executive secretary job when Pert was chosen, and in 1961, with Alton Lessard of Lewiston as chairman, he succeeded. Life at the *Sun* had become difficult after Schlick made an unsuccessful attempt to organize a Newspaper Guild unit, and soon found himself back writing obituaries, saying management saw him "as some kind of bomb-throwing Communist."

Schlick didn't have any early political affiliations; he told an interviewer he couldn't remember how he'd voted during the 1950s, but found, as a reporter, that "the Democrats, when they went to a convention, had a lot more fun than the Republicans." He worked on Frank Coffin's primary campaign against Roger Dube in 1956, but when asked about the "major planks in the party platform," he answered, "Not a clue." He lost his one bid for elective office, a House primary race in 1964. Nevertheless, Schlick remained party secretary until shortly before George Mitchell took over as chairman in 1966.

POLITICS MEETS POLICY

Not many elected leaders master both politics and policy, and in that sense Ed Muskie was the FDR of the Maine Democratic Party. In both aspects, his management of the Model Cities Act of 1966, the last of Lyndon Johnson's Great Society programs, outdid even his landmark environmental bills.

The bill was in dismal shape when Johnson chose Muskie as its manager. It had been drafted by a task force without input from Congress, and despite its assignment to Joseph Califano, Johnson's brilliant young aide, it neglected key constituencies on Capitol Hill and was getting nowhere. Johnson now appreciated Muskie's legislative abilities, and knew that a senator from a state with no major urban areas couldn't be accused of feathering his own nest. Don Nicoll began negotiating changes while Muskie vacationed in Maine. During a day-long meeting at Muskie's home in Kennebunk on July 6, Califano, Larry O'Brien and a Budget Bureau official settled the details.

When he returned to Washington, Muskie swiftly moved the bill through the Banking and Currency Committee, where he served. It was then called "Demonstration Cities" — finally changed, at Muskie's behest, to avoid the association with contemporary war protests. Southern Democrats were still opposed, and Muskie placated them by cutting the funding period from three years to one, without reducing the annual appropriation, and having a conservative Democrat, Thomas McIntyre of New Hampshire, sponsor the amendment. The bill moved to the floor on August 18, and Muskie spoke about cities, saying "Men have been drawn to cities as if by magnets. Cities have used the power and imagination of their people to create states, nations and even civilizations." Yet he acknowledged decay and slums, saying, "Our cities contain within themselves the flowers of man's genius and the nettles of his failures."

Al Gore Sr., from Tennessee, was impressed by Muskie's analysis of how Model Cities differed from post-war "urban renewal" programs, which focused on "blighted" downtown buildings that were torn down and replaced by new buildings and parking lots. Muskie said communities would plan their programs, and its features — such as the Historic Preservation tax credit that still aids downtown redevelopment — allowed restoration rather than destruction of downtowns. Gore said Muskie's answer "has given more life and meaning to the program than any explanation I have yet heard."

Entering final debate, Majority Leader Mike Mansfield expected the bill to fail, with Democrats divided and most Republicans opposed. He'd never seen votes changed as Muskie somehow managed on Model Cities; it was enacted, 53-27. Robert Kennedy called Muskie's speech the finest he'd heard in the Senate, while New York's other senator, liberal Republican Jacob Javits said, "The cities are strangling. They are in the gravest danger. It is wonderful to me that a barefoot boy from Maine could say it as eloquently as he has."

Model Cities resulted in 150 projects nationwide, and lasted for six years before being dismantled by the Nixon administration. There were many critics, and some programs were ineffective. There were successes, too, including one in Portland, which got an early grant. Caroline Glassman, a future state Supreme Court justice, was then a young lawyer asked to oversee the Portland application.

When it became clear everyone was welcome, the response was overwhelming. Glassman said, "The city council was kind of shocked because they were not accustomed to having welfare mothers, taxi drivers and everybody else come into city hall and meeting with lawyers and architects and bankers, and hospital directors." The application letter from Barney Shur, acting city manager, said, "Never in the history of Portland and I suspect in the recent history of urban America have the citizens of a community and the professionals in its public and private agencies joined in such a concerted, intensive and frank discussion of the problems which beset its residential neighborhoods and the development of innovative pathways to the permanent solution of these problems."

Some of Portland's least neighborhood-friendly features—Interstate 295 and the Franklin Arterial—were already under construction, but the city's focus soon changed. The revival of Portland from a decaying seaport to today's thriving, vibrant place, attracting visitors and residents from around the country, took years and traveled down many byways, but its genesis is rightly traced to the Model Cities program.

FIRST PRINCIPLES

In his 1954 convention speech, Ed Muskie roused the delegates by proclaiming, "For too long we of the Democratic Party in Maine have permitted ourselves the luxury of apathy and discouragement. We have found it easier to say, 'What's the use!' and then sit back while a mere handful has sought to retain at least the shadow of an organization. It is time for us to get up and go, and there will never be a better time than right now. The means and methods of organization are not nearly as important as the will to organize." He balanced the partisan appeal by saying "The success of a political party is not an end in itself. It is merely a means of service to our state and our country."

After he succeeded Muskie in the Senate, George Mitchell provided a formal tribute on Muskie's seventieth birthday, in 1984, saying, "Ed Muskie created a living, effective Democratic Party in the state of Maine for the first time since the founding of the Republic. He not only gave a voice and a forum to those left out by the old Republican Party, he laid the groundwork for the reinvigoration of that party in Maine as well. He has helped give us a state with some of the nation's most enlightened legislation and some of the nation's best young legislators—men and women of both parties. Ed Muskie saw . . . that a democracy can function only so long as new ideas and new blood are allowed to rise to the surface to challenge the old, to surprise the complacent, and to renew the jaded."

Ed Pert made the point more simply, saying Muskie "helped Maine people to understand that change was possible and that Maine people could have a better life. And that Maine could change without being spoiled."

Despite contrasting temperaments, Muskie and Frank Coffin were only rarely in conflict. For Don Nicoll, both were equally capable of "drawing people in, engaging them, and then putting them to work." When he worked for Coffin, at the beginning, "It was much more collegial, and much more a partnership of equals," although he said Coffin "was in a different category of intelligence and ability than I." When he worked for Muskie, "Ed was clearly the boss and I was his trusted lieutenant."

In a recent interview, Mitchell emphasized similar points. While the disarray of Maine Republicans, and the presence of a charismatic leader—"and clearly Ed Muskie was that leader"—were important to the Democratic revival, he said, "It was our good fortune that both Muskie and Coffin could distill and convey a message to people in a way they could understand. They were true intellectuals."

Jerry Plante said, "Both Coffin and Muskie were very issue-oriented. They knew that good issues could overcome personalities . . . for the Democrats to become a majority party, we had to have a better caliber of candidates than we'd had prior to 1954, but you still had to bring people into your organization with issues." For himself and others, "There were plenty of opportunities." Plante was a floor leader at twenty-three, House clerk at twenty-eight. Until the 1990s, most Democratic candidates for Congress and governor were in their early forties.

Nicoll observes that Coffin and Muskie, unlike some of their successors, never sought worldly success. They lived modestly, and never aspired to wealth. "Frank's devotion to the law and a democratic and just society was unconditional," he said. "If you agreed to become a judge, it was almost like taking priestly vows."

Near the end of his life, Coffin bemoaned what had become of political parties, writing, "The political party itself is an endangered species." Yet he said, "I have not given up hope for a resurgence of interest in making political parties more effective instruments of government, midwives, so to speak, between the mass of citizen-voters and their elected leaders and the policies for which they stand." He harked back to his Bates College Chapel speech in 1950, where he described politicians as "to a great extent decent people, generally trying to do the right thing, besought by a host of pressure groups . . . more broad-minded than the average citizen, possessed of an immeasurably greater ego, generally underpaid for their untiring energy, constantly subjected to abuse, and capable once in a while of doing a brave or wise deed."

Coffin said the antidote to party decline wasn't to register as an independent, which he compared to "a spectator sport confined to watching the game only in the final few minutes of play." Progress, he said, is achieved through parties, "even if you have to hold your nose on some issues, by good and bad people working together, for good and not-so-good motives." He recommended a political apprenticeship, "even more for the millions of young people who boast a far better education than those in mid-twentieth century, who have given themselves to many worthwhile causes, but who have notably absented themselves from the political scene."

THREE

Reform Governor

1966-1974

"Republicans generally regard government at any level as an alien force, something to be feared and opposed. We Democrats, on the other hand, look upon government, if properly directed and efficiently operated, as a means to improve the general welfare."

—Ken Curtis, Maine Action Plan

After the dismal 1960 election that followed Governor Clauson's death, Democrats had much better fortune in 1964. In addition to the Lyndon Johnson-fueled legislative sweep—there were now twenty-nine Democrats and just five Republicans in the state Senate—William Hathaway, state party chairman, parlayed that position into a winning bid for the 2nd Congressional District seat. His successor as party chair, Peter Kyros, repeated the strategy in the 1st District two years later. The 1964 state elections brought a host of Democrats into various offices— Dick Dubord, Maynard Dolloff, Denis Blais, Joe Brennan, John Martin, Ed Pert— and Ken Curtis.

The electoral successes followed a slow, but steady climb in party enrollment that had begun with the 1954 campaign and was to continue for more than two decades. From 1954-66, Democratic enrollment grew by 50 percent in what was now the 2nd Congressional District, and by 70 percent in the 1st District, as programs espoused by Ed Muskie and Frank Coffin won over voters in every major town and city, while maintaining the mill town base. From fewer than 100,000 Maine Democrats, the party now enrolled 158,000. It wasn't enough to consistently win legislative elections—there were still 233,000 Republicans—but parity was just a decade away. During Ken Curtis's two terms as governor, Democrats added 55,000 voters; Republicans, just 4,400.

Party organization was strengthened, too. In 1966, George Mitchell, returning to Maine after serving in Muskie's Senate office under Don Nicoll, was elected party chairman, and threw himself into the job with characteristic energy. While his closeness to Muskie was undoubtedly the reason he was acceptable to all sides, Mitchell supplied an attention to detail the party office hadn't seen since Frank Coffin stepped down ten years earlier. By the end of Mitchell's brief tenure—he moved to the DNC in 1968, to further Muskie's national ambitions—he had set new standards for statewide recruiting, platform writing, and communication with party groups and the press.

After Ed Schlick stepped down as executive secretary, the job was filled by Ralph Barnes, Peter Kyros's political director, who then left when Kyros was elected to Congress. Mitchell chose Ed Bonney for the post, who provided stability in the party office, which moved in 1968 from Lewiston to Augusta—and headed the political operation for seven years. Bonney, Cumberland County chair, knew both Curtis and Mitchell, and was working for the W. T. Grant department store when Mitchell offered him a raise to work for the party.

Mitchell hired a third staff member, for legislative research, and was an excellent fundraiser. With Bob Dunfey, owner of Portland's Eastland Hotel, "he raised a lot of money—a lot of money," Bonney said. "I would ask some of the same people for money, and they'd give me money, but not at that level." The Curtis campaign was an early beneficiary. Ed Schlick had founded the "500 Club," for those who'd give at least $500, almost as a joke, but Mitchell took it seriously. The 1968 state convention program listed more than seven hundred members.

Bonney found Mitchell at times too serious, but "admired his ability to think on multiple tracks about a problem . . . Sometimes the resolution is not really evident at first, and you've got to figure out how are we going to get around these people and get what we want. George had a wonderful knack for doing that."

In 1967, Mitchell predicted at a Cumberland County meeting that Democrats would become the "majority party in Maine within the next few years." He said the party had gained an average of 7,300 voters a year since 1954, "because we offered better candidates and better programs," and because of "the failure of the Republican Party to meet its responsibility to the people of Maine." Republicans' complacency, and their rejection of any idea proposed by a Democrat "has resulted in their identification as the party of blind opposition, the party of the status quo." The Democratic Party, he added, "in the position of the underdog, has been the party of innovation, of challenge, of ideas. Our link to the academic community has been strong, and we have not been reluctant to draw upon it." Mitchell also warned against complacency by Democrats. "We must recognize that change is inevitable, and that our task is to accommodate to that change," remembering that "our only standard must continue to be the public interest—not our political interests, not any private interest." The Republican Party "has forgotten this, and they are paying dearly for it now. We cannot permit the Democratic Party to make the same mistake." By 1968, for the first time, Democrats had active committees in all 16 Maine counties.

Mitchell was also the first party chairman to recruit his own successor since Coffin chose John Donovan. Severin Beliveau's ebullient personality was on display from the beginning. Bonney said Beliveau was "very gregarious, he was funny, and he wasn't married at the time." Beliveau chaired the Oxford County committee, was already a successful attorney, and became a State House lobbyist after stepping down from the state committee in 1973. It was his idea to charter a plane to take the entire Maine delegation to the 1968 Democratic National Convention in Chicago, and to host a big party for Muskie as the vice presidential nominee, despite last-minute suspense about whether Hubert Humphrey would actually pick him.

While the national party nearly came to pieces that year, leading to the election of Richard Nixon as president, Maine Democrats were beginning a new period of growth and prosperity, with Beliveau as dealmaker and builder. With the move to Augusta, the party acquired its first real estate,

Home of the Maine Democratic Party from 1968-1976, the federal-style building at 62 State Street in Augusta has since been converted to apartments.

at 62 State Street, and expanded the federal-style residence to accommodate a printing operation producing campaign brochures and constituent mailings for all Democratic legislators, and many county officers as well. Charlie Micoleau, a key Muskie staffer, got his start in the Democratic office, as did Tony Buxton, later Mitchell's campaign manager in his 1974 bid for governor. The staff grew to seven full-time employees, and recruitment efforts attracted young Democrats, both men and women, many just out of school.

ON THE RISE

In 1958, Ed Muskie's plan for a successor went awry, as Frank Coffin declined to run and the Democrat who was elected, Clinton Clauson, served less than a year. In 1966, however, Democrats found a true heir.

Ken Curtis grew up in Curtis Corner, a small hamlet in the town of Leeds, the last of five generations of Curtises, beginning with William Curtis, who moved north from Massachusetts in 1800. They were mostly farmers, and, until the Great Depression, successful ones. Curtis, born in 1931, remembers his childhood as similar to families around him, telling his aide and early biographer, Kermit Lipez, "We were comfortable, but, like a lot of rural families, we didn't have any money, and we didn't have a lot of clothes, or modern cars." There was enough to eat, and his one-room school had a good teacher. "It wasn't bad academically," he said, and when he later attended Cony High School in Augusta, found he was "ahead of the other kids, but socially behind them."

Curtis's first paid work was as school janitor, "when I was hired at a dollar a month. There was no running water, and it was my job to get a bucket of water and pour it into the bubbler for the kids, and to build and tend the wood fire to heat the school building. That was when I started saying, 'You know, there's got to be more to it than this.'" His classmates seemed resigned to small town life, but Curtis was not. It felt like defeatism. "I didn't like the town I was growing up in. I didn't like the conservatism. I didn't like the attitudes . . . and that kind of internal turmoil growing up leads you down the path to some political action." He had an example from his father, Archie, who "was one of 16 Democrats in town," and made no secret of his support for the New Deal and Franklin Roosevelt.

Leeds didn't offer any vocational courses, so Curtis got to attend Cony for free, but switched to the college track after two years. He then decided to attend Maine Maritime Academy in Castine, with free tuition in exchange for a ten-year commitment to the U.S. Naval Reserve. "I'm not saying I was the smartest person in the world, but I figured it would be a lot better to go into the military as an officer than as a buck private," he said.

At Cony, he had chaired "Chizzle Wizzle," the high school's biggest social event—his first elective office—and was a lineman on the varsity football team, despite weighing 145 pounds. He also played football at Maine Maritime, trumpet in the band, and earned money cutting hair with his best friend, Larry Sparta. There was plenty of business because Castine had no barber, and haircuts were required to pass inspection.

Curtis's Navy service began after graduation in 1952, and included a mine detection school in Key West, Florida. After completing active duty, he arrived back in Maine in October 1955. Portland University School of Law's semester had already started, but he didn't stop to apply. "I just walked in and said I would like to sign up," he said. "They thought I was crazy but they let me in."

The GI bill covered tuition, but not expenses, and Curtis worked at Sears, at the office of an admiralty law attorney, and, with a friend, started a short-lived doughnut shop in Wells. "We didn't do very well because we didn't stay open as late as we should have," he said. But he did hire Pauline "Polly" Brown from Kennebunk for the weekend shift; they were married in 1956 while he was still in law school.

Curtis saw his legal degree much as Ed Muskie came to, as an entrée to politics, which began when he sought out Don Nicoll, then Democratic Party executive secretary, for advice. He joined the South Portland Democratic Men's Club, and, after hearing Jim Oliver speak, volunteered. "Next thing I know, I'm driving him everywhere he went," Curtis said.

Oliver was a former three-term Republican congressman from 1937-43 whose unorthodox views, including support for the "Townsend Plan," led to his defeat in the 1942 1st District primary by Robert Hale. Hale was still serving in 1954 when Oliver, now a Democrat, first challenged him, and was running again when Curtis joined his campaign in 1956. Oliver lost that 1st District race by just twenty-nine votes at the same time Frank Coffin won the 2nd District. Oliver was finally victorious in 1958, when he ended Hale's sixteen-year tenure, and he invited Curtis to become his Maine district representative.

The same year, Ed Muskie moved from the Blaine House to the U.S. Senate. Curtis had met him during Muskie's 1956 re-election campaign, and was impressed, calling Muskie "a great speaker for young people. He could explain the political process in a way that was very inspiring . . . He was almost like a teacher. His speeches were really teaching, and I learned an awful lot."

Curtis learned from Oliver, too. "He was an old-school politician who used to talk an awful lot. He used to figure he had to fight for publicity, fight to get mentioned in the papers, and of course you did in those days as a Democrat." Oliver supported public power, increased Social Security benefits, and federal aid to education. "He was a man really ahead of his times politically, and coming from Maine that's very difficult." But after his exclusion from the Republican Party of the 1940s, Oliver couldn't forgive or forget. "He never tried to appeal to Republicans," Curtis said. "Instead, he'd give it to them." When he began campaigning himself, Curtis followed Muskie's example, rather than Oliver's.

Curtis's first political job lasted only two years, with Oliver swept out in the 1960 Republican tide. But Curtis, with assistance from Muskie's Senate office, worked briefly for the Legislative Research Service. Since Curtis never served as a legislator, it provided useful insights, as well as political contacts. Next was a Kennedy administration appointment as Maine director for the Area Redevelopment Administration (ARA), a parallel with Muskie's work for the Office of Price Stabilization. A jobs and economic development program, ARA focused on underdeveloped regions, of which Maine was a prime example. Curtis's statewide travel introduced him to the state's power structure, coordinated by the Republicans, "the utilities, the paper companies, the banks," that Curtis saw as a "stranglehold," but one that "was starting to weaken and give way . . . and you could see some hope of breaking it." Curtis stayed longer than Muskie had at OPS, nearly three years. He found the work rewarding. "I got a tremendous practical education," and, "I learned more in that job than I could have anywhere about the thinking of Maine people and their problems."

Maine lost one of its three congressional seats following the 1960 census, and in the new two-district alignment that pitted two incumbents against each other, the 1st District race was won in 1962 by a liberal Republican, Stan Tupper, who had defeated Peter Garland in a primary—the Republican who had ousted Oliver. Curtis, who was thirty-three, and itching for his own political race, challenged Tupper in 1964.

His announcement sounded themes he would use throughout his political career: "For the past several years I have been working in many economically depressed areas in Maine, and I know that far too often our attempts to grow and expand run headlong into entrenched obstructionism created by political, financial and industrial leaders who promote the status quo for their own selfish interests. Maine workers are the most productive and conscientious in the country, asking only for a day's work and a day's pay. Yet they are rewarded with few jobs and low wages . . . Maine has always been a wonderful place to live and raise a family. Yet its young people are forced to leave to find job opportunities . . . the time has come when special interest groups and political kingmakers can no longer block our progress, control our industrial growth, and dictate wage levels."

Curtis easily won the primary, but, as Kermit Lipez observed, "It is unlikely that Republican leaders . . . feared a candidate who had to be his own driver." While his volunteers were enthusiastic, Democratic Party leaders were not. Curtis said, "Party people looked at me with wonderment, to be polite about it, and rightfully so. I wasn't a very polished candidate. I had a homemade campaign, and Tupper was unbeatable."

Yet Curtis had made an impression with his ARA work, his call to action attracted young people and, when Barry Goldwater won the Republican nomination for president, GOP liberals like Tupper were on the defensive.

Curtis found, though, that he "couldn't get to the left of" Tupper, who had voted for the 1964 Civil Rights Act. Labor unions endorsed Tupper, and the Democratic Congressional Campaign Committee didn't provide significant help. But discontent with the Republican ticket was growing, Curtis gave a strong performance in the single TV debate, and finally, national Democrats provided some support, with ads linking Curtis with Lyndon Johnson and Ed Muskie, who was on his way to his first re-election triumph. The Tupper-Curtis contest was close; a recount gave Tupper a 203-vote margin from more than 190,000 cast. Curtis wasn't disappointed by the outcome. "I didn't think I could beat Tupper," he said. "I ran for Congress because I wanted to run for governor . . . I almost screwed up my plans by winning that seat."

Since Democrats had swept the legislative races for the first time since 1910, they selected the "constitutional officers" — attorney general, secretary of state and treasurer. After his strong Congressional campaign, Curtis had his pick. He considered attorney general, but decided on secretary of state. "You had nothing but controversy as attorney general," he said, but "Who can get upset about you running all over the state talking about highway safety?" And indeed, Curtis became such a traveler, to "any service club or organization that would invite him," that he earned unfavorable attention from Republican House leader Harrison Richardson, who charged Curtis with being "a part-time secretary of state and a full-time candidate for governor," and said "mature Democrats should come forward and curb Curtis's excessive political activity." None did.

PLAN OF ACTION

Harry Richardson wasn't wrong about Ken Curtis's intentions. Curtis openly used his office as a platform to run for governor. He was among the youngest candidates ever, and focused on depicting this as a strength, not a weakness. He was flattered by quiet support from former Governor Percival Baxter, a Republican who'd served from 1921-25, and was better known as donor and founder of Baxter State Park, Maine's wilderness park surrounding Mount Katahdin. Baxter had also welcomed Ed Muskie's 1954 campaign, and wrote many personal notes to Curtis, in one observing, "Since I left Augusta the importance of having a wise and friendly governor is far more important than I realized."

Curtis made an issue of John Reed's lengthy tenure. Since he'd become governor in 1959 through Clinton Clauson's death, then defeated Frank Coffin in a special election, Reed's first three years didn't count toward the constitutional two-term limit. He narrowly defeated Maynard Dolloff in 1962, winning by just 483 votes, and had faced opposition in the 1966 Republican primary from Jim Erwin, who got 37 percent. The issue was more potent then than it might seem today; until Reed, no governor had served more than four years. Had he won again, Reed would have served 11 years. Curtis made the slogan "seven not eleven" memorable to voters.

Curtis's primary was a three-way race against Senate President Carlton "Bud" Reed and House Speaker Dana Childs, who both gave up posts as the first Democratic presiding officers since 1910. Curtis mostly ignored them, campaigning full-time while Reed and Childs were busy at the State House. He took 55 percent of the primary vote, far outdistancing both rivals. Curtis also sensed Republican dominance could again be an effective theme. In his announcement speech, he said, "Years of one-party government in Maine have meant, for the most part, government by drift and indecision, without leadership or direction." His intensity prompted the *Maine Sunday Telegram* to observe, "If there is one emotion that Ken Curtis does not evoke from the voter, that emotion would be indifference. No one, Republican or Democrat, is neutral about Curtis."

Kermit Lipez described Reed as "a lucky politician," and he did seem to lead a charmed life. He was the last Senate president to become governor, and Coffin's challenge had been swamped by Republican turnout. In 1962, he barely beat returning Democrat Maynard Dolloff, who'd won the primary over Dick Dubord of Waterville, former DNC member and attorney general, by just 200 votes. Many thought Dubord would have been a stronger nominee. Still, Reed was just 45, the economy was in good shape, and 1966 was a good year for Republicans nationally.

Curtis said recently, "Part of my problem was I was young, and people doubted whether I had the experience to be governor." He was aware not just of his youth, but of his reputation for impulsiveness, and aimed to moderate his language. "I tried not to be quite so blunt—used special words that depicted thoughtfulness and moderation. My big problem was moderation. At least that's what everybody said." His ultimate answer, though, was the Maine Action Plan, a remarkable campaign document that, through its introduction and ten "points," took a comprehensive look at Maine, its problems, and opportunities for change.

The plan is little known today, in part because it was presented point-by-point, during appearances from Portland to Presque Isle, starting on October 5 and continuing through Election Day; it never appeared between covers. Yet its eighty-seven pages would constitute a short book, and in scope, specificity and imagination, it has never been equaled by any candidate for governor.

The Education section is the first, and longest, point. "From my experience as Maine director of the Area Redevelopment Administration, I am sure that full educational opportunity is a necessary condition to high economic achievement," Curtis wrote. "It is high time to strike at this link between poor education and poverty." Maine then had a 40 percent drop-out rate, and only 30 percent of high school graduates attended college, compared with 50 percent nationally; it lagged all other New England states. The recommendations pointed to "a remarkably close correlation between the annual expenditure of a state per pupil and its ranking in terms of per capita income," and suggested a major increase in state education spending, then 60 percent of the national average. Curtis pushed for regional vocational centers available to all students, and suggested "reorganizing the relationship between the University of Maine and the State Colleges"—a prelude to the University of Maine System, created in 1968.

Curtis presented Labor, Point Three, to the Portland Democratic City Committee on October 15, where he said, "The past has not always been kind to labor in Maine. Although there have been periods . . . when enlightened governors have been friends of labor and far-sighted legislatures have passed progressive legislation, the opposite has generally been the rule." He took aim at the "Estey bill," passed by Republicans under John Reed in 1961, which Curtis said created "untold hardship" by reducing unemployment benefits, and was eventually repealed by Democrats in 1965: "The suffering caused Maine's working men and women during those four years was unnecessary."

The points are nothing if not sweeping. Under Transportation, Point Four, Curtis advocated expanding Interstate 95, then under construction, to four lanes to Houlton; incorporating the Maine Turnpike into the Interstate System and eliminating tolls; and extending an interstate route north to Fort Kent. The first aim has since been achieved; the latter two have not.

In Utilities, Point Five, Curtis said the fledgling Dickey-Lincoln hydro project on the St. John River, just authorized by Congress, had provided "a prospective yardstick" for rates charged by private utilities such as Central Maine Power and Bangor Hydro. He counted on "the prospect of public power to shake them out of their lethargy," but added, "I detect no similar shakeup in the Public Utilities Commission," which, after Muskie's reforms, "has lost its steam; it has become the servant of the utilities rather than the protector of consumers." This was to become a major focus.

Conservation and Natural Resources, Point Seven, was presented in Presque Isle. Curtis highlighted the Allagash Wilderness Waterway, on the ballot that November, and credited Reed with creating municipal conservation commissions. But he faulted Republicans for ignoring water pollution. While predicting ultimate success for Muskie's Clean Water Act in Washington, he said, "Maine must have and will have clean water." To Curtis, the issue was simple: "None of us would live in a filthy house. Yet in many respects we are living amid filthy rivers that are little more than open sewers."

Point 8 opened up a discussion of the elderly that was new at the time. A year after enactment of Medicare and Medicaid by Congress, Curtis pointed out that Social Security retirement benefits averaged only $53 a month in Maine, and he wrote, "Neglect, poverty, loneliness, a feeling of hopelessness, of uselessness, have been the reward of those in later life whose only crime has been to grow old."

Point 10, on state government, concludes the series with a blizzard of recommendations; it was drafted by George Mitchell. It includes points familiar since Frank Coffin's 1954 platform, such as abolition of the Governor's Council, the eighteen-year-old vote, and election of a lieutenant governor. It also drew upon recent party platforms, advocating a Cabinet-style government to replace Maine's maze of state agencies; and appointment by the governor of the attorney general, secretary of state and treasurer. Many features, however, are Curtis's own. He advocated annual legislative sessions and professional management of the State Retirement System. He wanted collective bargaining for state employees, and a forty-hour work week. A line item veto for the governor, expansion of cultural agencies tied to approval of a bond issue for the state library, museum and archives complex, and "home rule" powers for municipalities were all on his list. He proposed consolidation of county jails into the state prison system, and securing discretionary federal grants that then amounted to only $53 per capita in Maine, but $103 in Vermont.

There's one problematic element at the very end, where, discussing financing, Curtis relies on "accelerated growth," administrative efficiencies and increased federal funding. "Financing state government for the next two years without a new major tax will not be easy but I do not feel our economy can stand another new tax at this time," he said. Kermit Lipez concluded that Curtis "was boldly progressive on everything but government spending."

Though there were barbs about John Reed's alleged penchant for ceremony over substance, Curtis depicted a broader contrast between the way the two parties operated: "Republicans generally regard government at any level as an alien force, something to be feared and opposed. We Democrats, on the other hand, look upon government, if properly directed and efficiently operated, as a means to improve the general welfare."

The Maine Action Plan did not receive rave reviews, with some editorial writers, surprisingly, faulting its "lack of specificity" and "threadbare" research. Curtis, however, was convinced it transformed him from a candidate with a fresh face and vigorous campaign style into something more. Making well over one hundred specific recommendations for state government, he drew a strong contrast with Reed, who made no such commitments. Curtis ads soon talked about "The Man with a Plan."

Curtis said recently of the Maine Action Plan, "We got involved in it for political reasons, feeling that we needed to add some depth. But once we got into it, we recognized what an important thing it was, because you were, in an educated way, developing your program, so you already had your platform to run on."

Curtis had another problem: labor union loyalties. Ben Dorsky was still in charge and, once again, he tried to swing the Federated Labor Council behind Reed. He was fiercely opposed by Denis Blais and the textile unions, but he secured the council's recommendation.

Jerry Plante, elected to the House at age twenty-one, had become House clerk in 1964, opposite Ed Pert in the Senate, and offered to help. His research showed that Reed had compiled an "atrocious" labor record, and he produced a Maine Labor Manifesto for the council's convention. Dissenters staged a floor fight, and won, with 2,817 delegates for Curtis and 2,569 for Reed. Plante said, "It proves again that issues and research can overcome anything."

Campaign funding was important to Curtis, but even more vital was the sense working people were behind him. As a neophyte candidate for Congress in 1964, the loss of labor backing wasn't crucial, but as a Democrat seeking to lead the state, it was. As Curtis put it, "It was winning something I wasn't supposed to get that would establish me as a major contender in the minds of voters."

Though in Maine the Kennedys were not quite the golden boys they were elsewhere in the Northeast, Curtis sought out the support of Bobby Kennedy, now senator from New York, who came to Maine on October 31, speaking to a packed house of 3,000 in Portland's City Hall Auditorium. Kennedy said, "Ken Curtis is doing in Maine what John Kennedy did across the country in 1960." Reporters noted the personal warmth of the endorsement, and the comparison to his brother, something Kennedy rarely did.

Polls still showed Reed leading, though with a substantial undecided factor. Reed pressed Curtis about paying for his many ideas, and Curtis held a press conference. His staff's budget review showed there would be enough economic growth to avoid a significant tax increase. Then, in answer to a reporter's hypothetical question about future revenues, he said, "I would favor an income tax."

The answer was candid, reflecting Curtis's beliefs, but ill-timed. Reed pounced, even though he'd earlier signed a sales tax increase, to 4 percent. With headlines blaring, Curtis approved full-page ads headlined, "Curtis Stands Firm Against New Taxes." There was no mention that Curtis was "taking the pledge" for two years, and his 1970 opponent, Jim Erwin, later featured this ad in his attacks.

The election wasn't as close as Curtis anticipated; he got 53 percent, comparable to Muskie's first election, with an 18,000 vote margin. Reed's political career was over, and Curtis became the first Maine governor to serve two four-year terms. The Allagash and state cultural building bonds were approved, and Democrats won both congressional seats. The 1966 ticket, with Curtis, Bill Hathaway and Peter Kyros at the top, was almost uniformly successful. Kyros's campaign was long considered a model, managed jointly by David Flanagan, later Joe Brennan's legal counsel, labor leader John O'Leary, and the candidate's son, Peter Kyros, Jr. There was only one loss. Margaret Chase Smith defeated Elmer Violette for her fourth and final Senate term, but Democrats had three seats in the four-member Congressional delegation.

Legislative losses were sobering, however. Speaker Childs and Senate President Reed had left their posts to run for governor, and Democrats hadn't expected to retain all their gains from 1964. They'd held a commanding 29-5 majority in the Senate, and a comfortable 81-70 edge in the House, but only ten Senate and fifty-six House seats remained. This was a large obstacle for an ambitious governor seeking to carry out many campaign promises.

A ROCKY START

When Ken Curtis became governor, Maine was in many ways closer to the nineteenth century than to the twenty-first. Duane Lockard, whose 1959 book on New England politics remains insightful, said of Maine, "In few American states are the reins of government more openly or completely in the hands of a few leaders of economic interest groups—power, timber, and manufacturing." Writing in 1974, Kermit Lipez identified further obstacles to the Curtis agenda: "The natural opponents of these ruling groups, the workers and the poor, though eager for economic gain, also harbored a suspicion of change that was not shaken by their hostility toward the rich." Seasonal residents "from away" also had an outsized effect. Lipez wrote, "These summer people, many of them wealthy and vocal, have power beyond their numbers. Whenever they see their stake threatened—usually by industry—they can inspire passionate opposition." For Curtis, economic development definitely included industrial development, and his vision encompassed sweeping changes.

His administration got off to a rocky start. Some of the conflict was inevitable. Curtis was seen by Republicans, as Muskie had been, as a young upstart. And Curtis was far more brash; where Muskie was deliberative, Curtis was impetuous. He favored causes unpopular with most Mainers, and rarely chose caution over candor. His inaugural address was highly anticipated.

He told listeners, "I have traveled to every corner of every county in this state. Everywhere I encountered the same conflicting attitudes. I found a genuine appreciation of our Maine way of life; but, at the same time, I found a great concern over the lack of opportunity that seems to go with that way of life. But this need not be so." Addressing the Legislature a few weeks later, he advocated opportunity for every citizen, saying, "The whole of our state cannot know true well-being as long as a part of it is suffering and in want."

Allen Pease, a college professor who served as chief of staff throughout the administration, wrote later, "Curtis assumed office determined that his would be a compassionate administration. Translated into new laws and a new philosophy of service, compassion would become the hallmark of the Curtis years."

Pease was an essential figure. As Maurice Williams had done for Muskie, Pease crafted the budget and efficiently ran the Governor's office. He had some of the cachet of Colby Professor Paul Fullam, the 1954 nominee for U.S. Senate, and Bowdoin's Herbert Ross Brown, so adept at putting together Democratic platforms. Pease studied with Fullam at Colby, where Don Nicoll was a classmate; Nicoll calls Pease "a quintessential public servant." Like Curtis, Pease came from a farming family, born on Pease Hill in Wilton. His "folksy charm" was disarming with lawmakers, while his "penetrating mind" analyzed financial and political problems. Pease had, with John Donovan, co-chaired Curtis's 1966 campaign, laying the groundwork for the Maine Action Plan.

Curtis looked for talent wherever he could find it. Al Mavrinac, a Colby political science professor, worked on legislation. Walter Corey, federal-state coordinator, was from Yale Law School. Other Yale graduates hired by Curtis included Kermit Lipez, who replaced Corey, Andy Nixon and Peter Bradford. Nixon was the point person for numerous energy projects that enlivened Curtis's two terms—Dickey-Lincoln, the hydroelectric dam complex proposed for northern Maine, and several oil refinery plans. Bradford, a sharp observer of the Maine scene, worked on the energy projects, and was delegated by Curtis to shake up the Maine Public Utilities Commission; he later chaired the PUC for Joe Brennan, after serving on the federal Nuclear Regulatory Commission. Another notable staffer was Neil Rolde, press secretary until 1972, when he won a House seat from York, a solidly Republican town, serving 18 years before he ran for U.S. Senate in 1990 against Bill Cohen on a platform of universal health care. A Maine historian, Rolde wrote nearly a dozen books.

Curtis had few Democratic votes in the 1967-68 legislative sessions, and had several Republican adversaries. Harry Richardson, House majority leader, called himself the "designated hit person," though he claimed it was just for show: "I was the one who suggested that Curtis wasn't smart enough to pour piss out of a boot, but actually we worked very closely together." But not at first.

Curtis and Republican lawmakers deadlocked on the budget. Inflation was rising, revenues lagged, and Republicans tried to outflank Curtis by increasing the sales tax to 5 percent. Richardson declared, "The governor wants us to be a caretaker legislature, and we're just not going to be."

Curtis wasn't amused. Saying government reform must precede tax increases, he vetoed the budget. The session dissolved in acrimony. The *Bangor Daily News* said, "The governor and Legislature had one thing in common: partisanship," and the *Sunday Telegram* denounced "six months . . . of name-calling and political infighting." A young, inexperienced governor who'd never served in the Legislature confronted Republican leaders reasserting their prerogatives after two years of minority status.

Curtis knew he had to do better. In addition to his new staff team, Democrats began winning more legislative seats. Although Democrats didn't gain a majority, they neared parity. Curtis also decided to confront the tax issue head-on.

The Curtis administration became known for dramatic increases in local school aid and teacher pay, higher salaries for state employees, founding of the University of Maine System, robust conservation and environmental protection efforts, and more generous benefits in unemployment, worker's compensation and welfare. None of this would have been possible without a state income tax.

TAXING PROGRESSIVELY

As Curtis surveyed prospects for the 1969 legislative session, he knew that the income tax, his own strong preference, had brought down governors elsewhere who advocated or enacted one. Of forty-three states with income taxes, most followed the federal income tax's passage in 1913, or came during the Great Depression, when several states neared default. In New England, Massachusetts's flat-rate tax dates to 1916, followed by Vermont in 1931; Vermont's tax later became progressive, starting in the 1950s. New Hampshire has taxed only interest and dividends since 1923. Maine ultimately became part of a third wave of income tax adoption, along with Rhode Island, Connecticut, Michigan, Illinois, Ohio, Pennsylvania and New Jersey, but Curtis had no way of knowing that.

He met with Ed Muskie, who urged him to accept the Legislature's proffered sales tax increase, based on his own experience as governor. Curtis also had the report he'd commissioned from the Task Force on Municipal and State Revenues in 1967, concluding that "the most equitable and flexible new tax to meet state needs is the combined personal and corporate income tax." He agreed: "Economically, the income tax was the only tax that made any sense for raising money for the future. There was no alternative."

Curtis kept almost all Democrats on board, though it wasn't easy, and he needed many Republicans; as part of "emergency" budget passage, it required two-thirds. When Curtis unveiled his plan, House Speaker David Kennedy was "shocked," while Senate President Ken MacLeod called it "incredible." But other Republicans held their fire.

Harry Richardson became an ally, and the bill's author; he was a strong supporter of the University of Maine, and knew it needed more funding to keep pace with other expanding public university systems. Richardson so angered other Republicans that when Curtis nominated him to the new university system board of trustees, the Governor's Council blocked it.

In the Senate, Curtis convinced Majority Leader Bennett Katz, a reluctant convert, to help. Katz also believed in the university system, and a new Augusta campus for his constituents was included. In later years, Katz sometimes expressed doubts about the income tax, but at its inception, he was essential.

Curtis wanted to make the tax simple, with individuals paying 25 percent of their federal income tax obligation. This backfired when people got the the idea they'd pay 25 percent of their income to the state; Republicans rejected any such link. Richardson devised six brackets, steadily rising from 1 to 6 percent, with the 1 percent applying to adjusted income up to $2,000 and the top rate beginning at income of $50,000. It was a more progressive structure than what exists today, and Curtis liked it. For many years, the sales tax remained the largest source of state revenue, but the income tax financed the expansion of services Curtis championed.

Although the budget initially fell one vote short of two-thirds in both House and Senate, votes were switched, and lawmakers adjourned in a better mood. Curtis, however, knew his greatest test still lay ahead.

DISASTER AVERTED

If the early polls against John Reed in 1966 had been discouraging, those for the 1970 race looked catastrophic. Curtis's opponent in the June primary, Plato Truman of Biddeford, had served a single House term. His signs read, "Stop Curtis Taxes," and his slogan was, "Two great names, one great candidate." Truman got 37 percent, further discouraging Curtis.

In July, he and his wife, Polly, were devastated by the death of their older daughter, Susan, from cystic fibrosis; she was eleven and had just completed fifth grade. The campaigns were briefly suspended. Feeling uncharacteristically adrift, Curtis again met with Muskie, and asked if he should withdraw "for the good of the party." Allen Pease, who attended, remembers Muskie saying, "You have to run. It's the party's responsibility to defend the program." Curtis got back to work.

At times, Curtis seemed to court political trouble. Following the assassinations of Martin Luther King Jr. and Bobby Kennedy in 1968, just five years after John F. Kennedy was killed in Dallas, the National Governors Association asked its members to submit bills complementing federal legislation that banned mail-order sales. Curtis's modest measure was attacked by Republicans, abandoned by Democrats, and denounced by 1,200 sportsmen who attended a public hearing as "confiscation."

Vietnam had fractured Democratic unity in 1968, and Curtis opposed Lyndon Johnson's policies well before his withdrawal from the presidential race. He sympathized with student protesters, and was joined, at a lower rhetorical level, by Bill Hathaway, the 2nd District congressman, who in 1972 used the issue to defeat Margaret Chase Smith, possibly the U.S. Senate's most hawkish member. But Ed Muskie, on the 1968 ticket with Hubert Humphrey, and George Mitchell, state party chair, supported Johnson for what younger Democrats thought was far too long. Still, Curtis's outspokenness on guns and the war was overshadowed by the more pressing matter of state taxes.

Curtis's November opponent was Republican Jim Erwin, John Reed's primary opponent in 1966, now state attorney general. Erwin campaigned on cutting state spending and repealing the income tax, but was first too specific, then not specific enough. Erwin said he'd cut state spending 10-20 percent, details to follow, but they never did. He began hedging, and five days before the election claimed $34 million in "administrative savings," without reducing services. Newspaper editorials lampooned the claim.

Curtis tried a different tack. New York's Republican governor, Nelson Rockefeller, had come under fire for raising taxes from his own party during his 1966 re-election campaign. He focused on what the new funding had achieved. Curtis followed suit, and sketched detailed second term plans. After the summer trials, he was more poised and focused, and scored a clear victory in a September televised debate, while Erwin gave a performance worthy of Burton Cross in 1954—Lipez called it "all starch and wooden gravity."

The Erwin forces then spotlighted Curtis's 1966 ad on taxes, where he appeared to prevaricate, and the governor responded with a five-minute paid ad, arguing that since both parties had agreed taxes needed to be raised, the income tax was fairer than another sales tax increase.

In the Curtis files is a clipping of a letter to the editor making the case perhaps better than he could himself. D. B. Robbins of Rockland asked, "Is honesty the best policy in politics?" and answered that, "If Governor Curtis should lose, it would seem he has been too frank and honest for his own good . . . I don't like the income tax, the pouring of money into the University of Maine and the Maine Maritime Academy," yet "in the face of disaster at the polls, Curtis speaks out and is criticized for telling the truth . . . and for that reason alone, he should be re-elected."

On Election Night, early returns were dead even. The next morning, Curtis had a tiny lead, and with more than 325,000 votes cast, a recount was inevitable. Curtis hired George Mitchell to represent him, and the election night count held. On November 23, Curtis was declared the winner by 890 votes. It was easier for other Democrats, as Ed Muskie's election to a third six-year term carried Bill Hathaway and Peter Kyros to victory in the two House races. Curtis had been fearless, he had survived, and was about to embark on a second term far more productive than his first.

OIL AND WATER

No account of Ken Curtis's tenure would be complete without acknowledging what now seems his eye-opening support for a major hydro-electric dam on the St. John River, in northern Maine, and for an oil refinery in Machiasport, far up the Downeast coast.

Dickey-Lincoln started as an attempt to bring public power to Maine. Ed Muskie had done battle with the electric utilities as governor, and Curtis was determined to find ways to lower Maine's energy prices closer to those of other Northeastern states. As Muskie and Curtis saw it, Maine was doubly disadvantaged. It had missed out on the rural power initiatives of the New Deal. Franklin Roosevelt had been intrigued by the potential of harnessing the Bay of Fundy's tides near his summer home at Campobello, but the project never got off the drawing board. Dickey-Lincoln was itself an alternative to several "high dams" that would have flooded both the Allagash and St. John. It was paired with a revival of the tidal power idea that would together have produced efficient electricity generation.

Maine, by the 1960s, was more dependent on fuel oil for heating than any other state, and prices, as Curtis saw it, were kept artificially high by preferences for domestic oil drilling. Complicated import quotas resulted in Maine prices at least 10 to 15 percent higher than other East Coast states.

Muskie got initial authorization for Dickey-Lincoln in 1965, and the Army Corps of Engineers worked on plans. After Richard Nixon's election, funding dried up, although the economics looked better after the oil price shocks of the 1970s. Legislative attempts, and then a 1973 state referendum led by state Senator Peter Kelley to establish a Maine Power Authority, both failed. In 1980, the Senate witnessed an unusual debate between Maine's two senators, with Democrat George Mitchell trying to advance Dickey-Lincoln, and Republican Bill Cohen emphasizing its taxpayer and environmental costs. At the outset of the Curtis administration, Democrats thought it made good sense to protect the Allagash River, while damming the even more remote upper St. John. Environmental groups later turned sharply against Dickey-Lincoln, and today Mitchell says he's glad the dams were never built.

Curtis's role centered on attempts to site a refinery at Machiasport, near the mouth of the Machias River. Washington County already had the state's highest unemployment rate, as fishing and canneries faded. Curtis assigned Andy Nixon and Peter Bradford to spearhead the effort, and the two became experts in oil industry economics and federal regulatory schemes. Bradford's 1975 book, *Fragile Structures: A Story of Oil Refineries, National Security and the Coast of Maine* tells the whole unlikely saga of millionaire oilmen, Washington politics, and pioneering environmental legislation in exquisite detail.

The developer was Armand Hammer, a swashbuckling industry iconoclast who'd made deals with Vladimir Lenin before the U.S. banned trade with the Soviet Union. Late in life, he made Occidental Petroleum the world's twelfth largest oil company. The Johnson administration was asked to designate a foreign trade zone in Maine to provide oil quota exemptions, and, for a time, the scheme appeared near success. The logical place for the trade zone was Portland Harbor, where tankers had fed pipelines to Montreal since World War II, but no one expected approval of a refinery in Portland, so Machiasport became a subzone.

Curtis, meanwhile, insisted on tough environmental safeguards. In a dramatic special session, lawmakers enacted a Site of Location bill to regulate placement of new industrial facilities—the nation's first such land use law. Oil spill monitoring and cleanup, financed by industry, was also enacted for Portland Harbor, furnishing the model for George Mitchell when, as U.S. Senate majority leader, he pushed through national regulations following the 1989 Exxon Valdez tanker disaster in Alaska. Curtis's environmental planning board later became the Board of Environmental Protection.

The Machiasport plan fell apart when the Johnson administration ended and the Nixon administration withheld support. Armand Hammer's plan was followed by a succession of increasingly farcical attempts to build a refinery. Plans were unveiled for Sanford, Searsport and a wide variety of Washington County sites. The most egregious was the Pittston Corporation's plan for Eastport, on treacherous Cobscook Bay, far less navigable than Machias Bay. Pittston, even in the early days of federal environmental law, was a frequent violator.

The numerous refinery plans were a boon for the new *Maine Times*, which covered hearings extensively, while the daily newspapers mostly ignored them. As Curtis somewhat ruefully noted, Maine never saw any major new coastal industrial development, but enacted some of the nation's toughest environmental laws while anticipating such projects. He always saw it as his responsibility to balance development with environmental protection. Responding to the Sierra Club's opposition to Machiasport, he said, "The poor housing, insufficient education, and present pollution which result in large part from the inadequacy of our present tax base are more of an environmental blight than a modern refinery and terminal operating under the strictest possible regulations."

Curtis ultimately felt vindicated by the OPEC oil embargo of 1973, which drove prices sky-high and led to another state budget crisis in his final year. "It was a foolhardy policy to deplete domestic resources of oil when foreign resources were cheaper and when you could see a time when both foreign resources and domestic resources could become short," he said. Dickey-Lincoln would also have helped, instead of utilities "becoming 70 percent dependent on oil." That was a prime reason behind building the Maine Yankee nuclear plant in Wiscasset, which produced electricity from 1972-96.

BUILDING A LEGACY

As Republicans, and some Democrats, fought against the income tax, business groups were also mobilizing, and qualified a 1971 referendum question for the ballot—the first time voters anywhere could have repealed an income tax already being collected. Curtis reluctantly stayed out of the fight, relying instead on a coalition of school, municipal and citizen groups to make the case for the tax. The issue cast a shadow over the start of his second term, though it didn't deter him, or lawmakers, from enacting sweeping changes to state government, despite the potential loss of $64 million in new revenue. When Election Day arrived, the results were stunning—Mainers rejected repeal by 3-1, casting 190,229 votes for the income tax and just 63,403 against it, an extraordinary turnout for a referendum-only election.

Ed Muskie then kidded Curtis that "the income tax is more popular than you are." Curtis had a simple explanation: "People could see that the tax worked exactly the way we said it would." The primary burden fell on corporations and upper income taxpayers, not on wage-earners. Looking back, Curtis said, "Of all taxes, the income tax . . . was progressive, fair and, most importantly, based on ability to pay . . . Maine's tradition of caring people was at its best when many of its wealthiest gave their support."

Curtis did have one setback on taxes. He endorsed, and the Legislature enacted in 1973, the Uniform Property Tax that effectively merged school assessments into a single statewide rate, regardless of the value of assessed property in each municipality. Critics mobilized a referendum against the tax, claiming it took away local control. The repeal effort succeeded in 1977.

Government reorganization was the keystone to Curtis's last four years, and he had a strong bipartisan cast of allies, who realized that a four-year governor's term might accomplish little if the governor couldn't actually direct the government. "In the past we really had four branches of government," Curtis said. "The executive, the judicial, the legislative, and the state department heads, who were sacred. The governor wasn't supposed to interfere."

In Allen Pease's compendium, *The Curtis Years: 1967-74*, there are two fold-out charts depicting government in 1966, and the structure after reorganization. The first shows a welter of more than 200 independent agencies, many reporting to the Legislature, or to no one. Curtis never had effective control over department heads, though each governor since then has had the benefit of a Cabinet. By 1974, most state services were consolidated to sixteen Cabinet-level departments, a lineup that remains substantially intact. There were hard-fought battles. The Maine Forest Service, once the largest state agency, resisted inclusion in the new Department of Conservation, along with state parks and lands, but lost.

Governor Ken Curtis, official portrait.

Separate departments for Indian Affairs and Manpower Affairs were later eliminated.

Independent agencies remained, some large and important, from the University of Maine System and Maine Turnpike Authority to the Maine State Housing Authority, Municipal Bond Bank, and Maine State Retirement System. Curtis also won legislative approval for several teams within the Governor's office, including the State Planning Office, Federal-State Coordinator, Office of Energy Resources, and Office of State Employee Relations. None remain in their original form. Nor did Curtis have the votes to repeal the Governor's Council; that waited until the Longley administration.

However dazzling these accomplishments might seem, Curtis was always aware of work undone. Allen Pease described the limitations of any administration, saying, "There are lessons to learn: that power unused may be power abused; that one often fails in spite of good intentions; and the public, the press and especially political opponents each interpret the facts of public life quite differently."

Still, Curtis's ability to enact sweeping reforms while working with a Republican Legislature and Governor's Council was impressive. He took his cue from Lyndon Johnson, who bridged a seemingly intractable Democratic divide between southern conservatives and northern liberals. Though Curtis broke with Johnson on the war, he admired his legislative abilities. He said recently that Johnson "knew how to count votes. He knew how many votes he needed, and he knew where they all were. He'd get a Republican to sponsor a bill, and suddenly he had 12 more votes." In the Legislature, Curtis said, "You've got to know those you'll never get, and those you can work with. We romanced the heck out of the people who were interested."

Curtis understood, as Muskie had earlier, that one reason Republican lawmakers were willing to center future authority in the governor's office was that he himself wouldn't run again. "That's fine with me," he said at the time. "These are things that are going to knit the family together and allow the next governor to walk into a much more workable situation than I found."

Reorganization was just the start. Considering the loggerheads lawmakers and the governor reached in 1967, their performance during Curtis's last session, from 1973-74, was remarkable; he vetoed only one bill. Like Muskie, he convinced lawmakers to amend bills to meet his objections. Even after bills reached his desk, "in many instances the legislative leadership simply recalled the bills," he said.

The scale of Curtis's legislative accomplishments remains staggering. A complete list takes many pages in *The Curtis Years*. He delivered ten special messages to the Legislature on programs he wanted enacted, most preceded by a study group or task force with detailed recommendations.

Among the many agencies and programs that began during the Curtis administration are the Maine Public Broadcasting Network, Land Use Regulation Commission, Department of Environmental Protection, Human Rights Commission, and Capitol Planning Commission. Curtis led a dramatic expansion of state parkland and public recreation. He advanced municipal sewage treatment plants even before the federal Clean Water Act; passed consumer finance regulation and established a new consumer protection office; and launched the "circuit breaker" property tax relief program. Statewide shoreland zoning regulations were enacted, and Coastal Zone Management rules were adopted.

Curtis undertook Corrections reform, finding that "the traditional system of incarceration and punishment of the public offender has been a failure, and an expensive one." Pre-release and work release centers were added, the Women's Correction Center in Skowhegan was closed and relocated to Hallowell's Stevens School, and average confinement for males was reduced from nine to six months. Inmates in the state system dropped from 1,029 to 695, a 32 percent reduction.

General fund bond issues were a vital part of Curtis' programs; forty-five bond issues went to voters in eight years, with more than three quarters approved. The largest, $50 million for pollution control, passed in 1969.

Public employment and spending increased markedly, fueled by the baby boom that increased school enrollment. Students attending kindergarten through high school increased by 20,000 and teachers by 2,600. Enrollment in higher education rose by 4,000, with out-of-state tuition students increasing nearly 50 percent. More than 2,000 state government jobs were added.

Richard Barringer, who came to Maine as the first director of Parks and Lands for Curtis, served as Conservation commissioner for James Longley, and State Planning Office director for Joe Brennan—all positions created under Curtis. He took Curtis's measure in 2013: "It is fair to say that no person is more responsible for the government we enjoy in Maine today, and that some would seek to dismantle. When he became governor . . . Maine ranked at or near the bottom among 50 states in virtually every important indicator of social, economic, and racial well-being; in economic diversity, in personal income, in education attainment, in spending on public education, in social services, in transportation, and in regulation of environmental excess and abuse. All this would change for the better during his term of office, in large part due to the force of his personal character and his ambition for all Maine people."

CENTER STAGE

The Curtis years saw increased prominence for many other Maine Democrats. Ed Muskie shrugged off his rough start with Senate Majority Leader Lyndon Johnson to use his seemingly obscure set of committee assignments in building an impressive resume, culminating in landmark environmental legislation. As early as 1964, he was mentioned for vice president, and in 1968 got the call from Hubert Humphrey. Amid the split over Vietnam and a disastrous convention in Chicago, Muskie helped bring the Democratic ticket back from the brink of oblivion. Though Humphrey and Muskie fell short to Richard Nixon and Spiro Agnew, the senator from Maine emerged with his reputation enhanced; Senate Majority Leader Mike Mansfield said that, had Muskie been atop the ticket, Democrats "would have won." President Kennedy's speechwriter Richard Goodwin, who later wrote Muskie's "election eve" talk to the nation in 1970, said he "was the only guy who didn't sound like a political hack."

Later that year, Muskie passed up running for Senate majority whip, second in command to Mansfield, even though he had the votes. He was already thinking about a presidential race. Instead, Ted Kennedy got the job, but his less-than-stellar performance led to his ouster by Robert Byrd of West Virginia, a much more conservative Democrat, in 1970, and it was Byrd who became majority leader in 1976. Had Muskie focused on Senate advancement, he might have been the first Maine Democrat to lead the Senate, rather than George Mitchell.

Muskie's campaign for president in 1972 was less fortunate. His inability to raise significant money before federal campaign financing became available, post-Watergate, was a major problem. Muskie's calm, reasoned demeanor didn't appeal to an increasingly radicalized student movement, in the first election where eighteen-year-olds voted. And his early campaign efforts were undermined by the Nixon-Agnew forces, though the scale of the disruption has never been fully plumbed. Still, Muskie performed on the national stage in a way that made most Mainers proud. Ken Curtis observed about 1972, "I don't see him as a failure. I see him as a finalist. He earned tremendous acclaim for a senator from a small state."

Another up-and-coming senator from Maine was Bill Hathaway, in 1972 defeating Margaret Chase Smith, who'd achieved near-legendary status during four terms in the Senate. From a working class family in Massachusetts, and a decade younger than Muskie, Hathaway served in the Army Air Corps and was a brilliant student at Harvard and Harvard Law. He started in Frank Coffin's office, who called him an "able and astute lawyer." Hathaway also followed Coffin's path in running for Congress in 1962, and, after falling just short to incumbent Republican Clifford McIntire, chaired the Maine Democratic Party for the next two years, as he prepared for his next campaign. In 1964, with McIntire running, unsuccessfully, against Muskie in his first re-election bid, Hathaway easily defeated Republican Ken MacLeod. Hathaway then served four House terms before embarking on his Senate challenge to Smith.

At one time, Hathaway was seen as likely to inherit Muskie's mantle. He was more outspokenly liberal, and the two clashed as early as the 1968 Democratic Convention in Chicago, when Hathaway attempted to block the Maine delegation from nominating Muskie as a "favorite son." Hathaway backed down, but there was a sense of rivalry, especially after Hathaway moved to the Senate and Maine was represented, for the first time, by two popularly elected Democratic senators.

The same year Hathaway won his Senate seat, a Democratic stalwart from Van Buren, Elmer Violette, suffered a bitter defeat at the hands of Republican Bill Cohen in his attempt to succeed Hathaway in the 2nd District. Violette's father was a log driver on the St. John River, then a grocery store owner and three-term legislator. In 1942, when he was just twenty-one, the minimum age, Violette succeeded his father, but had to resign after being drafted. Following World War II, he returned to the House in 1946, where he met Ed Muskie and stayed just one term.

Violette, with a law degree from Boston University, was among the wave of Democratic state senators elected in 1964, where he helped preserve the Allagash, and testified in Washington in favor of Dickey-Lincoln. He ran against Margaret Chase Smith in 1966, appearing frequently with Ken Curtis and getting 41 percent of the vote; he also worked on Muskie's vice presidential campaign. In later years, Muskie considered recommending him for a new judgeship in Maine's Federal District Court, even though the post seemed designed for George Mitchell, who was selected. Violette was appointed by Curtis to the Superior Court in 1973, after his nomination to chair of the Maine PUC was blocked by the Governor's Council. He ended his career on the Maine Supreme Judicial Court.

The 1972 defeat pained Violette; he was the early favorite and thought he should have won. But Republicans outraised Democrats by 2-1, and Violette witnessed a new form of campaigning, as Cohen's youthful energy, campaign consultants, and fundraising took hold. "Campaigns were becoming less and less unified," Violette told an interviewer. "It was the man and not the party . . . up front." Violette's defeat came amid less than universal support in Lewiston, showing cracks in the Democratic base.

Another Franco from the St. John Valley began his legislative career during these years. John Martin, like Violette and Severin Beliveau, traced his roots to the Acadian migration from defeated French Canada, and not the Quebecois farmers who worked in the mills. The Acadians were less socially conservative than the Quebecois, and politically better established in their communities, and more self-confident. Like Violette,

Martin followed a relative into the Legislature, at age twenty-three in 1964, but stayed for much longer than a single term.

At the time, legislators from Aroostook County generally served few terms. Even though sessions were shorter, serving at the distant State House was a big sacrifice, and few could pull it off. Martin, as an ambitious young House member, found a way. He taught high school, and later at the University of Maine at Fort Kent, and, during summer months, worked for Ed Muskie's Senate office in Washington. Martin was staying with Don Nicoll's family in suburban Maryland while Nicoll accompanied Muskie on his national campaign tour, and was able to regale the family with the latest developments over the dinner table.

Like Muskie a generation earlier, Martin seemed marked for advancement. He got significant committee assignments—Democrats were more numerous than in Muskie's day—and he ran against Louis Jalbert for floor leader in 1970, pitting the Franco past against the Franco future. Martin won by two votes. Jalbert, with his lifetime of political baggage, was eclipsed, and John Martin began his rise.

THE GENERAL WELFARE

During the 1974 campaign for governor, it wasn't unusual to hear Mainers say they wished they could vote for Ken Curtis again; the two-term limit was taking effect. No governor who's sought re-election since then has been defeated. Curtis could have run for Congress—there was no Senate seat available—but he had no interest. He wanted a break from politics, and created a law practice, now known as Curtis Thaxter Stevens Broder & Micoleau.

Of all the initially unpopular causes Curtis fought for—the income tax, gun restrictions, opposition to the Vietnam War—perhaps the most enduringly controversial was his attempt, mostly successful, to increase welfare benefits to levels closer to those of other New England states, what Kermit Lipez called "the constantly exploited welfare issue."

Curtis said, about his objective: "We're so far below the standard of what we need in Maine that we don't have the luxury to kick welfare around. Sure, there are abuses of the system, but there really aren't that many. And if you eliminate all of those you still haven't solved the problem. You're better off focusing your time on trying to solve the problems than focusing on the 2 or 3 percent who are abusing the system."

He also believed Maine possessed the means. In the Maine Action Plan, he wrote, "The social cost of crime, poverty and sickness dwarfs the marginal funds that must be raised by the state for the programs I propose. We can no longer afford to ignore the disadvantaged who live among us. In short, our social, economic, and religious values compel us to the same conclusion: We are our brother's keeper, and consequently, we must help those who cannot help themselves."

It was to be forty-four years after Curtis's first campaign before Maine elected a governor who preached and practiced the opposite.

DECLINE

FOUR

Prosperity

1974-1986

"Every successful politician values his or her own independence, and will insist upon that independence."
— Kermit Lipez, Interview

Violet Pease had been Democratic Party vice chair when she succeeded Severin Beliveau as chair in 1973. The recruiting tour for candidates, from the Legislature to county offices, had reached its peak. "We went to every town in the whole state," she said. "We went to Aroostook, we went to Washington County, and it was like a county meeting. We'd present issues and talk about campaigning, and of course hope to secure some- one then and there that might be interested in running, and telling them what we could do for them and what it's all about to be a candidate . . . We really managed to fill every position. It had never been done before."

The 1974 election closely followed the resignation of President Rich- ard Nixon, and was turbulent, both in Maine and the nation. In the pri- mary for governor, Democratic voters chose from a field probably un- equaled in either party, featuring four well-qualified candidates—George Mitchell, Joe Brennan, both living in greater Portland; state Senator Peter Kelley, from Caribou; and Lloyd LaFountain of Biddeford, former York County attorney and U.S. Attorney. Each of them could have been a capable governor. Brennan, given his experience as Cumberland County attorney—where he hired Mitchell as an assistant—and in the Legisla- ture, where he'd served as Senate minority leader, was the presumed front-runner. Mitchell had helped manage Ed Muskie's two national campaigns, and was nearly elected Democratic National Committee chairman in 1973, but his political profile in Maine was low, largely con- fined to Portland and his native Waterville.

Mitchell was meticulously organized, however, and got to know every county and most town chairs. By the time of the state convention, he'd won support from the greatest number of delegates. He translated that backing into a surprisingly easy primary victory, with 38 percent—10,000 votes more than Brennan, who finished just ahead of Kelley. For the first time, Democrats nearly reached parity with Republicans in turnout, with 87,612 votes cast against 96,794 for Republicans.

The Republican primary ended bitterly, with Jim Erwin, who'd challenged Governor John Reed four years earlier, beating Harry Richardson, Ken Curtis's legislative antagonist, by 1,351 votes. It wasn't a margin likely to be reversed by a recount, but Richardson insisted on one, making clear his disdain for the party's nominee.

George Mitchell seemed perfectly positioned, but he was not the candidate he later became, during his extraordinary comeback in the 1982 U.S. Senate race. In 1974, as he himself admitted, he had a hundred position papers, but didn't pick a few key issues, a method that had served Muskie and Curtis so well. As someone who grew up "literally at the bottom," along the stinking Kennebec River in Depression-era Waterville, Mitchell had transformed himself, building on his experience in Muskie's Washington office, after joining the Portland legal fraternity. A newspaper profile observed, "Mitchell's image remains that of the neat, unruffled lawyer with a briefcase," while Joe Brennan was "the big-hearted Democrat who'd use government to cure all ills, including the common cold."

The key factor was not even in view, however, until after the primaries. Jim Longley, a conservative Democrat from Lewiston, was a successful insurance agent who regularly joined the Million Dollar Round Table; he'd insured thousands of Mainers. He backed Muskie, and fancied himself a close friend of Ken Curtis. As a governor implementing ambitious new programs during the first 1970s bout of inflation, Curtis felt pressure to contain costs, and launched the Maine Management and Cost Survey, later known as the Longley Commission.

Longley wasn't Curtis's first choice, and the governor thought he'd extracted a pledge from Longley that he wouldn't use the commission as a platform for political office. Yet that's exactly what he did. When Longley insisted on what Republican legislative leaders thought were highly unrealistic savings estimates, he started running against the "professional politicians" and "entrenched bureaucrats," filing as an independent. He didn't stop until he left the Blaine House four years later. Because he had commissioned it himself, Curtis felt constrained to praise Longley's work, noted recommendations the Legislature had adopted, and said nothing about the eye-popping savings Longley predicted.

Many close to Curtis were surprised he picked Longley and then trusted him to stay out of politics. Some described the decision as "naïve." Curtis called it his "biggest mistake," and the presence of a

Democrat, and a recently former Democrat, together on the ballot for governor created an unfortunate dynamic that's been repeated many times since. Still, Vi Pease felt comfortable, after the primary, saying, "In Maine our political system has never witnessed an independent win any major election, and I don't expect there'll be much change this year." Longley was the first independent governor elected anywhere since North Dakota in 1936, and national reporters wondered if it would spawn a trend.

Mitchell was hindered by other factors. Post-Watergate, Jim Erwin's candidacy sank like a stone. Never popular with the rank-and-file, he was hampered by Republican infighting. Joe Sewall of Bangor, about to become Senate president, was among those who began seeing Longley's attractions. Mitchell and Erwin ignored Longley, even during televised debates, but this cost Mitchell more votes, even though he still led the final polls. He misread the situation in Lewiston, whose voters produced Longley's winning margin. Socially conservative Francos there were upset about the "culture wars" then raging, and with mills shutting down, the union vote wasn't what it was when Muskie ran for governor.

Mitchell responded tepidly to Gerald Ford's unconditional pardon of Nixon, while Longley denounced it. This was also the first gubernatorial election without the "Big Box" for party-line voting, a feature that once buttressed Republicans, but might have helped Mitchell. In the end, Longley's confident demeanor, and promises of cost-cutting efficiency in government—and perhaps fatigue with Ken Curtis's activism—won out.

Mitchell's wasn't the only surprising defeat. Four-term Congressman Peter Kyros lost by 680 votes to Republican David Emery, a twenty-six-year-old legislator, supposed to be another sacrificial lamb, who instead scored a huge upset in a year when, nationally, Republicans lost forty-eight House seats. Kyros, however, had a primary opponent in every election, and, though an effective representative, had flaws. One was his habit of insisting on his own intelligence, which didn't wear well with voters. Another was that he "went Washington," enjoying a little too openly the perquisites of power.

Earlier, Kyros was considered a likely candidate for governor in 1974. Columnist Jim Brunelle wrote of Kyros, "I have never known a public figure so bitterly disliked by his partisan comrades," with "an unfailing knack for rubbing people the wrong way." Yet Emery's campaign shows how little distance there was between these nominees on the issues. In October, Emery said, "I favor a comprehensive national health insurance program that would cover costs of hospitalization, surgery, medicines, examination and treatment by doctors, and convalescent care. Medicare for the elderly and Medicaid for low-income families should be incorporated into the system."

THE LONGLEY YEARS

Jim Longley was an inveterate letter-writer whose screeds filled many single-spaced pages, and whose syntax left recipients baffled. The transition was especially painful for Curtis, who received many missives about the impropriety of signing contracts or spending money before the governor-elect took charge. Things didn't improve when Longley took office.

Longley was a dynamic campaigner, but devoted little time or attention to what he'd do after assuming office. He asked Allen Pease, who'd intended to return to teaching, to help with the transition, and then to become State Planning Office director, a position that would later assume great significance. Nonetheless, Pease realized he was in for a rough ride, saying of Longley, "He really intimidated people, including people in the Cabinet." Longley decided to hold Cabinet meetings at 7 a.m., "not to take time out of your busy schedule," but that was just the beginning. He called department heads often, and always wanted to know where they were. "Big brother was watching you," was Pease's assessment.

Longley was the beneficiary of Curtis's creation of a Cabinet, but a key point had been finessed. While governors now could nominate commissioners, they couldn't fire them except for cause. Longley decided to ask the entire Cabinet for undated letters of resignation. One of them, Roberta Weil, commissioner of Business Regulation, refused. Described as "confident, keen, aggressive, independent and committed," Weil, appointed by Curtis, was the first woman to hold a Cabinet position in Maine; she was married to Gordon Weil, an experienced Democratic hand in Augusta and Washington, who later was a key adviser to Governor Joe Brennan. After months of harassment, Weil left, though she later became director of the Maine State Retirement System. Future governors were allowed both to hire and fire.

Longley's first formal Blaine House meeting with legislative leaders and lobbyists, in March, was a disaster. Incensed by a leak to reporters that one of his Cabinet picks had been paid before taking up his duties, he startled the gathering by saying, "Anyone who would leak such a thing to the press without foundation is, to use the street jargon, a pimp." When House Majority Leader Neil Rolde, Curtis's former press secretary, expressed incredulity, asking "Are you calling legislators pimps?" Longley's response was "If the shoe fits, wear it."

Things never really improved, and by the end of Longley's term, lawmakers were routinely overriding his vetoes, sometimes on important issues, such as an income tax increase well beyond the levels Curtis and Republicans agreed to in 1969. Aiming to increase school subsidies and teacher pay, the School Finance Act of 1976 added two new tax brackets and raised the top rate from 6 percent to 10 percent.

One day, Longley found an unwelcome guest in his office, a Republican banker from Bangor. Longley threw him out, and decided to lock the door, reversing the policy of Ken Curtis and most of his predecessors. Longley later compromised with a half "Dutch door," locked, which is still there, adjacent to the governor's inner office.

Longley did have press conferences, but they, too, were hostile encounters. One persistent reporter questioned Longley's decision to order a Lincoln Continental limousine to replace the Plymouth sedan Curtis had used—it seemed incongruous with Longley's cost-cutting reputation. After several stories, the limousine was returned and Longley used the Plymouth.

While Longley gave large raises to his closest aides, he attacked "the bureaucracy" at many points. Staff at the Department of Economic Development, which Curtis had retooled, was cut from 44 employees to nine. Longley locked horns with Don McNeil, the chancellor of the University of Maine System, who later departed, and he insisted on reducing funding to the fledgling seven-campus system, from which—by some estimates—it has never recovered. While agreeing that the university cuts were "the most lasting damage" from the Longley years, Don Nicoll said that Longley "did not so much reverse the Curtis program, as disrupted it."

Without a party, Longley in 1976 tried endorsing a variety of independents, Republicans and a few Democrats. Most lost, however, including his sister, Connie, running for a Lewiston Senate seat. Longley remained popular with his base, and, as the nation's only independent governor, got frequent attention from the national press corps. He completed his political evolution by registering as a Republican.

Democrats never quite believed Longley's promise to run for only a single term, and in his last year as governor, Longley often hedged. It was not until the filing deadline passed that speculation ended. Longley had been given a cancer diagnosis, which became terminal. He died in August 1980, less than two years after leaving office.

MARTIN TAKES CHARGE

Though the 1974 election was a big setback for Democrats at the top of the ticket, there was one big winner: John Martin, who had led the House caucus for four years, and now became House speaker, beginning an unprecedented nineteen-year run. Before Martin, no presiding officer in either House or Senate had served more than eight years. For only the third time in the twentieth century, Democrats achieved a legislative majority, and this time it was lasting. In the forty-four years since, House Democrats have been in the minority only once, from 2010-12.

Martin was later resented for his unyielding grip on power, but in the beginning he benefitted from the wave of young Democrats, energized by their opposition to the Vietnam War, who ran for, and won, many House seats. They were likely the difference in his narrow victory in the 1970 contest for minority leader against Louis Jalbert, "making Martin the first Maine politician whose success can be traced to the politics of protest," as one observer put it.

In some respects, the situation invited Martin's moves to centralize power. With an independent governor who had poor relations with both parties, Martin had a free hand in reshaping his own office. In 1982, Democrats won a majority in the Senate as well, and Martin's authority grew apace. He substantially increased both partisan and non-partisan staff. For the first time, the Legislature had teams of non-partisan professionals, staffing both the fiscal office and policy office, increasing the Legislature's influence and making it less dependent on the Executive Branch. Martin also assumed from the state party the function of recruiting House candidates, which led to the separation of legislative campaigns from top-of-the-ticket races. The post-Watergate creation of political action committees provided another means of influence, through the "leadership PACs" most legislative leaders still use to donate to other campaigns.

Following the Curtis Cabinet reforms, however, Martin found he had less influence than some of his predecessors, such as Louis Jalbert during his long tenure on the Appropriations Committee. The Executive reorganization removed the tight links between legislative committees and the state agencies reporting to them, and the lobbyists focused intently on Governor's offices as much as legislators.

Ken Curtis had succeeded in changing the Legislature's biennial meetings to annual sessions, and special sessions were regular occurrences. Curiously, annual sessions never led to annual budgets. The change took effect in the middle of his administration's last biennial session, and the replacement budget caused such confusion the effort was dropped. Then, in the Longley administration, annual budgets were abandoned. Martin won significant increases in legislative pay during the second Brennan administration. Once nearly on a par with New Hampshire, which pays lawmakers $100 per year, plus expenses, Maine now offers a higher salary, and benefits, though lawmaking is still paid as a part-time job.

Legislative sessions were also extended, to mid-June the first year, and late April in the second, which had fateful consequences. Because legislation voted on less than ninety days from a session's end must be passed as "emergency," it's taken two-thirds of both chambers to enact the biennial budget, though subsequent "supplemental" budget bills are often passed by a simple majority.

REPUBLICAN REVIVAL

The 1978 election saw the arrival on the national stage of a Republican who seemed to embody what Frank Coffin foresaw when he said the Democratic Party's rebirth, starting in 1954, had "changed the whole cast of Maine politics, and improved both the Democrats and the Republicans."

Bill Cohen had run a skillful and novel campaign in 1972 against Elmer Violette for the 2nd District Congressional seat vacated by Bill Hathaway, who was making his successful Senate run against Margaret Chase Smith. Republicans took note of more conservative Democrats offended by the radical anti-war movement and student rebellion against conventional morality, which displaced the "regulars," and led to the nomination of George McGovern that summer. They were members of the "silent majority" Richard Nixon wove into speeches, and who, a few years later, were described as "Reagan Democrats."

Nixon's "Southern strategy" to turn conservative Democrats into Republican voters had at least a faint echo in Maine. Cohen didn't carry Lewiston, but he won enough votes in the Democratic stronghold to score a convincing win at a time when there were fewer Republicans in the 2nd District than the 1st. Some Democrats, early on, thought Cohen campaigned more like a new-wave Democrat than a traditional Republican. He leaped from high school basketball stardom and a seat on the Bangor City Council into congressional politics, and sometimes said one reason he became a Republican is that there was more room for advancement; he was thirty-two when he went to Washington.

Cohen then achieved the near-miraculous feat of becoming a household name as a freshman when, on the House Judiciary Committee, usually a backwater, he cogently grilled Nixon administration witnesses during the Watergate hearings, then voted for articles of impeachment against a president of his own party. His Watergate performance, Cohen later confided, ended his chances for advancement in his Senate caucus, but made him among Maine's most reliable vote-getters, setting the pattern for later successful Republicans, including John McKernan, Olympia Snowe, and Susan Collins. When Cohen moved to Washington, he shared a house with Bill Hathaway, and the two became as friendly as representatives of different parties can be.

Cohen considered running against Ed Muskie for what proved to be Muskie's last campaign, re-election to a fourth term, in 1976; early polls were encouraging. Cohen did nothing to discourage speculation, and said he'd decide by year's end. On January 2, he called Muskie, his fellow delegation member, to say he wouldn't challenge him. Cohen had spent a weekend at a Maine ski resort and found himself thinking about a passage from *Zen and the Art of Motorcycle Maintenance*, a counter-cultural classic, that suggested to him that "You can achieve your ambitions, just not at the top of the mountain. Most of life takes place on the side." The dalliance with a Muskie challenge led directly to what some thought was Cohen's more likely objective: a race against Hathaway, who was seeking his first Senate re-election in 1978.

Hathaway had been in Washington for fourteen years, but got mixed reviews from other Democrats. Leon Billings, Muskie's last chief of staff, provided a harsh assessment, saying Hathaway "gave away his seat," through neglect of his Senate duties and lackluster campaigning. It might have been that, given his friendship with Cohen, Hathaway didn't take the challenge seriously enough, or respond to the new campaign techniques Cohen pioneered.

As he had in the 1972 race against Elmer Violette, Cohen adroitly turned several issues without an obvious partisan slant to his advantage. He criticized the Dickey-Lincoln project, which Muskie and Hathaway backed to bring low-cost public power to Maine, as a boondoggle and environmental disaster. He stood four-square against a claim by Maine's Indian tribes to some two-thirds of the state, based on rediscovery of a 1795 federal law that appeared to maintain their land titles in perpetuity. Many Democrats were more sympathetic to the tribes, and, on a presidential visit, Jimmy Carter spoke about settling the case, suggesting $40 million could do it. The cautious response, as one Democratic staffer put it, "was to welcome the visit but not comment on the offer." Hathaway embraced it, though, alienating voters. Hathaway lost in a landslide, getting just 34 percent to Cohen's 57 percent. An independent, Hayes Gahagan, took 7 percent.

BRENNAN'S COMEBACK

For Democrats, the 1978 governor's race turned out to be a better opportunity. George Mitchell, the 1974 nominee, focused on trying again for a long time. He passed on running for Congress in 1976, when freshman 1st District Congressman David Emery would presumably be ripe for a challenge, as did Joe Brennan, although seven Democrats did enter, with Rick Barton losing to Emery in November. Mitchell recalls meeting his old colleague and recent rival at the Roma restaurant in Portland to discuss the race. When Brennan said he was in, Mitchell decided he was out; he then accepted appointments from Jimmy Carter as U.S. attorney in 1977 and federal judge in 1979, on Muskie's recommendation, and told a friend, "my political career is over."

Brennan, after falling short to Mitchell, was undeterred, and his political career was about to make a major advance. He grew up in an Irish Catholic neighborhood on Munjoy Hill in Portland. With a political biography that became well known across the state, he was the first Maine governor to grow up in a homogenous immigrant neighborhood. Both his parents emigrated from Ireland—a northern branch of a movement that brought tens of thousands of Irish families to Boston, and forever changed the political life of Massachusetts.

The Portland community was smaller, but equally cohesive. Brennan, the fifth of eight children, grew up in a Kellogg Street tenement—he still lives nearby—and attended Catholic schools before entering the University of Maine School of Law. His political career reflected both the strengths and insularity of a tight-knit ethnic community, but he says he never encountered any overt prejudice until he applied to teach at Oxford High School, where the superintendent asked if he intended to proselytize non-Catholic students—though he got the job anyway. As an adolescent, Brennan played pool, took bets and could easily have fallen in with the "wrong crowd." It gave him a life-long appreciation of the struggles of working people, and the role of public policy, from criminal justice to human services, in improving their lives.

Brennan's main competition in the 1978 primary came from Phil Merrill, who had made a mark in the state Senate after Brennan left in 1974 to run for governor. Merrill competed for Brennan's former Senate seat, defeating George Mitchell's aunt, Jane Kilroy, in the primary. Kilroy held a Portland House seat even when Republicans dominated city politics, and Merrill said of other potential candidates, "they figured they couldn't beat Jane." Merrill was young—just thirty-three—and progressive, in the Curtis mold. Curtis was then serving, unhappily, as Democratic National Committee chairman at Jimmy Carter's behest. He made it clear, without a formal endorsement, that he favored Merrill over Brennan, departing from Muskie's neutrality. Based on his 1974 showing, Brennan figured to have the inside track, but Curtis's swerve "put a chill" on his prospects, said one Brennan insider.

Merrill also objected to Brennan's determination, as attorney general, to continue to litigate the Indian land claims rather than pursue a settlement. In an interview he gave in 2000, Merrill said he was popular with the "Muskie wing," contrasted to older constituencies, the ethnic Catholics, who Merrill said were so devoted to Brennan that, after 1974, he never lost a primary, spanning seven more races for governor and federal office. Brennan beat Merrill handily, taking 52 percent of the vote to Merrill's 36 percent, and Democrats pulled even with Republicans in total primary votes. But the Brennan-Merrill rivalry was to take a toll on party unity far into the future.

After the 1974 election, Brennan had won the important consolation prize of attorney general, which Democrats selected for the first time since 1964; Mitchell deferred here, too. Jim Erwin had tried to use the attorney general position as a stepping stone, and fell just short to Curtis in 1970. Brennan was successful in large part because of his vigorous legal brief against the Indian land claims. His approach blunted arguments that, with his strong anti-war stance and sponsorship of progressive legislation, he was "too liberal."

Brennan was also helped by the presence—the only time it's happened since Longley's 1974 success—of a Republican-leaning independent. Herman "Buddy" Frankland, a charismatic evangelical minister, had built a Baptist "megachurch" in Bangor with 3,000 members, and 14 buses drawing parishioners from the inland "Bible belt." Frankland urged Longley to run again, and when Longley declined, laid claim to his voters. The Republican in the race, Linwood Palmer, was a quiet, moderate former legislator who won respect but few votes. Frankland, like Longley, was endorsed by the *Bangor Daily News*, and took 18 percent. Brennan was the easy winner, with 48 percent against Palmer's 34 percent. Shortly after, Frankland was accused of adultery with a choir member, and faded from view.

A PLUM APPOINTMENT

In May 1980, a little more than a year after taking office, Joe Brennan was confronted with a decision that shaped his legacy, and reshaped the Maine Democratic Party. Ed Muskie decided to leave his Senate seat to become Jimmy Carter's Secretary of State, and for the first, and so far only time, a Maine governor appointed a U.S. senator. Though the track record for "replacement" senators winning election wasn't promising, unlike most states, Maine has no special election provisions, so Brennan's choice would have 2½ years to serve.

For most Democrats, the obvious choice was Ken Curtis. Since serving as governor, he'd been DNC chair and ambassador to Canada. Brennan, however, told Muskie at a private meeting at Brunswick Naval Air Station that he wouldn't pick Curtis. Curtis had favored Phil Merrill in 1978, and Curtis and Brennan had sharply contrasting views of the Indian land claims case. It was a third point, that saw Brennan "really heated," said Kermit Lipez, recalling a meeting Curtis backers had with Brennan.

Morris Pilot, a Bangor District Court judge, appointed by Curtis in 1966 and reappointed by Longley in 1973, sought another term from Brennan in 1980, who decided the judge didn't measure up. A *Bangor Daily News* reporter called Curtis in Canada, and, apparently without mentioning the controversy, got Curtis to say he generally reappointed judges when asked. Brennan found the resulting headline embarrassing, and perhaps for all these reasons, looked elsewhere.

Brennan adviser Gordon Weil advocated a "placeholder" appointment of James Russell Wiggins, retired editor of the *Ellsworth American* and *Washington Post*, whom Brennan knew and liked. The "placeholder," Weil said, would allow Brennan to run in 1982. Governors elsewhere had appointed themselves, but that wouldn't work in Maine. "People wouldn't stand for that," he told Brennan. "They'd never re-elect you." Weil soon found that Brennan had already focused on George Mitchell. Weil continued to get calls from others, including Bill Hathaway, but could see Brennan had decided: "Once he made up his mind, he didn't change it." Brennan did eventually run for Senate, though not until 1996, ten years after leaving the Governor's office.

Brennan and Mitchell had worked together when Brennan was Cumberland County attorney. They jointly prosecuted two Portland police officers who'd beaten up a suspect, a case that produced threats, and a bullet—fired into Brennan's home—that landed on the bed where his young daughter was sleeping. The rivals from 1974 remained collegial. Mitchell had supported Brennan's desire to be attorney general, then to run for governor again, and Brennan thought highly of Mitchell's abilities.

The appointment flabbergasted political hands, but cemented a political friendship that long survived their public careers. Their Democratic ticket in 1982 was among the most successful in party history, producing landslide victories by Mitchell and Brennan and a Democratic state Senate, which, like the House majority, proved lasting. How Brennan and Mitchell dealt with each other remains unique in party annals—a model for how to lose gracefully, and how to bide one's time.

In the Senate, Mitchell exceeded everyone's expectations, possibly including his own. Despite arriving just before Democrats lost their majority for the first time in 26 years, Mitchell used his committee assignments to continue Muskie's environmental work. He led the Democratic Senatorial Campaign Committee in 1986, recapturing the majority, and took the national stage, as Bill Cohen had during Watergate, through his performance at the 1987 Iran-Contra hearings. He won the 1988 majority leader race over two more senior senators. Though he stepped down as leader after six years, Mitchell left behind a long list of bipartisan accomplishments, including a new Clean Air Act, oil spill protection, federal housing tax credits, the Americans with Disabilities Act, and a five-year bipartisan federal budget plan, the last such occasion where Republicans and Democrats came to agreement. After leaving the Senate in 1995, Mitchell led the talks that, through the Good Friday Agreement, brought peace to Northern Ireland in 1998. He became prominent in legal and business circles, both nationally and internationally.

For Ken Curtis, the U.S. Senate appointment decision was his political finale. After Ronald Reagan won the presidency, his ambassadorship lapsed, and though he returned to Maine to practice law, he seemed unsettled. With Mitchell, still little known to voters despite his 1974 run, trailing far behind David Emery in early polls, Curtis explored a primary challenge Mitchell feared he would lose. Given their closeness dating back to 1966, when Mitchell was party chair and Curtis ran for governor, Mitchell found it a painful prospect.

Curtis's bid didn't inspire the old enthusiasm, though, and after a mild heart attack he left the race. Since then, Curtis and his wife, Polly, have lived mainly in Florida, recently returning to Maine. They lost their second daughter, Angela—"Angel"—also to cystic fibrosis. Brennan appointed Curtis president of Maine Maritime Academy in 1986. He served until 1994, and was credited with reviving a school whose future was in doubt. Curtis never assumed the role Muskie had played for the Democratic Party, but those who served with him still see the Curtis administration as Maine's golden age of progressive politics.

While Brennan sought the governorship again after leaving it, Curtis never did. A staffer, Rick Stauffer, recalls asking him some years later, "Would you ever want to be governor?" to which Curtis replied, "No, it wouldn't be fun." Curtis's years at the Blaine House had shown a dramatic increase in federal funding, which continued into the Nixon administration, though scaled back. Lyndon Johnson's incentives to states encouraged creation of the State Planning Office and the Cabinet reorganization Curtis championed. His administration, Stauffer said, "demonstrated the positive aspects of government." After the 1970s, he added, "It would have been a job of telling people no, and that certainly didn't fit his personality."

FIRST TERM RECOVERY

When Joe Brennan took office in January 1979, the national economy was in an alarming state. Unemployment was 7.5 percent, but inflation was even higher, peaking at 12 percent. The following year the Federal Reserve raised interest rates to unprecedented levels, causing a sharp, but short recession that lasted through 1981.

If possible, things were even worse in Augusta. The Longley administration had left behind a shambles. The administration had purchased, with federal funds, a Medicaid computer billing system literally unable to process a bill. When Frank McGinty, deputy commissioner of the Department of Human Services, started work, his first phone call was from the state fire marshal, who wanted to shut down DHS headquarters on State Street. Boxes of unpaid bills—six months in all—were stacked so high the fire marshal considered the building a fire hazard. There was no money in the budget to pay the bills, totaling $50 million.

At the Department of Transportation (DOT), then the largest state agency, it was equally dire. Roger Mallar, Brennan's first commissioner, was a highway engineer in the traditional mold. Because of the recession and soaring gasoline prices, travel was down, as were Highway Fund revenues. Without a two-cent gas tax increase, he'd have to lay off staff, Mallar told the governor, but Brennan refused. When Mallar persisted,

Brennan said, "You don't know me. I am not going to increase those taxes."

Brennan, during a 1978 primary debate, had taken a "no new taxes" pledge, as he tells it, on impulse. Brennan decided that Phil Merrill, a skilled debater, was beating him badly, so he "made a call at the line of scrimmage." Brennan figured, correctly, that reporters would focus on the no-tax pledge, and "a bad day turned into a good day." It also limited his options. The income tax was bringing in plenty of revenue, with the new top rate of 10 percent, with inflation pushing taxpayers into higher brackets, not yet indexed for inflation. With no obvious funding solution at DOT, however, Mallar resigned.

Brennan turned to a young town manager, George Campbell, who'd served in Old Town, Greenville and Dexter, but had no transportation experience, as Mallar's successor; they met during Brennan's 1978 campaign. Campbell initially worried he wouldn't be confirmed, as lawmakers began lining up against his appointment. He knew Joe Sewall, the Republican Senate president, well from his time in Old Town, and discovered that Sewall had been absent when the nomination was posted— on vacation in Ireland. On his return, there was an initially hostile meeting in Brennan's office, where the Senate Transportation chair, a Republican, denounced Campbell. Brennan sat silently, waiting. Sewall finally said to Brennan, "The Republicans have no objection. It's not our problem if you can't control your Democrats," then led his delegation out of the room. A negative committee recommendation was overturned by the Senate, 32-1.

David Flanagan, Brennan's legal counsel, who was present at many such meetings, said that Brennan "drove his staff crazy" with his deliberate approach, and said, "He wouldn't make an unequivocal commitment to anything." He also said of Brennan, "There's never been anybody who was more prudent, careful, and concerned about doing the right thing." Brennan's relationships with Republican leaders, Flanagan said, were "cordial," especially with Joe Sewall, and with Linwood Palmer, his opponent in the 1978 governor's race. On the other hand, "He got very frustrated with leadership of the Democratic caucus. There were people there who thought they should be governor."

On Campbell's first day at the new DOT building—part of the Curtis building boom—he entered the conference room to find "a big cardboard box filled with pink slips." The layoff notices were ready to go out, but he told his staff, "Let's find another way to do this." What he discovered was that DOT's local road assistance programs, some unchanged for seventy years, were so inflexible most towns were unable to use their allotment, and nearly $50 million had accumulated, making it hard to convince legislators more money was needed; the programs also cost $5 million annually to administer. Campbell approached the Maine Municipal Association, whose legislative office was led by John Melrose and

Kay Rand—Melrose was later DOT commissioner under Angus King, while Rand is now King's Senate chief of staff—and came up with a new, integrated program that allowed towns to draw money annually. It was timed to start a year later, which freed $20 million for immediate use; the layoffs were averted.

There was another issue, however, that Campbell couldn't finesse. Jim Longley had backed legislation requiring tolls to be removed from the Maine Turnpike, but the Legislature decided instead to keep the tolls, but eliminate the Turnpike Authority and require DOT to take over maintenance. By 1981, though, lawmakers, responding to constituents, wanted to abolish the tolls as well as the Turnpike Authority. To do that would require five cents more on the gas tax, which had been at nine cents since 1971—a 55 percent increase. Citing his pledge, Brennan said no, and that was that. "Look what happened to George H.W. Bush," was Brennan's response some years later when asked about why he wouldn't go back on his word.

When Brennan was re-elected in 1982 without renewing the pledge, one of Campbell's first tasks was to request the two-cent increase Roger Mallar had sought—something Brennan agreed was overdue. Democrats had just won a Senate majority, and Peter Danton of Saco, a Brennan confidant, co-chaired the Transportation Committee. Danton told Campbell, "I didn't get elected to raise gas taxes for you. Give me a program that means something, and I'll give you a nickel."

Campbell figured out how much construction and maintenance the new money would buy, and Danton had him prepare two index cards for every senator and representative showing what projects their districts would receive with the five-cent increase, and without it. After Campbell finished presenting his budget, he lingered in the committee room, but Danton told him, "You go back to work," which Campbell interpreted as "showing they were going to take control." In late March, without a recorded vote, the Legislature approved the transportation budget with the five-cent increase intact. All the money went into the underfunded state road system, rather than the turnpike, and legislation also required the Turnpike Authority to make annual contributions to DOT's budget.

HUMAN SERVICES

When he was campaigning, Joe Brennan never tired of telling people that "the best welfare program is a good job, and the best social services agency is the family." He reminded listeners that, while he believed whole-heartedly in government's ability to improve their lives, there were limits in its ability to provide services, and pay for them.

The Longley administration's neglect of programs, and costs, was vividly on display in the Department of Human Services, and not just from unpaid Medicaid bills. As commissioner, Brennan picked Michael Petit, a former social worker and head of Portland United Way, who, like George Campbell, was just thirty-three, and had volunteered for his campaign. Petit led the drive for improved services, while Frank McGinty, his deputy, often provided a reality check on what could be done within available resources.

Brennan's speeches weren't as gripping as Ken Curtis's had been, but he made equally effective use of commissions and task forces, and used their recommendations to reshape policy. Petit had three task forces: on foster care, maternal and child health, and long-term care for the elderly. "Nursing home beds had quintupled over the previous 15 years, but nobody wanted to go there. There were few services other than custodial care," Petit said. "The state was approving CONs [Certificates of Need] without consulting the Legislature." Since the state was paying much of the bill through Medicaid, that needed to change, he said. A one-year moratorium on approvals for hospital and long-term care projects allowed tighter standards to be devised.

The same was true for boarding homes for the mentally ill and disabled, many released from state psychiatric hospitals during the wave of "deinstitutionalization." Those decisions fell to Kevin Concannon, Brennan's commissioner of Mental Health, who said there were "virtually no standards." Ultimately, hundreds of boarding homes were closed, and state funding was redirected to new facilities.

For the task forces, Brennan picked prominent Mainers, including Peter Mills, a Republican, former U.S. Attorney and state senator—the second of three generations of that name to serve in the Senate—and Tom Allen, a future Portland mayor and Democratic congressman. Perhaps Petit's favorite moment from the field occurred when he and Brennan visited "Mrs. McGillicuddy," a foster parent taking care of two children with cystic fibrosis in a Bangor tenement, who got a $120 monthly stipend.

Petit knew he'd be asking for significant increases, despite a bleak first-term financial picture, and asked to present his budget personally, thinking about the scene with Mrs. McGillicuddy. When Rod Scribner, the finance director, "a little irritated with me," Petit said, objected to "the 100 percent increase he's proposing," to $240 a month, Brennan looked at them both, then said, "It's OK, Rod."

Concannon also appreciated Brennan's hands-on attention. It became traditional, between Christmas and New Year's, for the governor to visit all the mental health and youth facilities, starting in Presque Isle or Bangor, and heading through Augusta and Pownal to Portland, and the Maine Youth Center. "Often, our public institutions don't get attention until they're in the middle of scandal or problems," Concannon said, "I certainly appreciated that he led those visits, and he enjoyed them as well." Brennan's accessibility to "people who were ordinary, who didn't have power," set him apart. Concannon knew that Brennan "would soon be making final decisions about budget recommendations. It really helped." Concannon was later DHS commissioner for Governor Angus King, headed Medicaid programs for Oregon and Iowa, and served as DHHS assistant secretary for nutrition in the Obama administration.

When Brennan took office, he'd received a confidential report from Don Allen, chosen by Governor Longley to run corrections, saying the Maine State Prison in Thomaston had essentially been taken over by guards and certain inmates, with no central control, and daily intimidation of prisoners not part of the ruling clique. Relying on Arthur Stilphen, his administrator as Cumberland County attorney and now commissioner of Public Safety, Brennan ordered State Police to restore order. It became known as "the lockdown," and the operation's aims were accomplished without injuries or loss of life. It was risky; memories of the 1971 Attica State Prison uprising in New York, where ten hostages and twenty-nine inmates died, were still fresh. Concannon was heading both Mental Health and Corrections, which were then separated into two departments, with Allen becoming the first commissioner of Corrections, serving through the McKernan administration.

Brennan took another risk when he delayed plans for a 250-bed Veteran's home in Augusta that had overwhelming legislative support and was about to be approved. Petit pointed out that a single facility would force some families to drive seven hours to visit. A revised plan eventually included an Augusta site, and five others, including South Paris, Calais and Caribou.

Considering his reputation for caution, Brennan regularly took positions without regard for their political popularity. After hearing an opponent of a short-lived federal search for a nuclear waste depository north of Sebago Lake argue, "If we can't safely store nuclear waste, why do we keep making it?" he supported a 1987 referendum to close the Maine Yankee plant in Wiscasset, which voters rejected for the third time. A stalwart backer of gun control, he was willing to fight for priorities on a national stage. To express his opposition to Ronald Reagan's efforts to arm the Contra rebels in Nicaragua, and prop up other military regimes, Brennan denied permission for the Maine National Guard to train in Central America; Congress later voted to "federalize" the Guard.

Brennan hosted a meeting of the National Governors Association in Maine in 1983, where staff had produced a ten-point agenda to support children and families, including a national minimum wage increase. The NGA chairman, long-time Illinois Governor James Thompson—a Republican known as "Big Jim"—insisted the increase be removed. Brennan stood his ground, saying, "There are 200 members of the press here. You explain why we took it out." The recommendation stayed in.

At times, fiscal prudence prevailed. When the Legislature passed a state minimum wage increase, Brennan let it become law without his

Governor Joe Brennan, first term.

signature, rather than sign it—an action he later regretted. After the free-for-all of the Longley years, Brennan earned a reputation for being tight with a dollar. His legal counsel, David Flanagan said Brennan's first term restraints were "what the state needed after four years of rock 'n roll." Flanagan saw the tensions in the administration as "a very healthy balance . . . as a good CFO, he knew the state budget and was very conservative. There was always a grain of skepticism, especially when we had some commissioners who were willing to spend all the money we had."

Brennan disappointed the Maine State Employees Association by taking a tough line on salary increases; there were numerous petitions to the Labor Relations Board, and disputes between the union and personnel director David Bustin. Brennan's 1978 rival, Phil Merrill, was MSEA's legal counsel, and later, executive director.

Brennan kept his own staff's pay below legislatively authorized levels. When George Campbell complained, Brennan told him, "That's why they call it public service." Budget restraint did pay dividends; in the Longley years, the Legislature convened three times in special session to increase the DHS budget. Under Brennan, Mike Petit said, "We never had a supplemental. We lived within our means."

Another first-term achievement was creation of the Finance Authority of Maine, consolidating three existing agencies. It included the Maine Guaranty Authority, tainted by the failure of Freddie Vahlsing's sugar beet venture in Aroostook County and the bankruptcy of the Evergreen Valley Ski Resort in Stoneham, both creating significant losses. FAME, as it became known, is now among the most respected state guaranty and development agencies. When Ronald Reagan's first budget in 1981 dramatically cut direct federal support for subsidized housing, Brennan beefed up the Maine State Housing Authority. He appointed long-time legislator Elizabeth "Libby" Mitchell its director after her defeat by Bill Cohen in his first Senate re-election bid in 1984.

Relations with the Legislature were largely conducted by the chief of staff, Davy Redmond, who knew Brennan from their days on Munjoy Hill. A high school coach, Redmond was known for political hardball but, from his legislative days serving with Brennan, he had a keen sense of lawmakers' wants and needs. While Brennan and House Speaker John Martin weren't close, any clashes occurred behind closed doors and not in public. Brennan got on well with Joe Sewall, the Republican Senate president, who served eight years, including Brennan's first term. "We never had a problem with Joe," Brennan said.

DEMOCRATS UNITED

Brennan began his 1982 re-election campaign from a position of strength, with nothing like the income tax albatross Curtis had shouldered. His U.S. Senate appointee, George Mitchell, turned around his race with David Emery after a January 1981 poll showed Emery, an unannounced but certain candidate, with 61 percent support. With a lingering recession and unpopular federal policies, voter opinions had shifted, and Democrats capitalized. Brennan and Mitchell campaigned together through summer and fall; both seemed to gain strength from the partnership.

John Baldacci, future governor, won his first legislative race, for an open Senate seat in Bangor that most observers figured belonged to George Wood, a popular Republican, surgeon and city councilor. Baldacci said, "I remember what a powerful, dynamic ticket that was. That was a huge year in 1982, when George and Joe were on the ticket together. That was the strongest ticket we had as Democrats . . . a powerful one-two punch."

Brennan's opponent was Republican Charles Cragin, a Portland attorney who'd finished second to Linwood Palmer in the 1978 primary. Brennan ended up exceeding the most optimistic predictions, winning 61 percent and carrying all sixteen counties. The margin of victory remains a modern record, and a rare moment since the 1974 election that a governor has gained a majority. Mitchell also registered 61 percent, reversing where he'd been when his race with Emery began.

Democrats made huge state Senate gains. From a one-seat deficit, they achieved a two-thirds majority, winning twenty-three seats. Joe Sewall was retired as Senate president when he lost his seat to Michael Pearson of Old Town, Sewall's hometown. David Huber, head of a major family-owned forest products company whose wife, Sherry Huber, was a two-time candidate for governor, also lost. Another Republican moderate, David Ault, was defeated by Bill Diamond, who later became secretary of state and has now served eight Senate terms and three in the House. Gerry Conley, who'd aided Brennan's aspirations earlier, became Senate president, but announced he'd serve only one more term.

The 1982 election completed the Maine Democratic Party's long rise from irrelevance, surpassing Republicans in voter registrations and controlling the governorship, House and Senate for the first time since 1912. There were many reasons why Brennan's second term was more successful than his first, including an experienced administrative team, and a broader range of policy initiatives after a first term focused on righting the ship of state. There's no question, however, that having the votes, and reliable legislative leaders, played a large part.

SECOND TERM'S THE CHARM

Americans presidents are often less successful in second terms than in their first. As Maine governors, Ken Curtis reversed that equation, and so did Joe Brennan, who left office on a high note. Brennan was no longer hampered by the no-tax-increase pledge; though it wasn't necessary to raise either income or sales tax rates, Brennan made other revenue adjustments to keep the budget in balance. The economy was improving—thanks to the same forces that, nationally, led to Ronald Reagan's landslide re-election. Brennan's administrative team had gelled, with some members, such as Richard Barringer, Frank McGinty, and Gordon Weil, taking on new roles. The triage of the administration's first days was long past. Brennan could afford to launch ambitious new initiatives, and he did. He displayed both comfort and confidence in what he later called the best job he ever had.

Transportation was the first example of what new revenue could do. In Brennan's second term, and immediately after it, the state did more highway reconstruction, and maintained more miles, than in the decades before or since. Two bond issues to support a "three port strategy," developing state-owned piers and terminals at Portland, Searsport and Eastport, showed deft management, even though the most ambitious expansion, to more than double Searport's capacity with new piers on Sears Island, was thwarted by federal environmental law. Brennan had decided the 1970 federal Environmental Policy Act didn't apply to state-led projects, and authorized construction. A federal Appeals Court ruled against the state, the project was abandoned, and though another push was mounted by the King administration, the Sears Island cargo port has never been built.

Public support for bonds was critical when the Reagan defense build-up produced a sudden demand for warships, more than Bath Iron Works could produce in its own yard. Transportation Commissioner George Campbell remembers a tense meeting where he offered "everything we had" to support a new site, and Bill Haggett, the imperious BIW president, told him, "That's not enough. We're going to Boston." When Campbell returned with the news, Brennan told him he'd find a way.

Portland and the state each authorized voter-approved bond issues of $15 million to help BIW retrofit a surplus drydock that was towed from Virginia to Portland Harbor. For two decades, the sounds of shipbuilding again rang out along the Portland waterfront. The project added 1,000 workers to the BIW payroll, and was the first major use of state and municipal tax dollars to support industrial development, which prompted an unsuccessful lawsuit from Common Cause, claiming such aid to private businesses was unconstitutional. The drydock closed in 2001, and departed for Europe.

When Brennan took office, the Office of Energy Resources (OER) that Curtis had established had fallen into disarray. The governor asked Gordon Weil to leave Business Regulation and see what he could do; the state then had no legal authority even to manage energy shortages. Successes at OER encouraged Brennan to consider Weil for chairman of the three-member Public Utilities Commission (PUC). Weil had already convinced the Legislature to authorize a new position to better represent consumer interests before the PUC, where hearings were dominated by large industrial users. Brennan settled on Peter Bradford, who was leaving the federal Nuclear Regulation Commission, as public advocate—a title Weil invented after consulting the first pages of an unabridged dictionary.

Brennan, however, changed his mind and decided Bradford, who'd shaken up the utilities as a Curtis PUC appointee, should instead return to the PUC, this time as chair. Weil left the administration, and Paul Fritzsche, an attorney initially tapped as Bradford's deputy, became the first advocate, serving for more than a decade. The public advocate became so respected by all parties, including the commissioners, that the post is now ingrained in PUC proceedings. Like the commissioners, the advocate is appointed by the governor and confirmed by the Legislature, but serves a fixed term and cannot be removed except for cause. OER never achieved similar status, and was abolished in 1991.

There were shortcomings as well as successes. The PUC's orders for utilities to develop renewable energy sources through long-term, fixed-price contract for biomass and small hydro went awry. When oil prices plunged, the electricity contracts cost far more than new sources, chiefly natural gas, and customers had to pay the "stranded costs" in rates, along with lower earnings for utilities.

Brennan, a self-described "city boy," wasn't focused on land conservation, or environmental policy, and his first term had included cutbacks at the Maine Forest Service. He gave authority to appointees, such as Dick Barringer, to pursue these aims, however. Barringer, who'd come to Maine as Curtis's director of public lands, stayed on as Conservation commissioner under Longley. When Brennan took office in 1979, he renominated Barringer, who nearly lost a confirmation vote after House Speaker John Martin testified against him. Barringer said Martin was displeased by his consolidation of Conservation's many northern regional offices to Presque Isle; Martin had wanted the office in his district.

The Natural Resources Committee voted 6-5 against Barringer, and a Republican Senate was unlikely to muster the two-thirds necessary to overturn. Howard Trotsky, a committed environmentalist, had originally cast a protest vote against Barringer, but now was willing to switch. He'd been hospitalized, and had to be rolled into the committee room on a gurney to rescue the nomination.

Martin moved on from his initial opposition. In 1985, he and Barringer worked together to enact the Maine Rivers Act, which established state water quality classifications for all major streams, and funding for improvements. It's considered a national model, and fulfilled Ed Muskie's goal from the 1950s to ensure permanent protection for one of Maine's premier resources. Barringer came to appreciate Martin's legislative skills. "Whenever I had a significant bill, I offered sponsorship first to John Martin. He always accepted, and the bills always became law. It was like magic." Martin also played a key role in enacting, and defending, the Land Use Regulation Commission, which acted as a zoning board for the unorganized territories, and whose decisions were often resented by those who had previously enjoyed a free hand.

Brennan later asked Barringer to become State Planning Office (SPO) director, the post Allen Pease held under Longley. Brennan wanted SPO to become his "think tank" for policy initiatives. Barringer resisted; Conservation had many perks, including an "air force" of planes and helicopters. But he recognized Brennan needed him at SPO, and his successor as commissioner, Dick Anderson, was highly qualified, having turned the Maine Audubon Society into an influential force at the Legislature.

Another signature second-term initiative was the Maine Health Care Finance Commission, an attempt to study, then contain, hospital costs, which were driving up Medicaid expenses and producing an insurance company exodus that left Maine Blue Cross the sole insurer for much of the state. Brennan wanted Frank McGinty to run the program, but first had to convince the Legislature, over solid opposition from hospitals, to authorize it. McGinty remembers no less than 125 meals at the Blaine House, where he and Brennan met with every legislator, in small groups, by day; and with providers, hospital executives, insurers, and business leaders in the evening. Blue Cross, initially an opponent, came around, and the legislation garnered support from major businesses such as L.L. Bean, Unum, and BIW. McGinty recalls that, at the end of House debate, a legislator abstained, saying she was married to a hospital board member; a third of House members followed suit. "That showed the influence the hospitals had, and how they extended into every community," he said.

During the commission's existence, it produced markedly lower cost increases, restored a "highly competitive" private insurance market, with improvements in the quality of care. McGinty said it represented Brennan's overall approach to state programs: "Tax revenue through the income or sales tax is derived from people who work very hard. It needs to be put to good use, so we can look taxpayers in the eye and say we used those funds wisely and effectively. That was imperative."

The commission didn't specify rates for each procedure, as the federal government does for Medicare. Instead, it set a revenue cap for each hospital, with expenses allocated as they saw fit. On Medicaid, the state committed "to providing 20 percent of the cap, in 52 equal payments," McGinty said. "Being paid on time was often as important as the rate." The system provided protection for rural hospitals that feared losing out in a system which rewarded larger, high-volume hospitals—something now done through the federal-state "critical access" program. While its rate-setting approach went out of favor, the commission's emphasis on global budgets remains an attractive alternative for containing health care costs, which have continued to soar in the decades since.

LEGACY

Brennan's education legislation may be his most important legacy. The 1984 Education Reform Act prompted the most far-reaching changes in public schools since the Sinclair Act created regional school districts, under Ed Muskie, in 1957. The reform act addressed three priorities: professional standards and salaries for teachers, a statewide assessment of learning, and an agreed-upon standard for state funding. The first two aims were accomplished; the third has proven ever-elusive.

Teaching standards had never been codified in Maine, and varied widely from district to district. The new law specified requirements for academic degrees and certification, and also set a statewide minimum salary, initially $17,000, adjusted only sporadically since then; it's now $30,000, lower in constant dollars than the original one.

Perhaps the most successful initiative was the Maine Educational Assessment, targeting six subject areas, and applied at three grade levels to establish a consistent baseline. The MEA, though sometimes confused with standardized tests like the SAT, ACT, and GRE, wasn't designed to measure each student's aptitude or achievement, but to provide an index of learning for each school. For nearly two decades, it provided valuable and sometimes surprising data about individual schools and districts, leading to curriculum and teaching changes to correct learning deficits. It's been praised by educators as Maine's most reliable and useful test, but its effectiveness has been blunted by revisions to cut costs, as well as competing, federally-required assessments from the "No Child Left Behind Act," which take a narrower focus.

The Education Reform Act also established as a "goal" that the state pay 55 percent of local school costs. The state has never reached this level, though it's come close twice, during the first McKernan administration, and then the first Baldacci administration, before recessions reduced revenue, and thus the proportion of school budgets paid by the state. In the original draft, several Republican lawmakers favored a 50 percent goal, but were outbid by Democrats, who proposed 55 percent. Despite two subsequent referendums to formalize and then fund the 55 percent share, in 2004 and 2016, it still hasn't been reached.

After re-election, Brennan also devoted considerable attention to the University of Maine System, with its seven widely separated campuses, still loosely structured. By executive order, he created the Visiting Committee in 1984, chaired by Colby President Robert Strider, and joined by Ed Muskie in one of his last major public roles. Its report in January 1986 defined distinctive roles for each campus, recommending that the University of Maine, as the "flagship campus . . . be strengthened as a research and doctoral institution," while the University of Southern Maine become "an urban comprehensive university" with "limited graduate programs," finding USM "overextended." The report urged that four former teacher's colleges, in Farmington, Machias, Presque Isle and Fort Kent, remain undergraduate institutions, with faculties working more closely together given their modest enrollments. Finally, it suggested the University of Maine at Augusta coordinate the system's two-year programs. The bulk of the committee's recommendations were achieved.

After finding that enrollments trailed national averages, with high tuition and low faculty salaries, the Visiting Committee called for an immediate $15 million "down payment" to bring the university's state appropriation back closer to its original level after the funding drought of the Longley years. Brennan accomplished this during his final year in office. The supplement vanished, however, following the 1990-91 recession, and the system has since been "flat funded"—with no allowance even for inflation—for years at a stretch.

Brennan's last year also saw appointment of Robert Woodbury, then USM president, as university chancellor. Woodbury served until 1993, before stepping down to run for governor, and is widely acknowledged as the system's most successful leader, attaining good relations both with legislators and administrators within the system. The system also achieved peaks in enrollment at nearly every campus that haven't since been equaled.

ACHIEVEMENT AND PROSPERITY

Joe Brennan's two administrations lacked the fireworks that Ken Curtis often created. He's sometimes been seen more as an administrator than an initiator. He had a loyal cadre from his Portland days known as the "Brennanistas," a circle some Democrats found hard to penetrate, but he was also willing to recruit and utilize talent from many sources, especially when the stakes were high in terms of policy and dollars. Among those who know him well, Gordon Weil described him as a "careful person," who was willing "to do nothing" rather than act rashly. "As governor, he made not a single mistake . . . his only mistakes were of omission rather than commission, things he didn't do." Yet Frank McGinty sees a Brennan who was willing to take risks, who emphasized "the importance of progress, of finding a way to compromise . . . even if it wasn't a perfect solution." He recalls a speech in which Brennan said, "An imperfect plan, boldly articulated and vigorously implemented, will succeed."

Brennan did act decisively on many occasions. The "lockdown" of the Thomaston prison, and his refusal to deploy the Maine National Guard to Central America, had plenty of downside risks. His initiatives to reform public education and revamp the University of Maine System were among the most substantive and far-reaching of state responses to the 1983 "Nation at Risk" report. And the Maine Health Care Finance Commission's efforts to regulate hospitals were unique, and accomplished much despite strong initial resistance.

Brennan's departure marked the end of a political era where Democratic governors, and one former Democrat, led Maine for twenty years. A Democrat at the helm no longer seemed unusual, and establishment of a House majority in 1974, and Senate dominance in 1982 provided a strikingly different governing style than the stand-pat Republican administrations preceding Ed Muskie's election in 1954. In broad terms, Muskie was the pioneer, while Ken Curtis reorganized from top to bottom, increased revenues, and set new missions for state agencies which, however, took years to realize. Brennan administered and refined the new system, providing spending restraint, regulation in health care, energy and environmental protection, and support for education at all levels.

Maine improved its ranking on national indicators of health, education, and taxation during Brennan's administration, and reduced the gap between Maine incomes and national averages. He achieved this despite continued job losses in older industries such as poultry and shoe-making, and a challenging economic landscape. During the 1970s and again in the 1980s, Maine—for the first and only time since just after statehood—saw its population grow faster than the nation as a whole. Maine grew by 12.3 percent during the '70s, and by 9.9 percent during the '80s—from 993,553 residents to 1,227,928. Since then, population growth has been just a third of the national average and, in 2010, turned negative.

Objectively, these achievements should have created confidence in state government, its impact on the economy, and appreciation of the role of the Democratic Party. Instead, Maine was soon to enter a period of conflict, division, and economic decline that has lasted until the present moment.

FIVE

Disaster

1986-1994

"Measured against the needs of the country it was a modest result. Measured against the difficulty of adopting anything that inflicts sacrifice . . . it was a significant accomplishment. I hoped that from the pain and bitterness of our experience we all had learned valuable lessons . . . But obviously that didn't happen."
> —George Mitchell, on the 1990 federal budget agreement

John Martin was born, grew up, and still lives in Eagle Lake, a small town in Maine's northernmost House district, variously District 1 or District 151; the number switches from north to south each time redistricting takes place. Eagle Lake, home to fewer than nine hundred residents, is small even compared to nearby Fort Kent—with a population of 4,097— but has long been a seat of local political power. Martin's great uncle, Michael Burns, represented the district from 1918-34, and his uncle, Claude Martin, from 1942-56. Both were Democrats, when there were just a dozen or so in a chamber of 151. By the 1980s, John Martin had built the House Democratic caucus into an overwhelming force with commanding majorities, while Republicans became a largely ineffectual minority, much as Democrats once were.

Martin displayed assurance and self-confidence at an early age. John Crabtree, a childhood acquaintance and later a Maine Warden Service lieutenant, got to know Martin when, as teenagers, they worked at the Eagle Lake grocery store. He described Martin as "cocky," and added, "He let it be known that if he didn't like the way things were going, he was going to change it. He had his sights set" on larger things.

In Eagle Lake and at Fort Kent High School, Martin's classmates were headed south, as traditional industries disappeared. In a 1998 interview, he said that from 121 students, "There were only five left in the St. John Valley. I was the only one in Eagle Lake." He considered leaving, too, but instead enrolled at the University of Maine. There, he encountered prejudice from a professor who mangled the names of French students so badly Martin offered to help pronounce them. The professor retaliated by lowering Martin's grades, and Martin pursued the matter all the way to the university's board of trustees, where former Senate President Bob Haskell served. Claude Martin approached Haskell on his nephew's behalf, who lent a sympathetic ear; they'd served together in the Legislature. The next year, the professor was gone.

After receiving his degree, Martin stayed on for a new graduate program in political science. Fellow student Herb Marsters from Westbrook challenged him to join him in running for the Legislature. Marsters dropped out—he had three children and couldn't afford it—but Martin ran, and won amid the 1964 landslide. He entered the House from Eagle Lake, age 23, the same time as Joe Brennan, from Munjoy Hill in Portland.

John Marsh, who later headed the Maine Warden Service, was teaching high school in Greenville when Martin started teaching in Fort Kent. They shared an interest in the Allagash region, where U.S. Interior Secretary Stewart Udall had paid a visit, and Senator Ed Muskie sought either federal or state protection. Marsh invited Martin to bring his students to Greenville—"in those days, they never saw kids from another part of the state," he said. The students toured the Allagash and Moosehead Lake, and in Greenville formed two teams to debate whether the Allagash should have state or federal ownership. The state provision prevailed, as it did at the Legislature, where Martin, as a freshman, supported the bill.

"I was glad he was in the Legislature," Marsh said of the early days. "He was the kind of leader we needed to have." And Marsh agrees with Martin's assessment of his students' destinations: "As soon as they graduated, they'd move south to work at Pratt & Whitney."

Since 1964, Martin has divided time between politics and teaching, later moving to the University of Maine at Fort Kent, where he's a tenured professor. It's as a student of the Legislature, however, in all its history, traditions, rules and procedures, that he is unique. When he bested Louis Jalbert to become Democratic floor leader in 1970, Martin called it his "toughest race." He had closely observed Jalbert, by that time an aging, widely resented Franco from the Lewiston branch, and Martin moved up quickly in committee assignments, from State Government to Taxation to Appropriations.

As the 1986 election approached, John Martin had been House speaker for six terms; reporters frequently speculated about a run for governor. Maine then had a half dozen political columnists, and Martin was always grist for the mill. His poll results, however, showed that, while at least as well known as his leading rival, Attorney General Jim Tierney, who'd succeeded Brennan, his favorable ratings were barely above single digits.

Not for the first time, a legislative leader wielding power through force and persuasion, making deals without regard for ideological consistency, found his route to the governor's office blocked by public opinion. Martin never announced his candidacy.

Severin Beliveau became the Franco candidate that year, and finished second to Tierney. Beliveau had followed his service as party chairman by building a leading lobbying practice at Preti Flaherty, along with Tony Buxton, George Mitchell's 1974 campaign manager; Harold Pachios, a close friend of Mitchell's; and others from the party's recent successes. Martin, however, still saw himself as the best qualified, and his ambition was not relinquished so much as redirected.

Joe Brennan was headed to Washington. He ran for Congress in the 1st District, while incumbent Republican John McKernan returned to Maine to run for governor. The press dubbed it a "job swap," and it actually happened. McKernan won the 1st District in 1982, when David Emery stepped down to challenge Senator George Mitchell, defeating Democrat John Kerry in a result many attributed to McKernan's "pro-choice" stance. Kerry, an Irish Catholic, opposed abortion, and the race ultimately helped produce consensus in both parties. Olympia Snowe and Susan Collins also used the abortion issue to establish their moderate credentials.

McKernan, then thirty-eight, and the youngest governor since Ken Curtis, was born in Bangor, and graduated from Dartmouth College and the University of Maine School of Law. He'd shown a libertarian streak in the Legislature, sponsoring the bill that decriminalized marijuana possession, and worked with Snowe to repeal mandatory helmet use by motorcyclists. Like Bill Cohen before him, he appealed to Democrats and, in 1986, won votes across the political spectrum.

After his political days, Jim Tierney became a Columbia Law School professor and director of the National Association of Attorneys General—where he helped negotiate the landmark tobacco settlement with cigarette manufacturers. In 1986, however, Tierney was a scattershot campaigner, without the single-minded focus Brennan used in all his campaigns. He came from a similar background, Irish Catholic, but in a fractured family where both parents worked. He remembers a strong class division in Brunswick, where he grew up. His earliest political memory is of organizing an impromptu "Muskie for Governor" torchlight parade in 1954, where, however, the candidate lingered inside so long after giving his speech that the torches went out. After attending law school and marrying, Tierney moved to Durham, representing a rural district in the Legislature, and became House majority leader, with Martin as speaker, from 1976-80, then attorney general.

Don Nicoll called Tierney "one of those political figures who combined a grass roots feel of what the Democratic Party is with a brilliant mind, but ultimately lacked the discipline to focus on one of the many

issues he'd been pursuing." Nicoll said teaching and lobbying, not politics, are Tierney's strengths.

In November, McKernan won easily, with 40 percent in a four-person
race to Tierney's 30 percent. Two independents split the remainder but
didn't materially affect the outcome. Former Republican Sherry Huber
ran on an environmental platform, while a business-oriented former
Democrat, John Menario, who'd been Portland city manager, emphasized
efficient government. The new governor, the first Republican since John
Reed's defeat by Ken Curtis twenty years earlier, was athletic, handsome
and—to critics—lightweight, as summed up by his nickname, "Jock." His
most important detractor, it turned out, was John Martin.

A SUPPLY OF GAVELS

Early on, Martin established himself as a force to be reckoned with. Tony
Buxton, who worked with Martin frequently, said he did it through detailed knowledge of Mason's Rules, which guided floor debates, and by
overhauling the closed system he inherited. As minority leader, Buxton
said, Martin often huddled with the state law librarian "on the finer
points of disputes." Use of Mason's Rules "brought greater openness and
procedural fairness to the House, and thus to the legislative process that
requires agreement between the House and Senate for any bill to be
enacted," Buxton said. "Every legislator could speak on any matter."
Each day, the "horse blanket," a record of the previous day's proceedings, was available, bringing in the public as well. By Martin's second
term as minority leader, Buxton said his procedural mastery was so complete that though "the genial Republican Richard Hewes served as speaker, Martin virtually ran the House."

Although he often clashed with caucus liberals, Martin was devoted
to the cause of public power and vigorous regulation of private utilities.
He supported Peter Bradford throughout his tenure on the Public Utilities Commission. When McKernan tried to shift the PUC to a business-
friendly, less consumer-oriented stance, Martin convinced lawmakers to
reject not just one, but two PUC nominations before McKernan offered a
compromise choice.

As he set longevity records, Martin tightened his control. Both in public and private, he was something to behold. He could rattle through bills
with what seemed like reckless abandon when it suited him, only to slow
things to a crawl when he found something unsatisfactory. Chamber staff
kept an abundant supply of oversized wooden gavels; Martin might
break several in succession as he pounded through legislation. Martin,
the unchallenged House master, could conduct unrelated business while
presiding—phoning an errant journalist, or enlisting support for another
bill.

Don Nicoll met Martin when he began working for Ed Muskie in the legislative off-season. "One cannot overestimate the importance of his links to the St. John Valley," Nicoll said. "That's his world, and he keeps going back to it." Although he gained a wider perspective as speaker, Nicoll said, Martin "focused on winning the tactical battles in the Legislature, without appreciating the impact of his style and actions on the general public."

Where Martin was unequalled was putting his stamp on the state budget, down to the last detail. It was longer annual sessions, combined with still-biennial budgets, that created the need for enactment by two-thirds majorities, yet, until 1991, Martin had little difficulty winning enough votes. In private meetings, he could be mesmerizing even with Republicans who vowed opposition. A Democrat who witnessed these meetings said Martin "has an incredible knack even with his worst enemies. He will convince them that it's snowing green cheese." But his tactics did cause resentment. Martin's frequent use of the word "obviously" in explaining his position suggested his listeners weren't bright enough to keep up.

Even reforms for which Martin is often praised could be seen as two-sided. Before Martin became speaker, lobbyists were frequent visitors on the floor, where friends and acquaintances also came and went. Martin banished anyone not a member to the rear of the chamber and later had a wood-and-glass wall erected, so members could be observed but not approached while in session. The new policy also enhanced Martin's own authority, since he had members' undivided attention.

Early relations between the new governor and House speaker were wary. Martin, facing a Republican chief executive, was unconstrained in a way he hadn't been with Joe Brennan, who commanded deference. McKernan seemed less sure of himself, and Martin took note.

Labor lawyer Jim Case, who earlier worked on Muskie's Senate staff, said of Martin, "He did have a lot of power. Power tends to accrue to people who think they have it." Case thinks Martin "saw McKernan as a young, inexperienced member of the minority party. That's the way he was with essentially everybody." When Martin worked in Washington, Case said, "He had a lot of love and respect for Ed Muskie, but his approach was to be quite demanding." When the party queried Martin about his availability for the Congressional 2nd District race in 1978, when Bill Cohen ran for senator, Case said Martin's response was, "Put together half a million dollars and I'll run." Instead, Republican Olympia Snowe easily defeated little-known Democrat Mark Gartley.

There was restiveness within the Democratic caucus, though until Martin's last years as speaker it was kept under wraps. Neil Rolde, his first majority leader, served just one term, while Rolde's successors—Jim Tierney, Libby Mitchell and John Diamond—each served two. Each had their own ambitions, not content as second-in-command. Diamond was explicitly not Martin's pick. He favored another candidate, but Diamond was chosen anyway. It wasn't until 1988 that Martin had a deputy prepared to stay in the background—Dan Gwadosky of Fairfield, whose uncle, Dick McMahon, Ed Muskie's first campaign manager, gave him impeccable credentials. Gwadosky was chosen majority leader three times, and succeeded Martin during the turbulent year of 1994.

For major legislation, the Senate is traditionally a counterweight; some House members would call it an obstacle. That was rarely true for Martin. After Democrats took a Senate majority in 1982, their long-time floor leader, Gerry Conley, whose political career is entwined with Joe Brennan's, served one more term and was followed by Charles Pray, who'd been assistant leader, then majority leader for one term. Pray, from Millinocket, was something of a cipher. His nearly silent public demeanor put him in the shadows opposite the ever-quotable Martin. Mike Carpenter, later attorney general, who served with Pray, said "He got his feet under him, and established himself well in the caucus," but added that Martin "was more dominant, and Charlie struggled with that perception." It was rare that the two top legislative leaders came from northern Maine— reporters called it "the Allagash Alliance"—and the remoteness of their districts from Democrats' traditional voting strength may have contributed to rank-and-file discontent.

GATHERING STORM

John McKernan, meanwhile, got off to a tentative start. Those who expected an influx of Republican and business talent into the Cabinet were generally disappointed. McKernan did find a canny overseer of the Department of Transportation in Commissioner Dana Connors, a former Presque Isle city manager, whose department benefited from declining gas prices and a huge influx of federal funding, thanks to George Mitchell's work on the 1987 and 1991 federal transportation bills, which had many discretionary Maine projects. But McKernan's choice for Human Services, Rollin Ives, from Jackson Brook (later Spring Harbor), a private psychiatric hospital in Westbrook, raised eyebrows. Ives had run as a Republican against Joe Brennan for Congress in 1986, and wasn't shy about seeing Human Services as a political realm, too. Following the even-tempered Michael Petit, Ives's hard-edged demeanor also created an adversarial relationship with the press. When he didn't like a question, he called the assembled reporters "doorknobs." In public appearances, Ives was noticeably unwilling to defer to the governor.

McKernan's choice for Mental Health, Susan Parker, who replaced Kevin Concannon, was baffling. Though, at the time, she was a rare woman in Maine's Cabinet, Parker had no significant administrative experience, and was soon presiding over a virtual collapse of care at the

Augusta Mental Health Institute, or AMHI. Suffering from overcrowding, AMHI had eight different superintendents over the next eight years, and Parker seemed unable to lead. Nursing and other staffing shortages left patients unattended. In the summer of 1988, when temperatures reached record highs, there were five patient deaths in the aging main building—which had no air conditioning—though the cause has often been misunderstood. To escape the heat, patients taking medication that reduced their immunity began sleeping on the stone floors, became chilled, developed pneumonia, and died from complications. The hospital was decertified by Medicare, and in 1991 the administration signed the AMHI Consent Decree, providing judicial protections. A generation later, the AMHI decree remains in effect.

McKernan and the Legislature did agree that, despite a modest rate of violent criminal activity, Maine needed to get "tough on crime." The jail and prison population soared as lawmakers decided to double sentences for Class A felonies and limit sentencing discretion. After being reduced during the Curtis administration, the prison population more than doubled. McKernan asked for a major expansion of the prison system, which was turned down three times by the voters in referendum. The governor then claimed it was impossible to get the public to approve corrections bonds, even though two more modest bond issues were approved during the Brennan years. The standoff led to creation of the Government Facilities Commission in 1992, which bypasses the voters and has approved new courthouses and prison construction at an escalating rate.

Money wasn't a problem during McKernan's first term, and the governor was willing to spend. Aided by strong revenues, budgets rose faster than during the Brennan years, and McKernan agreed to fund the Maine Health Program for low-income residents not eligible for Medicaid, and proposed several welfare-to-work programs that became models for other states.

The state was actually over-collecting revenue, because Martin and McKernan couldn't agree on adjustments to the state income tax following 1986 federal tax reform, which dramatically lowered rates by eliminating tax shelters and deductions. The new top federal rate was 28 percent, down from 50 percent, and the bottom fifteen brackets were collapsed to a single 15 percent rate, billed as "simplification," which also reduced progressivity.

States needed to compensate, but the McKernan-Martin standoff meant Maine did nothing, while withholding took far too much from paychecks. Taxpayers got two rounds of rebate checks, and after the 1990 economic collapse, there was widespread anger and confusion when McKernan proposed tax increases. Ultimately, the only adjustment was to lop off the top, 10 percent bracket, leaving Maine's top rate at 8.5 percent, and the overall tax system even less progressive than its federal counterpart.

No event during the McKernan years inflamed passions more than the strike at International Paper's Androscoggin Mill in Jay. It began in June 1987, the administration's first year, and lasted seventeen months until Local 14 of the United Paperworkers International Union gave up; the mill had continued to operate with replacement workers, many from the South. International Paper was then the largest paper manufacturer in the world, and had decided it would make no more major investments in Maine, even though the Jay mill was just 20 years old. The previous year, workers at the Boise Cascade mill in Rumford had struck over many of the same issues—reduced pay and benefits—and Joe Brennan called union leaders and management into his office, much as Ed Muskie had during the Lewiston textile strike in 1955. The Rumford strike was settled. John McKernan made no similar effort during the Jay strike.

IP's decisions proved a bellwether, and Maine papermaking has declined, with several more old-line mills closing following the financial crisis of 2008. Only a handful of paper mills remain, most owned by foreign-based companies. In 1987, there were 1,250 strikers in Local 14 alone. Today, the Androscoggin Mill, after ownership changes and downsizings, employs just four hundred.

McKernan's relations with state employees had ups and downs. At the outset, some state workers who saw themselves as career civil servants publicly expressed disappointment that the new governor doubted their loyalty. In negotiating a new contract with the Maine State Employees Association, however, the administration offered a three-year agreement that would extend into 1991. While the first two years provided inflation adjustments, the third year would increase pay 7 percent. Partly as a result, MSEA remained neutral in the 1990 governor's race, as McKernan sought re-election against Brennan, who was seeking a return to his old job.

BEFORE THE FALL

As tensions rose, McKernan and Martin weren't the only players. Normally, the selection of assistant caucus leaders has little long-term significance, but the Republican Senate contest in 1986 was an exception. Barbara Gill, a moderate from Cape Elizabeth, was ousted by Charlie Webster, whose aggressive political style contrasted sharply with the Republican leader, Tom Perkins, or, for that matter, Martin's House Republican counterparts. Webster, an oil burner repairman from Farmington, billed himself as "the working man's Republican," and moved up to leader when Perkins retired in 1988. Despite the Republican delegation's small size in 1991—thirteen members, against twenty-two Democrats—it was just large enough to sustain a gubernatorial veto, and Webster was prepared to use it.

As John Martin began to play an outsize role, the Democratic Party leadership that once might have intervened no longer had that capability. Unlike the Frank Coffin-Ed Muskie days, and into the early 1980s, when party chairs were future candidates or veteran organizers, chairs during the McKernan-Martin years had little clout. The recruiting and organizing efforts Coffin designed, which had flourished under chairs like George Mitchell, Severin Beliveau and Violet Pease, were greatly diminished.

Authority in the party office devolved to the executive director, as the executive secretary post was renamed, and fundraising became the dominant task. The late 1980s were the heyday of "soft money," a federal campaign finance loophole that, upheld by the courts, became a floodgate of congressional campaign money. Post-Watergate finance reforms placed contribution limits on donations to candidates, but not to state parties. Large donors funneled contributions to the state parties, which recycled them to congressional campaigns, becoming "pass throughs." State parties had abundant cash flows and seemingly greater relevance, but in fact support for state candidates withered. "Soft money" was finally limited under the McCain-Feingold Act of 2002, but those restrictions, and many more, were swept away by the U.S. Supreme Court's 2010 *Citizen's United* decision.

As the 1990 elections approached, the two major parties contended in ways rarely seen before in Maine's normally low-key races. The McKernan-Martin standoff set the tone, but the main event was the challenge to McKernan by Brennan, who said he aimed to restore order. Brennan campaigned relentlessly on what he claimed was the Republican governor's inability to manage the state budget. Maine was in fact headed into a deep financial pit created by a national recession, induced by the savings and loan crisis, that extended into 1991. Many new banks, inexperienced at commercial lending, became dangerously overextended, and Maine experienced bank failures at a rate not seen since the Great Depression. The state budget had already been patched, and the "rainy day fund" emptied, with Martin's consent. Brennan thought if he could break McKernan's credibility—the governor was insisting things were manageable—he would win, and Brennan led all the polls, though not by a wide margin.

Elsewhere, the sands were shifting. In the June Democratic primary, an avowedly liberal state senator from Portland, Tom Andrews, won the Congressional 1st District primary, the seat Brennan left, over two more experienced rivals: Jim Tierney, who'd run for governor in 1986, and Libby Mitchell, who'd opposed Bill Cohen in 1984. In the 2nd District, state Representative Pat McGowan mounted the first serious challenge to Republican Olympia Snowe, seeking her 7th term, though reporters didn't take him seriously.

McKernan was anything but confident. During an editorial board interview, asked how he would prevent the House speaker from preempting his aims, he said sharply, "John Martin has to learn that he doesn't run the State of Maine." On election night, McKernan went to bed thinking he'd soon be an ex-governor. Instead, by morning he'd won re-election by 14,000 votes; an independent candidate named Andrew Adam, who barely campaigned, got 48,000 votes.

Why Brennan fell short has been much debated. Perhaps some voters, weighing their choices, were reluctant to return a governor who'd served the two-term limit; Maine's constitutional amendment, unlike the federal one limiting presidents, has no lifetime ban. Whatever the reason, Brennan never won another November election, though he kept trying.

Tom Andrews easily defeated David Emery, but Olympia Snowe held on to her seat by 5,000 votes over Pat McGowan; none of her previous challengers had gotten even a third of the vote. There were other surprises. Dale McCormick became the nation's first openly gay state legislator, winning a Senate seat. In Augusta, a pitched battle ensued over a House seat in District 90, where incumbent Dan Hickey, a former House chamber doorman and reliable vote for Martin, was seeking an eighth term against a prominent Republican attorney, Sumner Lipman.

The House Democratic Campaign Committee had gone to extraordinary lengths for Hickey, spending large sums on leaflets, mailings and advertising; when the *Kennebec Journal* endorsed Lipman, the committee produced a satirical newspaper insert in response. After a recount, Lipman won by seven votes, but Democrats weren't done. Augusta had three House districts, and about ten votes had been cast in the "wrong" district. Martin pushed through a resolution requiring a new election, which Lipman won by a wider margin. He took his seat almost three months after the session started.

There were two motivations. One was to prevent Lipman from becoming a legislator; Democrats suspected he wanted to run for governor, as he did in 1994. They also wanted to gain a two-thirds, veto-proof majority, which they'd achieved during McKernan's first term in the Senate, but not the House. The Augusta election feud seemed a tempest in a teapot, but it foreshadowed events two years later that led to Martin's fall from power.

GLOOM AND ANGER

The 1991 legislative session began amid a confounding haze of gloom and anger. The state's fiscal shortfall was staggering, and the Appropriations Committee met in emergency session for three days over the 1990 Christmas holidays. The House chair, Don Carter, who lived in Winslow, headed home late one night. Heading north along Route 201, his car left the road, crashed, and he was killed instantly. Carter had Martin's implicit trust, and had been a steadying presence. He'd served in the House since 1968, and had co-chaired Appropriations since 1982. During tributes, his nine-term Republican colleague, Don Strout, wondered why Carter wasn't driving on Interstate 95, a safer road. Majority Leader Dan Gwadosky recalled how he'd come into the House chamber many times to find Carter finishing a crossword puzzle. When he asked, "Do you think it's going to work out all right?" Carter always answered, "I think we will work it out." Martin, dissatisfied with Carter's successors, later removed an Appropriations chair who displeased him, temporarily appointing himself to the post, mid-session.

On January 14, Peter McKernan had just finished a two-mile jog during a preseason baseball practice at Dartmouth when he suffered a heart attack. Although his heart was restarted by CPR, he never regained consciousness and died nine days later. Peter, twenty, was the only son of John McKernan; the death recalled the time twenty-one years earlier when Ken and Polly Curtis lost their daughter Susan as Curtis campaigned for re-election. The lives of both men were never quite the same.

These personal tragedies didn't lead to compromise; instead, confrontation ensued, and longtime cross-partisan friendships began to fray, then disintegrate. John Marsh, retired after his long Maine Warden Service career, was elected to the House in 1990 as a Republican from West Gardiner. He went to see his old high school teaching colleague, John Martin, about the complexities of a bill. Martin explained things to his satisfaction, but when Marsh was observed leaving Martin's office, "I got a note to go to the Republican office," where two House colleagues, Appropriations Committee member Judy Foss and Assistant Leader Francis Marsano made it clear informal contacts with Martin were banned. "They chewed me up into little pieces and spit me out," Marsh said. "I was a pretty ineffective legislator from then on."

Democrats, for their part, were intensely suspicious of budget numbers supplied by the administration, and Finance Commissioner Sawin Millett in particular. Even before the December special session, lawmakers had been called back in August to fix the budget, each time with lower revenue projections. The "funny numbers," as Democrats called them, continued into 1991 and 1992, with more special sessions. McKernan conceded, after the election, that he'd underplayed the shortfalls, attributing it to the intensity of the re-election campaign, when aides screened out negative news. His opponents created the slogan that McKernan "lied to save his job."

The 1991 budget debate became open season on government agencies. The Maine Health Program disappeared. The Office of Energy Resources that Ken Curtis created and Joe Brennan revived was abolished. A 1988 growth management law, requiring comprehensive plans for every municipality to combat sprawl, was repealed because, at least in 1991, there "was no growth to manage." Attempts at savings often included forfeiting substantial amounts of federal funds. In legislative committee rooms and on the floor, the atmosphere often verged on chaos.

SHUTDOWN

In popular memory, the shutdown of state government that began July 1, 1991, was precipitated by an intractable budget dispute, but that wasn't the immediate reason. By June, the budget was nearly complete. McKernan proposed, and Democrats quickly agreed, to increase the sales tax from 5 percent to 6 percent and add income tax surcharges, producing $300 million to help fill the shortfall—$650 million in today's dollars. The budget also included a huge variety of gimmicks that swept unspent money from every department. It reduced municipal revenue sharing and school funding, and cut the university system and most major programs. The remaining problem was Maine's workers' compensation system, which Republicans insisted must be completely overhauled by sharply reducing benefits to injured workers.

The problem had been brewing for years. Peter Mills, as a lawyer who often represented injured workers, worked with Jim Case to find a solution. Mills later served seven terms as a Republican state senator, ran twice for governor, and is now executive director of the Maine Turnpike Authority. He wrote a succinct analysis in 1996 that lays out why workers' comp was such an intractable political problem.

"During the 1970s, worker's compensation benefits were dramatically expanded, not only in Maine, but in the rest of the nation," Mills wrote. "The impetus was bipartisan. The Nixon administration was a chief proponent for liberalization. It was widely, and correctly, believed that historical benefits were entirely inadequate to compensate workers for serious injuries. Because Maine's Legislature and the Governor's office were dominated by Democrats and labor, our benefit expansions were greater than those [of] most other states . . . many decent business owners agreed they were long overdue."

Mills also explained that, unlike most casualty insurance, it's inherently difficult for insurers to estimate future claims costs, which could require payments for a few months or an entire lifetime for injuries that appear similar, and administrative costs were high. By the late 1970s, premiums paid were nowhere near adequate to cover future costs, but the reckoning was deferred because, amid record-high inflation, insurers could earn substantial investment income. Things fell apart in the 1980s.

Maine had already made changes. Over objections from his labor allies, Joe Brennan had approved a 1985 law allowing payments to an employee's attorney only when the worker's claim prevailed. In 1987, McKernan signed a bill eliminating lifetime partial benefits. Insurers claimed it wasn't enough and began to stop writing the policies employers are legally required to have. A crisis atmosphere was fanned to white-hot intensity, particularly by Senate Minority Leader Charlie Webster.

Though the budget was ready, Webster convinced his twelve Senate Republican colleagues to withhold their votes until Democrats agreed to many more worker's comp concessions. House Republicans, led by mild-mannered dairy farmer Walt Whitcomb, were willing to deal with worker's comp separately. McKernan sided with Webster, and a state government shutdown began on July 1, a Monday that led into the Independence Day holiday on Thursday.

McKernan's planning for the shutdown, when it arrived, was minimal. State workers locked out of their jobs crowded the Hall of Flags outside the Governor's office. An Associated Press report said McKernan "was all but barricaded in his office. The outer door to the governor's suite was locked and the regular phone line went unanswered, with a recorded message saying, 'Due to the close-down of Maine state government, no one is available to answer your call right now. Please call again.'" Workers chanted "We want to be paid," and "We want a budget." To the governor, they added, "Stop hiding, Jock," and "Impeach McKernan."

Under Maine law, it fell to McKernan to define "essential services" that would continue, though the state had no overall authority to spend money. Police and other emergency agencies were obviously included, though workers weren't paid. There were gray areas. McKernan decided state parks weren't essential, nor were state liquor stores—at the time, the only source of hard liquor. He reckoned without thousands of tourists who flooded into Maine for the holiday. Few knew anything about the shutdown, and were outraged. After review, McKernan decided liquor stores, as a major revenue source, could re-open. Ultimately, 2,000 of 13,000 state employees worked during the shutdown.

And so it went. There was an apparent agreement on workers' comp, and agencies started up only to shut down again when Republicans rejected the deal. It wasn't until July 17 that McKernan finally signed a new budget.

If the legislative chambers were chaotic in June, it was worse during the shutdown, as the State House was filled daily with state workers more outraged than any tourist. Frustration mounted. Legislators remember shouting and the use of bullhorns by state workers whose zeal got out of hand. The workers believed they were justified. McKernan promised them a 7 percent raise, and they were instead locked out. Nor was the governor apologetic. He insisted that the money wasn't there, and the increases disappeared. Those who'd voted for him believing they'd receive better treatment than they had from Joe Brennan felt betrayed.

It's difficult, a quarter century later, to appreciate the impact the shutdown had on Mainers' thinking about state government. University of Maine political science Professor Ken Palmer had just completed a book, *Maine Politics and Government*, for which he was lead author, that was not published until 1992. In it, he paints a picture of Maine contrasted to other New England states: "Maine's style is generally moderate in political discussion and in government arrangements. Unlike neighboring New Hampshire, which is very conservative and very decentralized in its government operations, and Vermont, which is quite centralized and liberal, Maine tends to stay in the middle of the road. Personalities of candidates and specific issues have always received more attention during elections in Maine than ideology. Candidates, even incumbents, who are identified with the ideological left or right have been consistently defeated."

Just as the shutdown ended, Palmer provided quite a different impression to a reporter who surveyed academic opinion. "Right now we're seeing a Republican governor and a Democratic Legislature that utterly cannot work together," he said. "It could mean fundamental changes in the contours of Maine politics. We made the transformation from a one-party to a two-party system over 30 or 40 years fairly smoothly. We certainly didn't see the kind of confrontational politics that characterized this past session."

At the time, there had been no comparable event in memory in any state capital or in Washington. Plenty of states have had budget showdowns, but kept services running through continuing resolutions until agreement was reached. Maine had no similar legal authority. It was just four years later, in 1995, that U.S. House Speaker Newt Gingrich decided it would serve his interests, and those of Republicans after their sweep of Congress in 1994, to shut down the federal government. His rhetoric and strategy bore uncanny resemblance to the playbook pioneered by Maine Republicans in 1991.

Did the shutdown have to happen? Some Republicans believe it did, and not just the firebrands. Bill Vail, then commissioner of Inland Fisheries and Wildlife, close to the governor and respected around the State House, said recently the shutdown "was the only way to get what we needed on worker's comp."

Don Nicoll disagrees, saying McKernan agreed to a strategy he was unable to execute. The governor, he said, "became more partisan at a time when he was hit with a personal tragedy . . . he set a course, encouraging his compatriots to take a very partisan position, and then was ineffectual because of the tragedy."

Afterward, the principal objects of derision were McKernan, Martin and Senate President Charles Pray. Webster was rarely included, even though he devised the strategy, and was most enthusiastic about it. In a 2015 interview, Webster said, "I went down to Augusta a couple of months ago and had a discussion with some influential Republicans in the Legislature about the shutdown of '91, and . . . very few people cared. The average guy just did not care." He added, "Republicans should be willing to use this vehicle if needed," because "sometimes you have to draw a line in the sand."

Webster also claimed to be politically unscathed; he was re-elected in 1992. When he ran for governor in 1994, however, he finished seventh among eight Republican candidates; the primary was won by Susan Collins, with Sumner Lipman finishing second. The only candidate with fewer votes than Webster was Pam Cahill, Webster's assistant leader.

Pray was defeated in 1992, losing to Stephen Hall, a real estate broker from Guilford, an outcome that shocked some insiders. When several asked John Martin privately what had happened to his Senate counterpart, he said, "You have to understand that the voters in Charlie's district felt he was not really working for them, and felt he was rather arrogant." After a pause, Martin said, "I may be arrogant around here, but I'm never arrogant at home." Yet the reckoning was not far off.

Through the remainder of his second term, John McKernan seemed disengaged and remote. He stunned supporters from his legislative days when, in 1993, he vetoed a non-discrimination measure for employment, housing and credit, the so-called "gay rights bill," after urging by the Maine Christian Civic League. The bill had passed either the House or Senate several times, then finally was approved by both. Vetoing it seemed out of character, but by then the governor had few allies. McKernan had remarried, in 1989, to his former U.S. House colleague, Olympia Snowe, and while Snowe's House and Senate career lasted until 2013, McKernan never took another public role.

EMPLOYER IMMUNITY

Despite the travails of producing a new worker's compensation law, the 115th Legislature wasn't finished. An early interim report tracked insurance rates following benefit reductions across the board. Since it takes years for new cases to be reflected in rates, immediate savings were small. Wrote Peter Mills, "Any changes to the benefit structure might require five to ten years to take meaningful effect." That didn't deter Republicans, energized by the shutdown, from demanding more changes. As one of Webster's colleagues put it, worker's comp "was too good a political issue to let go."

Martin and Pray reluctantly authorized the Blue Ribbon Commission to Examine Alternatives to the Worker's Compensation System, whose report in 1992 would be voted on in special session. The commission took a recent Michigan law as a model, which embraced unorthodox strategies, but in a state unlike Maine in industries, size, demographics and union membership. The special session was largely pro forma; the report could be accepted or rejected as a whole, but not amended. And amid continuing shutdown fallout, rejection was not an option.

There was one unquestionable advance: Maine Employers Mutual Insurance Co., the state-chartered, non-profit company that now writes most worker's comp policies. The 1991 law at first did little to prompt for-profit insurers to return, and high insurance rates were assessed across the board, providing no incentive for improved workplace safety. MEMIC turned things around quickly, and provided lower rates within a few years; Maine worker's compensation costs are now among the lowest in the nation. The Democratic chairs of the Legislature's Banking and Insurance Committee, Senator Judy Kany and Representative Libby Mitchell, had advocated for a nonprofit insurer in the 1991 law, but Republicans rejected the idea.

The rest of the 1992 Blue Ribbon law was a disaster for injured workers. Among the key changes was a new Worker's Compensation Board of eight members, equally divided between management and labor, under the theory the new board would be forced to reach consensus. Instead, it deadlocked repeatedly on key issues, some not resolved until twelve years later, when the Legislature made the director of the Worker's Compensation Board the tie-breaking vote. As Mills notes, the 1992 law required removal of "every single worker's comp commissioner," who heard and decided cases, replacing them with novices. The existing legal text, with rules developed through years of administrative findings and court decisions, was repealed, replaced by hastily drafted language from a consultant unfamiliar with Maine's system.

The irony was that, left alone, and with MEMIC added, the 1991 law might have been the best solution. Mills said, "I doubt the state saved any money by repealing the 1991 law," which "represented the best and most successful compromise of competing interests forged in the heat of political tension." Jim Case called the 1992 replacement "very harsh," providing benefits "well below the national average." In retrospective descriptions, MEMIC's considerable achievements are regularly celebrated, but hardships for workers are mostly ignored. Mills calls the current statute "an employer immunity law."

BALLOTGATE

The second, shorter session of 1992 was perhaps even more dysfunctional than the first. Budget woes continued, along with rising acrimony and frustration. Behind the scenes, Democrats were beginning to question Martin's leadership. His legislative expertise was unrivaled, but he was the most unpopular politician in Maine, and many wondered aloud whether he could ever be dislodged. Martin could have stepped down as speaker, or announced his retirement. He had an experienced majority leader, Dan Gwadosky, who was a plausible successor. Martin never seems to have considered leaving, though one of his long-time partners did just that.

Ed Pert had become a trusted and admired figure in the party, and in the House since his early days as a lonely Democrat in 1950s Bath. He'd served as Senate secretary, from 1964-66, and when Martin was elected speaker in 1974, became House clerk. The speaker and clerk have an unusually intimate relationship, and are almost always together on the floor. The House clerk helps keep legislation moving, settles disputes, and explicates fine points of procedure. Pert had worked with Martin for seventeen years when, abruptly, he resigned in the middle of the 1992 session. Pert never spoke publicly about his reasons, but in a 1998 interview, he said that while serving his last years as clerk, Ed Muskie had asked him during several different conversations, "if I thought that John Martin might be thinking of moving on."

Joe Mayo, who'd been the assistant leader, or whip, for Martin and Gwadosky, decided he wanted the job, and went to see Martin. Martin was gone for the day, leaving word that he'd already appointed Debbie Wood, the assistant clerk, as Pert's acting replacement. Mayo then campaigned for the job, and was selected by the caucus as clerk before the 1993 session began.

The election of 1992 produced changes both nationally and in Maine. For president, Bill Clinton carried Maine on his way to defeating incumbent George H.W. Bush, a summer resident of Kennebunkport who finished third in Maine, behind Ross Perot. Charles Pray was ousted, and the Senate presidency passed to the only remaining member of leadership, Dennis Dutremble of Biddeford. Otherwise, the legislative lineup changed little. Republicans gained two Senate seats, but the Democrats retained a 20-15 majority. The GOP picked up five seats in the House, with Democrats still in control, 91-60.

Some Democrats still seemed bent on a two-thirds majority, but the prospect was fading. Shortly after House recounts began, however, it was apparent not everyone had given up. The resulting scandal, dubbed "Ballotgate," was at first, like Watergate, so improbable it seemed unbelievable. Those involved found themselves marked forever by the experience.

One of them was the new attorney general, Mike Carpenter. Jim Tierney, after his defeat in the 1986 primary for governor, had run for attorney general again that fall, even though other Democrats, including Carpenter, were already campaigning. When Tierney finally stepped down in 1990, Carpenter, a former state senator from Houlton, tried again. After surveying the Democratic legislators who'd decide, Carpenter decided he was third in a three-way race. A career assistant attorney general, Jamie Kilbreth, was Tierney's choice, while Barry Hobbins of Biddeford, a House and Senate veteran, was favored by Martin. But on the second ballot, after Kilbreth was eliminated, Carpenter won by a single vote.

He assumed an office run for most of the previous two decades by Tierney and Joe Brennan, who'd entertained large political ambitions. Carpenter had endured the state shutdown along with everyone else, and after he won a second term, it proved even more eventful. He got a message late Friday evening, December 11, 1992, from Secretary of State Bill Diamond, whose department oversaw elections. He phoned Diamond at home, and was told a room had apparently been burglarized at the State Office Building, where ballots involved in a House recount were stored. Diamond said Capitol Police had examined the room, and the locks had been changed, though there were few signs of disturbance. They did find a Coke can with a cigarette butt in it. The recount would resume the following week.

Though the fallout from "Ballotgate" dominated the 1993 session, the story behind it is less familiar than the Watergate break-in and subsequent cover-up. It was told most comprehensively in a 115-page investigative report Carpenter filed jointly with U.S. Attorney Richard Cohen, a Republican appointed by George H.W. Bush, who'd served as state attorney general from 1978-80.

What they discovered was, with minor variances, confirmed by the principals in the case, including the malefactors. The scheme was devised by John Martin's chief of staff, Ken Allen, who convinced a committee clerk, Michael Flood, to help him add enough ballots to the boxes, stored in Room 122, to make it appear Democrats won two races they trailed in the Election Day count.

Allen was known as Martin's enforcer, his eyes and ears on occasions from fundraisers to committee hearings. He attended every recount. Allen had a serious drinking problem, and, at Martin's insistence, had gone to an Arizona rehab center, then returned to his job. Soon after, his co-workers noticed signs Allen had resumed drinking.

Flood told Allen he knew how to get a spare key from the Office of Legislative Information. When they entered Room 122, Allen went to work, while Flood kept watch. Allen took blank ballots from two different races, marked them for the Democrat, and added them to the boxes, secured by tape, which Allen then resealed with leftover tape. The burglary was discovered, almost inadvertently, by election division employee Anthony Noonan who, while Allen was still inside, brought in additional boxes from his car. By the time Noonan entered, after being delayed by Flood, Allen had left, but Noonan smelled cigarette smoke, and thought he heard a window closing.

From the beginning, there were Keystone Kops aspects to this attempted election-fixing. In one race, the recount was complete and no further inspections were due. In the other, Allen, late Friday night, called candidate Deborah Rice, saying she had "nothing to worry about," and that she would win. He gave Jonathan Hull, the House legal counsel, who was acting as Rice's attorney, the same news. Both said they thought Allen had been drinking heavily.

That Friday, John Martin attended a meeting of the National Conference of State Legislators in Washington, D.C., with several staff members and Mike Michaud, whom Martin had trained as a speaker pro tem, along with Dan Gwadosky. After Jonathan Hull called him about the phone call with Allen, Martin decided to suspend Allen, and did so on Monday. Over the weekend, Martin returned to do after-hours work at the State House, which could only be accessed through the State Office Building. Electronic records showed Allen was also in the building, though the two said they hadn't seen each other. Allen returned to Room 122, intending to disguise what he now recognized as clumsy ballot-tampering, but with the locks changed, he couldn't get in. On Wednesday, the recount resumed and the altered ballots were discovered; Allen had put them in boxes marked "empty." Counting was suspended, and the investigation began.

The State House was thrown into turmoil. Unlike other states, Maine had never seen such a serious attempt at election fraud, at least not one involving recounts. The investigation showed that security could be remarkably lax; in one recount, numerous ballots had been inadvertently left behind at a municipal office. Afterwards, the Legislature designated State Police the custodian of ballots in all contested races, impounding ballots at polling places.

Michael Flood confessed first, as did Ken Allen, a week later. Flood, on a misdemeanor guilty plea, was sentenced to probation. Allen pleaded guilty to two felony counts, was fined and served several months in jail.

After the Legislature convened, the question soon became, as for Richard Nixon during Watergate, "What did the Speaker know, and when did he know it?" Few felt they got satisfactory answers. In their March 16 report, investigators sharply criticized ballot handling procedures, but also said, "There is no evidence that Kenneth P. Allen and Michael T. Flood acted in concert with any other persons . . . Their actions were not the result of a well-planned criminal venture nor was their conduct undertaken with the knowledge of others . . . The criminal conduct . . . was restricted to the events of Dec. 11 and their subsequent attempts to conceal that criminal conduct." Their crimes, it said, "were the actions of two partisan operatives bent on corrupting the outcomes of two specific Maine legislative elections."

Finally, the report addressed the "elephant in the room," whether others bore any responsibility. It found "no compelling evidence" anyone had assisted Allen and Flood, or had advance knowledge. It concluded, however, that, "Whether government officials or other persons participating in the election recount process acted reasonably and responsibly in detecting possible criminal conduct . . . are not questions which the criminal justice system is designed to address. The final judges of such conduct must be those in positions of public trust and, ultimately, the People of the State of Maine."

Mike Carpenter knew he was in a tight place. He owed his position to the same Democratic majority that John Martin had led for nearly two decades. In addition to calling in Richard Cohen, he delegated the investigation, and initial drafting of the report, to his criminal division deputies. He said recently there's no reason to doubt the main findings: "In terms of the speaker's role, there were no phone records, no State House logs, no testimony, nothing that would tie him to Ken Allen's actions."

It didn't end the controversy, however. Martin's opponents denounced the report as a whitewash, claiming Martin "must have known," and even some members of the caucus were angry Martin had allowed Allen to stay on despite his erratic behavior. Other Democrats thought Martin should have been exonerated, given the evidence, but Carpenter said that was not the report's purpose.

During the session, Republicans brought a "no confidence" motion that Martin said had no legal standing. He prevailed, 75-68, but some Democrats voted against him, and others supported him only because he assured them he'd step down after the session.

As winter approached, Martin showed no sign of leaving, and he told his staff he expected to preside when lawmakers reconvened in January 1994. Whether Martin could be removed wasn't settled, and a Democratic House member, William Lemke, a college professor from Westbrook, sought an Attorney General's opinion, and on January 3, got it. Signed by Carpenter, it found that "The provision of the Maine Constitution providing for the choosing of the Speaker neither specifies a fixed term . . . nor a particular time at which the Speaker is to be chosen. In consequence . . . the Speaker must be viewed as serving at the pleasure of the House of Representatives, and therefore may be removed and replaced at any time."

As lawmakers returned, Martin offered a "compromise." He'd serve through 1994, but then not seek another term; opponents dismissed it. Martin found he no longer had a majority, and resigned, with Dan Gwadosky becoming speaker for the final year of Martin's tenth term. Though Martin's resignation ended his time as speaker, voters had just cast a verdict on his tenure, along with the Maine Supreme Judicial Court.

TERMED OUT

The term limits movement began in the 1980s, as Republicans and business interests looked to break what they perceived as immutable Democratic majorities in Congress and many state legislatures. U.S. Term Limits, a financial clearinghouse for dozens of state bills and initiatives, helped launch a nationwide movement. The early 1990s recession and bank failures provided fertile ground for anti-incumbent rhetoric and turning out "career politicians," whether their constituents wanted to or not. Before the movement waned, twenty-one states voted for legislative or congressional term limits, or both, and in all but four, where courts found measures unconstitutional, legislative limits took effect, though legislators later repealed them in two states. Newt Gingrich made term limits the centerpiece of his "Contract with America," though Congress never enacted them. In 1992 alone, twelve states voted on legislative term limits. Maine's turn came the following year.

The Maine campaign was launched by Owen Wells, who headed the Libra Foundation for Elizabeth Noyce, an heir to the Intel fortune who'd settled in Maine. She wanted to contribute to political reform, and Wells convinced her term limits would do that. He then recruited a Republican, and a Democrat, as spokesmen. The Republican was Ted O'Meara, who'd won the 1988 nomination for the 1st District Congressional seat, and lost to Joe Brennan that November. The Democrat was Rick Barton, party chair from 1986-88, who'd also run unsuccessfully for Congress in 1976, winning a seven-way primary but losing to David Emery.

The two toured the state, visiting civic and social groups, nonprofits and editorial boards, while Wells authorized a sophisticated media campaign; John Martin was the target. Yet incumbency isn't as powerful in Maine as in other states. Senate presidents Joe Sewall and Charles Pray were "retired" by their own constituents. Asked why term limits should apply to every lawmaker, not just leadership—many rank-and-file House members had served for years—they said it would be "fairer" to have limits apply to everyone. Libra, they said, had considered various reforms, from shrinking the Legislature to electing the attorney general and secretary of state. Since all these ideas would involve constitutional amendments, an arduous process, they settled on term limits, arguing they could be adopted by statute, via referendum.

Not everyone agreed. John Martin was sure term limits would require a constitutional amendment. The state Constitution lists several conditions for House or Senate service: age, residency and citizenship. House members must be twenty-one; senators can serve at age twenty-five. Under this reading, limiting re-election would be a new condition requiring an amendment. Secretary of State Bill Diamond requested a ruling from the Attorney General, and a September 6, 1991, opinion confirmed this legal theory. Citing several cases, and a 1975 ruling by the Maine Supreme Court, it stated, "It is clear, therefore, that when an office is created by the Constitution, restrictions on the ability to hold that office may be imposed only by amendment to the Constitution."

Martin then convinced the House to petition the Supreme Court on March 10, 1993, for a "solemn occasion," to provide an advisory opinion on the constitutionality of voter-enacted term limits, for which signatures had already been filed. A court majority accepted the case, but the ruling wasn't what Martin anticipated. Two of the seven justices, Caroline Glassman and Robert Clifford, both Democratic appointees, said the case wasn't ripe for decision because there had been no vote yet. The five-member majority, with three appointed by McKernan, said there was no constitutional bar to term limits by referendum, since revising qualifications by statute "only incidentally involved constitutionally guaranteed right of suffrage." The opinion was written by Chief Justice Dan Wathen, appointed to the Superior Court by Jim Longley, to the Supreme Court by Joe Brennan, and promoted to chief justice by McKernan; Wathen resigned in 2001 to run for governor as a Republican.

John Martin again took no hints. When voters enacted term limits by 2-1 in November 1993, Martin was still speaker, though he resigned two months later. The limits became effective in 1996. Since then, only one speaker has served for more than two years, as leaders are regularly "termed out."

One curious aspect of the Maine term limits decision was underlined when the Massachusetts Supreme Judicial Court ruled in a case involving virtually identical constitutional language, which Maine had adopted when it separated from Massachusetts in 1820. Despite a 1994 referendum vote for legislative term limits, Massachusetts lawmakers had declined to implement them, citing constitutional concerns. In a 1997 case, the court ruled unanimously that legislative term limits were unconstitutional. There are no legislative term limits in Massachusetts, nor are governors limited, though since the four-year term was adopted there in 1966, no one has served more than two consecutive terms.

SIX
The Long Decline
1994-2010

"Power tends to accrue to people who think they have it."
                                        —Jim Case, Interview

Maine's 1994 elections were thrown into upheaval when U.S. Senate Majority Leader George Mitchell announced on March 4 he would be stepping down from his post and leaving the Senate. No one besides Mitchell's intimates realized this was coming, and it left the Democratic Party he'd served for so many years in a state of shock. Mitchell's Senate career had been shorter than those of Margaret Chase Smith and Ed Muskie, and later the tenures of Bill Cohen, Olympia Snowe and Susan Collins, but in fifteen years he'd made at least as large a mark in Washington as anyone from Maine.

In what was, to date, the last flowering of federal bipartisanship, Mitchell had a leading role, steering to passage a long list of substantive legislation, from transportation to the environment, housing and disability rights. Working with Republicans, including Minority Leader Bob Dole and President George H.W. Bush, then with Democratic President Bill Clinton, Mitchell produced agreements in 1990 and 1993 that balanced the federal budget and set the economy on track for its strongest growth since the 1960s. When he retired, Mitchell knew about contrary forces in the national Republican Party—previewed by Pat Buchanan in his 1992 challenge to Bush's re-election, then taken up by House Minority Leader Newt Gingrich—but it's doubtful he or anyone else foresaw the reaction that ensued in November 1994.

The lateness of Mitchell's announcement, a month before Maine's filing deadlines, set off a mad scramble among those who'd planned to run, had been thinking about running, or to whom it suddenly occurred for the first time. Within hours, the two congressmen, Democrat Tom Andrews in the 1st District and Republican Olympia Snowe in the 2nd District, decided to seek Mitchell's seat. This opened up both House seats, something that hadn't happened since the delegation shrank from three to two in 1962. Within a few weeks, nineteen major party candidates jumped in, four Democrats and four Republicans in the 1st District, and seven Democrats and four Republicans in the 2nd District.

With just three months to stand out, candidates struggled even to get their names known, yet the primary results were to shape state politics for two decades. In June, Jim Longley Jr., with his famous surname, won convincingly among 1st District Republicans, while Senate President Dennis Dutremble, with barely a year at the helm since Charles Pray's re-election defeat, won the Democratic nomination with a third of the vote. The 2nd District contests were even more consequential. John Baldacci, former state senator from Bangor, won the seven-way race with 27 percent, besting Jim Mitchell, also from Bangor, later a successful State House lobbyist, while Janet Mills, a District Attorney and future attorney general from Farmington, finished third. Both Baldacci and Mitchell were close relatives of the departing U.S. Senate majority leader, though they rarely mentioned it. George Mitchell is Jim Mitchell's uncle, and John Baldacci's first cousin, once removed. For the Republicans, Rick Bennett, then thirty-one and a two-term state representative, won over House Minority Leader Stephen Zirkilton. Bennett became state Senate president in 2000, and Republican Party chair in 2012.

The traffic jam for Congress also diminished attention traditionally focused on the governor's race. With John McKernan term-limited, the open seat attracted five Democrats and eight Republicans. Susan Collins won the GOP primary with 21 percent, followed by Sumner Lipman and Jasper Wyman, Maine Christian Civic League director. Three state legislators—Judy Foss, a four-term House member, and Senate leaders Charlie Webster and Pam Cahill—brought up the rear.

There were new faces among Democrats, perhaps their most talented field since George Mitchell, Joe Brennan, Peter Kelley and Lloyd LaFountain ran in 1974. Robert Woodbury, former University of Maine System chancellor, entered, as did Dick Barringer, commissioner in the Longley and Brennan administrations, and a party intellectual at the Muskie School. Former Portland Mayor Tom Allen had been a Rhodes Scholar and classmate of Bill Clinton at Oxford Univerity.

Then there was Joe Brennan. Despite losing to McKernan in 1990, Brennan decided to make a fifth run for governor. Some long-time supporters were already pledged to other candidates, and Brennan's presence, with his opponents' reluctance to criticize him, made for awkward moments at the few debates held before the primary. Allen had hired a former reporter, Dennis Bailey, as spokesman, and Bailey later said it was impossible to gain traction against Brennan; his base among primary voters was unrivaled. Allen did better than Barringer or Woodbury, but still earned only half as many votes as Brennan, who won with 56 percent. Allen wasn't finished, however.

Mike Carpenter had also planned to run. He realized his days as attorney general were numbered after the Ballotgate scandal and the fall of John Martin. He said recently he was unpopular with Democrats loyal to Martin, adding, "After all, I issued the opinion that cost him his job." He'd become known and respected statewide for his role in the drama, however. *Maine Times* caused a stir with a cover story on Carpenter headlined, "The Last Honest Man in Augusta." But when Brennan entered the race, Carpenter stayed out.

There were two wild cards. One was Jonathan Carter, candidate of the fledgling Green Party, formed in a schism with Democrats over the party's direction. Carter got plenty of press attention but only 6 percent in November. He'd also run in the 2nd Congressional District in 1992, splitting votes with Pat McGowan, who made a second run against Olympia Snowe; she won her eighth House term with 49 percent.

The fourth candidate, Angus King, was a different story. Though a long-time Democrat, King decided he had a better shot as an independent. He had a stronger claim than Jim Longley before him, and Eliot Cutler after him, to the label. Though King came to Maine as a Legal Aid attorney, and worked for Senator Bill Hathaway, he'd never run for office before, nor taken a role in the party. King possessed important assets. In a year when anti-incumbent strains reached a pitch not seen since Watergate in 1974, he was nonpartisan. He could finance his own campaign. Though unsuccessful in convincing regulators to permit new hydroelectric dams in the Penobscot basin—acquiring an aversion to government regulation in the process—he won energy management contracts with Central Maine Power, important in the "stranded cost" era. He sold the business before launching his campaign.

King was skilled at navigating print and broadcast media. As host of the public television program "Mainewatch," he'd met most of the state's political leaders. King was a careful and perceptive interviewer, a journalist who made his guests feel they were the center of attention. He scooped up Dennis Bailey after the end of Tom Allen's primary campaign. Bailey became a close adviser throughout King's two terms in the Blaine House.

Finally, King took a leaf from Ken Curtis's book, the ten-point "Maine Action Plan" nearly thirty years before, with twelve weekly installments of his "Making a Difference" tour. As a political outsider, King needed to project knowledge of state government to stand out in a way different from Longley in 1974; King's coolness was a far cry from Longley's fiery demeanor. King's tour summaries, collected in September as "Ideas: Initiatives to Develop Our Economic Advantages & Strengths," did have critics, who complained it was short on original thinking, but it clearly represented King's own thoughts and reflections on the challenges he'd face. And his substantive points, such as adding value to traditional exports from fisheries and forests, restructuring agencies and overhauling the budget process, won a hearing from those who cared about issues.

King drew from both sides of the political spectrum, advocating aid for children and the elderly while attacking the existing welfare system—an issue that worked spectacularly well for Gingrich that year. King advocated "abolishing" AFDC [Aid to Families with Dependent Children]—the main federal income maintenance program, now known, post-Gingrich, as TANF [Temporary Aid to Needy Families]—and replacing it with "welfare to work." King praised McKernan's ASPIRE program as a possible model. He advocated public land acquisition, after serving on the Land for Maine's Future Board, as well as "computerization" of state offices, and a robust, multi-modal transportation system.

Where he sounded most like Longley was on state spending, saying "Maine's state budget process for the last ten years has been a disaster," noting rising spending since 1968—though not acknowledging that other state governments had similar patterns, after taking on many additional tasks off-loaded by the federal government. King signed on to "Reinventing Government" and "a top to bottom review" he said would produce substantial savings, though not specifying the levels.

King's "Making a Difference" tour was a key facet of a campaign unlike any candidate's before him. No one else had a campaign book, and no Democrat has produced one since Curtis in 1966.

ELECTION DEBACLES

In 1994, Democrats had another handicap from a second judicial rebuke to John Martin's oversized role. In Maine, redistricting takes places four years after the U.S. Census. Under the Constitution, lawmakers get first crack. Gerrymandering is limited, though, because any new districts must be approved by two-thirds. If the parties fail to agree, the Supreme Judicial Court decides. Traditionally, the court splits the difference between Republican and Democratic plans, but for the House, that didn't happen. The court accepted the Republican plan outright, putting Democrats at a serious disadvantage because several new districts featured two Democratic incumbents. They lost half a dozen members in primaries.

In November, House Democrats nearly lost their majority. They emerged with a 77-74 margin, a loss of fourteen seats, and Speaker Dan Gwadosky had to fend off Republican gambits to get marginal Democrats to switch parties. They almost succeeded, though Democrats won two special elections that might have shifted control. Democrats lost the Senate outright, winning just sixteen seats, down from twenty, their first minority since 1982.

At the top of the ticket, things were no better. Though Susan Collins got a smaller proportion of the vote than any GOP nominee in the twentieth century, just 23 percent, Joe Brennan couldn't defend his home turf of Cumberland County, or Androscoggin County, against Angus King, who won with 35 percent of the vote, defeating Brennan by 8,000 votes, or 1.5 percent.

Olympia Snowe routed Tom Andrews, winning 60 percent. She'd prepared for this day for many years, and had a deeper and better organized political network than Andrews, beaten almost before he started. He'd won his Congressional seat as a critic of Pentagon spending, and when the 1991 base closing list included Loring Air Force Base in Limestone, Andrews, alone among the delegation, voted for it. This was unlikely to hurt him significantly in his southern Maine district, but was fatal to any hope of succeeding Mitchell.

The reverses continued. Andrews's 1st District Congressional seat went to Jim Longley over Dennis Dutremble. The only Democratic gain came in the 2nd District, where John Baldacci won a four-way race with 45 percent, defeating Republican Rick Bennett, independent John Michael and the Green Party's Charles Fitzgerald. Baldacci served in high-profile offices for the next 16 years.

Democrats lost the legislative initiative to Senate President Jeffrey Butland, who defeated moderate Jane Amero in the caucus. As freshman GOP Senator Peter Mills recalled, "I went down to Augusta thinking Jane would be our leader, and found out it would be Jeff Butland." It was a sign Republican moderates were losing their grip on the party and its nominees—the direction Charlie Webster pioneered, and not that of John McKernan.

Butland asserted himself immediately, saying there were too many committees for too few senators—his caucus had eighteen members to chair nineteen committees—and insisted on a reduction. Adoption of legislative rules, normally a one-day affair, took weeks. Seventeen joint committees remained; the Audit and Program Review Committee was disbanded, and the Aging, Retirement and Veterans Committee was awkwardly merged with the Legal Affairs Committee, renamed Legal and Veterans Affairs. Butland also insisted the 1991 tax increases had to go. Other legislative leaders, and the new governor, weren't so sure. Revenue growth was still weak, but Butland said he'd push things to the brink if what he called "temporary" increases weren't repealed. The income tax surcharges were repealed, and the sales tax rate dropped to 5.5 percent, later reduced to 5 percent later in the King administration, amid the biggest surge in tax receipts in decades.

The 117th Legislature was the last before term limits took effect. The 1996 election provided an opportunity, with Bill Clinton seeking re-election, for Democrats to restore their majorities, but they made only marginal gains, picking up four House seats, though they did retrieve a Senate majority with nineteen seats, gaining three.

The major event, however, was Senator Bill Cohen's decision to follow George Mitchell into retirement. Cohen had served three Senate terms and was a shoo-in for a fourth; his performance in the Watergate and Iran-Contra investigations had made him almost as popular with Democrats as he was with Republicans and independents. Cohen was just fifty-six, but Mitchell's departure, and Maine voters' adoption of congressional term limits in 1994, though overturned by the U.S. Supreme Court, seemed to weigh on him. As his chief of staff, Bob Tyrer, explained, "If you keep staying for six years at a crack, then the number of 62-year-olds people hire is smaller than the number of 56-year-olds people hire." Cohen was soon tapped as Bill Clinton's Defense secretary, serving through the second term as a rare Republican in a Democrat's Cabinet; he then formed a defense consulting firm, The Cohen Group.

Phil Merrill, seeking a political comeback, had announced he'd take on Cohen more than a year before the election. He toured the state in a 1972 car, dramatizing his claim that Cohen had held office too long; in the term limits era, it was a plausible approach, one that almost worked for Pat McGowan against Olympia Snowe. When Cohen announced he was retiring on January 16, 1996, though, everything changed.

That afternoon, a reporter called the Maine Democratic Party chair to check her reaction to Joe Brennan's announcement he'd be running for Cohen's seat. Her first words were "Oh, no." She wasn't the only one. Brennan had lost the last two governor's races, and previously expressed little interest in returning to Washington after his House terms from 1986-90. With Brennan in, however, Merrill departed, drawing the same conclusion Mike Carpenter reached in 1994; he was not quite done, however. In June, Brennan easily won a five-way primary with 57 percent; Bangor attorney Sean Faircloth, a freshman state senator, got 25 percent.

Brennan's November opponent was Susan Collins, who'd emerged unscathed from a Republican primary in which two rivals imploded. Collins, from a prominent Aroostook County Republican family, had worked for Cohen, and served in McKernan's Cabinet, while staying well clear of the State House wars. As the 1994 nominee for governor, however, she finished far behind Angus King, and Brennan.

The primary was the beginning of her comeback. One opponent was John Hathaway, an Alabama native, first-term state senator, and favorite of the right-to-life movement, which had picketed Collins in 1994. The second was Robert A.G. Monks, Ed Muskie's and Margaret Chase Smith's long-ago Senate challenger, also attempting a comeback. Monks, a corporate reformer, appealed to moderates; Hathaway attracted the growing conservative wing. Hathaway's campaign was rocked by child abuse allegations from Alabama that produced no criminal charges. Monks, it was reported, hired a private investigator to check the rumors.

"Opposition research" was controversial in Maine, and Collins's campaign benefited. She stayed above the fray and won easily. Good fortune continued, with Brennan an ineffective debater, and Collins depicting herself as Cohen's logical successor. Collins won by 32,000 votes in what was, finally, Joe Brennan's last campaign. For the first time since 1958, Republicans held both U.S. Senate seats.

SCHISMS

The failures at the top of the ticket were symptomatic. A generation of Democratic leaders who might have grown up behind Joe Brennan and John Martin, who'd occupied most of the political space for decades, failed to materialize; many left politics. Term limits was another setback, preventing legislators from developing skills in committee before seeking leadership posts. The Clean Election Act, adopted in a 1996 referendum, had a more positive impact, enabling a wider range of legislative candidates to run credible campaigns with public funding.

One traditional source of support for Democratic candidates, labor unions, were in steep decline. As a state marginal to the twentieth century's manufacturing boom, Maine's unions had never achieved the level of influence seen in the rest of the Northeastern and Midwestern states, though as party organization waned, Maine unions became central to get-out-the-vote efforts. National unions had, starting in the 1950s, focused on protecting existing jobs through work rules and international trade restrictions, rather than organizing new sectors. This proved self-defeating, as accelerating technological change eliminated entire manufacturing industries. Nor did public employee unions take up the slack. After the debacle of the McKernan years, the Maine State Employees Association's influence shrunk markedly, with the state increasingly relying on contracted services, not state employees, from the King administration onwards.

Progressive energy was also diverted as referendums that bypass the Legislature became an increasingly popular means of seeking political change. The three Maine Yankee referendums of the 1980s, all unsuccessful, were an early example. In the King years, a movement that at first seemed a way of uniting conservation and environmental groups ended in utter defeat.

The spruce budworm infestations of the 1970s and 1980s, which had defoliated fir and spruce across millions of acres of Maine's north woods, were followed by massive salvage cutting operations that fueled paper mill capacity. The multinational companies that owned most of the north woods began experimenting with planting techniques environmentalists feared would bring to Maine the tree plantations typical of Southeastern forests. One result was the 1989 Forest Practices Act, placing the first statewide restrictions on clear-cutting, and practices that reduced biodiversity and increased erosion into lakes and streams. The compromise was advocated by figures such as Roger Milliken, whose family-owned Baskahegan Company was a major forest landowner in Washington County, and who advocated long-term management to increase timber and environmental values, rather than the quick rotations preferred by paper companies.

After meager returns from Green Party runs for Congress and governor, Jonathan Carter embarked on a different venture, turning to the forest controversy for a referendum by his group, Ban Clearcutting. The 1996 ballot measure ignited a statewide debate that prompted an all-points bulletin from industry, claiming Carter's referendum would destroy their means of production. The charge had plausibility. In its final form, the initiated bill would have regulated cutting on nearly every forested acre—a compliance level that might have rendered large-scale harvesting uneconomic.

Governor King agreed with industry that Carter's campaign was an economic threat, and corralled mainstream environmental groups, the Natural Resources Council of Maine and Maine Audubon, together with industry moderates, to produce the Forest Compact, an alternative that went on the ballot as a competing measure. This is a legislative tactic that rarely works, but in this case did, after a fashion. The compact went beyond the existing Forest Practices Act, though Carter denounced it. Yet even some of his allies saw the initiated question as overreaching.

The competing measure got a plurality of votes in November, but fell short of a majority since, under terms of the state constitution, voters were allowed to vote "no" on both options. No one actively supported the Forest Compact when it returned to the ballot in 1997 and was rejected. The 1989 Forest Practices Act remains the only law regulating clearcutting. Roger Milliken, serving on the boards of Maine Audubon and the Maine Forest Products Council, remembers shuttling between the two and finding himself "in two separate universes." Industry spent more than $2 million contesting the referendum, and it hardened attitudes on both sides of the divide.

This ill-conceived proposal was on the ballot at the same time as the Clean Election Act, which provided a striking contrast in electoral tactics. The nation's earliest and perhaps most comprehensive system of voluntary public financing, it was the product of extensive discussions among a broad and diverse coalition, from the League of Women Voters to the Christian Civic League, with a legislative test and further revisions before being submitted to the voters.

Angus King's two administrations constituted an "era of good feeling"—the derisive term from the period of national politics in the early nineteenth century when the Federalist Party had collapsed and the Whig Party hadn't yet formed, leaving Democrats the only organized party.

Infighting and ideological confusion were rife, and though Maine's version was more benign, it represented a further decline in the Legislature's ability to respond to public needs.

As a man without a party, King had no dependable votes among legislators. He thought he might be able to use referendums to help govern, getting the idea after he successfully opposed a 1995 referendum to deny "gay rights." But he lost his taste for referendums after the Forest Compact. Although King acquired a reputation as an effective Executive Branch manager, his legislative accomplishments were few.

King's Cabinet was far more cohesive than McKernan's had been. Kevin Concannan, who returned to Maine after a successful stint as director of Oregon's Department of Human Services, was a widely praised choice for DHS. John Melrose, a planning consultant, was an effective Transportation commissioner, working with King to expand the state's commitment to rail, ports and pedestrian access as well as a beefed-up highway and bridge program.

Although one of Maine's most popular governors—King was easily re-elected in 1998 when Democrats fielded no serious challenger—there was a sense of drift that robust revenues and infrastructure spending couldn't quite overcome. It wasn't until King's final budget that he proposed a "legacy" program—an initiative to give every middle school student a laptop computer, reluctantly approved by lawmakers—that earned significant national attention.

Another leader confronting a disorienting new political world was House Speaker Libby Mitchell, the first woman to preside. Speaker Dan Gwadosky, along with every legislator who'd served four consecutive terms, had been removed by term limits in 1996. After losing her bid for the Congressional 1st District nomination in 1990, Mitchell rejoined the House as a replacement candidate. In 1994, she had become assistant majority leader, but now confronted a prospect nearly every speaker has since then: She had just two years before she was term-limited herself.

Mitchell enlisted King's cooperation on a budget stratagem to avoid a repetition of what Jeffrey Butland had done two years earlier, in vowing to withhold Republican budget votes unless taxes were reduced. The House and Senate passed a budget for current services by majority vote, which King signed, then reconvened in special session. Since it was enacted early enough to avoid the "emergency" designation, it took effect on time, with a supplemental budget covering a few new programs enacted later. Republicans, denied a role in budget negotiations, balked at other legislative priorities, and the maneuver has rarely been used since.

Mitchell had a reputation as a reformer from her earlier work on worker's compensation, but was unsuccessful in what she thought would be a signature initiative: a "thirteenth year" for high school graduates, offering one year of free tuition at any public college or university campus. She was inspired by the Hope Scholarship program pioneered by

Democratic Governor Zell Miller of Georgia, which provided full tuition for high school seniors maintaining a B average. While Maine's tuition rates were higher, and four years difficult to fund, Mitchell believed that if students spent a full year in college, they were likely to find the means to earn a degree. She told an interviewer in 2001, "It wasn't just the financial issue . . . it was a cultural issue." Students whose parents hadn't gone to college were reluctant, even though the skills required for most jobs were greater than for their parents' generation. These barriers to college attendance by Maine students have since been well documented.

Mitchell found it hard going. "There were [former] superintendents in the Legislature who told me, 'We already know who should go to college, and they're going,' " which Mitchell said "wasn't the point." Governor King showed no interest, and the coup de grace came when Representative George Kerr of Old Orchard Beach, whom Mitchell had appointed to chair Appropriations, publicly ridiculed the idea and said it wouldn't be in the budget. John Martin had removed an Appropriations chair for a lesser offense, but Kerr went unscathed. And though Mitchell later returned to the Legislature, becoming Senate president in 2008 and running for governor two years later, she never again offered a signature initiative in any campaign.

BACK TO THE BLAINE HOUSE

As Angus King's second term drew to a close, Democrats—after passing up the 1998 governor's race—were tightly focused on 2002. Two candidates announced, but John Baldacci was the frontrunner from day one.

Baldacci grew up in an Italian household in Bangor, was Lebanese on his mother's side, and moved comfortably between two worlds. "We would go to Waterville almost every weekend, and the people in Waterville would come up to Bangor, so there was a regular going back and forth," he told an interviewer in 2010. The Waterville visits always included the kitchen of Mintaha, or Mary, Mitchell—the mother of George Mitchell and his four siblings, though by then George had long since left home.

Baldacci's mother, Rosemary Karam, was part of the Mitchell clan and moved to Bangor after marrying Robert Baldacci; they had eight children. Robert Jr. was the eldest and John was the fourth of six sons. Although ethnic distinctions from earlier waves of immigration were fading, they were clear to Baldacci, who said, "Monday, Wednesday, and Friday would be tabouli, bulgur wheat, grape leaf zatr, and the Tuesday, Thursday and Saturday would be spaghetti and meatballs, and maybe pasta or some chicken parmesan. We didn't eat American food until McDonald's opened up."

In Bangor, the Baldacci family had opened an Italian restaurant in 1933 under the Joshua Chamberlain Bridge, Momma Baldacci's, that became an informal political clearinghouse under Bob Sr. Spaghetti dinners were the meal of choice whenever a Baldacci was running for office, and John often spooned out the meatballs. His father served on the Bangor City Council, and when John was twenty-three, decided it was time for him to take over. In 1980, John Baldacci ran for the House and lost, but in 1982, with a statewide ticket headed by Joe Brennan and George Mitchell, he won the Bangor Senate seat, where he served with the Democratic majority for twelve years.

Baldacci didn't stand out. He chaired State and Local Government, then Business Legislation, and in his final term, from 1992-94, Taxation. His friend and House compatriot, Jack Cashman—whom Baldacci tapped for the Governor's office and then the Public Utilities Commission—said they both thought of leaving the Legislature in 1990, but stayed because they expected Brennan to return as governor. Cashman left in 1992 after an eventful session as House chair of Taxation, but Baldacci stayed and co-chaired the committee. Neither found the assignment a comfortable fit.

When George Mitchell left the Senate in 1994, Baldacci was well positioned to run in the 2nd Congressional District, which Olympia Snowe was leaving behind. Bangor was the district's largest population center after Lewiston, and the Lewiston candidate in the primary, Jim Howaniec, drew votes only locally. Baldacci's task was complicated because Jim Mitchell, a Bangor attorney, was also in the race, as was Mary Cathcart, a legislator from Orono.

Baldacci's expertise in "retail" campaigning paid off, and he carried most of the rural counties, including Hancock, Piscataquis, Somerset, Waldo, and Washington. Mitchell took Aroostook County, while Janet Mills carried only Franklin and Oxford counties, from her prosecutorial district. Baldacci's decisive margin came in Penobscot County, where he bested Mitchell by 2-1, and 3-1 in Bangor; together, Penobscot and Androscoggin counties tallied half the vote. Mitchell was anything but a sore loser, and worked on Baldacci's campaigns in all his subsequent races. Baldacci had an easier time in November; his Republican opponent, Rick Bennett, came from Norway, in Oxford County, and had served just two House terms.

Baldacci arrived in Washington as one of just two Democratic freshmen. His Maine counterpart, Jim Longley Jr., one of seventy-three Republicans elected in the Gingrich tidal wave, was far more typical. Longley faithfully supported Contract with America bills until he realized, too late, how unpopular Gingrich was in Maine. Baldacci was fortunate to inherit members of George Mitchell's Senate staff, including Larry Benoit as chief of staff, who'd directed Mitchell's comeback in 1982. He served in the minority his entire time in Washington, under Gingrich and Dennis

Hastert, Gingrich's ineffectual successor, and without important committee assignments. As Joe Brennan had, it seemed Baldacci would welcome
a return to Maine, but he seemed ambivalent.

In entering the 2002 governor's race, Baldacci was treading the same
path John McKernan had, from Congress back to Maine, that originated
with Frank Coffin's ill-fated bid in 1960. Much more than Attorney General, the other popular proving ground for Democrats, Congress provides
staff, a political network, and major contributors, but doesn't necessarily
fit well with the administrator-in-chief role, where both McKernan and
Baldacci struggled.

Chellie Pingree, a four-term state senator and majority leader, opposed Baldacci for the open seat, but within months was persuaded she
wouldn't be able to compete in fundraising. Baldacci pointed out that the
nomination for U.S. Senate against Susan Collins, facing her first re-election test, was open, and Pingree switched, though she never seemed as
focused on the Senate as the Blaine House. It wasn't until 2008, when 1st
District Congressman Tom Allen ran against Collins, that Pingree got
another chance, and won the congressional seat. Baldacci had no primary
challenger, a test that might have—as it did for Frank Coffin in his first
race—sharpened his awareness of Democratic voters' views.

Republicans had trouble finding a candidate. With Collins and Olympia Snowe ensconced in the Senate, Democrats with legislative majorities,
and term limits in force, there were no established GOP politicians capable of challenging a four-term congressman. They picked Peter
Cianchette, from the Cianbro family, a company founded in Pittsfield by
four brothers that became the state's largest construction company. He'd
worked in the Dragon cement division, then moved to South Portland as
a management and business consultant. Cianchette served two House
terms, and was the last GOP nominee for governor from the party's moderate wing. He offered only muted criticism of Baldacci, who won easily,
with 47 percent to Cianchette's 41 percent, a 38,000 vote margin. Jonathan
Carter, making his final appearance in a statewide race, took 9 percent.

POLICY ADRIFT

Baldacci's return to the State House did not go smoothly. Several members of his Washington staff were willing to move to Augusta, but the
new governor didn't ask. The Cabinet remained unfinished until September, and Baldacci's appointments suffered by comparison to Angus
King's. Kevin Concannon offered to stay on at DHS, but Baldacci declined; he had decided to merge the Department of Mental Health into
DHS to become the Department of Health and Human Services, but the
new, even larger agency struggled. Baldacci had a succession of commissioners before a department veteran, Brenda Harvey, brought some sec-

ond-term stability. For Transportation, he picked David Cole, a late arrival, who lacked the panache with legislators of his predecessor, John Melrose. Lee Umphrey, a veteran of Senator Claiborne Pell's staff who'd also worked for George Mitchell in Northern Ireland, was Baldacci's first communications director, and an advisor on a par with Dennis Bailey for King. But Umphrey stayed only two years, and had three successors.

Despite Baldacci's years in the state Senate, relations with the Legislature were never warm, and became distant. Baldacci did have the handicap, as had King, of a revolving door among legislative leaders. There were four House speakers: Pat Colwell, John Richardson, Glenn Cummings and Hannah Pingree; and three Senate presidents: Beverly Daggett, Beth Edmonds and Libby Mitchell. Even in Baldacci's first year, though, House Democrats felt neglected.

When Baldacci took office, the state was experiencing a financial hangover after the 1990s revenue surge ended. Under King, general fund spending had reached nearly 7 percent of the state economy, but the revenue curve was down sharply. A shortfall of $1.2 billion loomed for the first biennium, but Baldacci immediately ruled out any tax increase. Instead, there were reductions nearly everywhere, some of the "gimmicks" devised in 1991 returned, with the state sometimes perilously close to running out of cash, and at one point issuing a $450 million tax anticipation note.

Opponents didn't trust Baldacci's fiscal intentions, however. The Maine Municipal Association unveiled its referendum proposal to write into law the previous goal that the state pay 55 percent of local school budgets. Baldacci asked MMA to delay the vote until 2004, giving him room to deal with school funding in his first biennial budget. MMA refused, the question went to the ballot, and Baldacci then convinced lawmakers to add a competing measure, essentially to reach 55 percent over four years, not immediately. The MMA question fell short of a majority, but outpaced the competing measure and went back on the ballot in 2004, when, unlike the Forest Compact, it was approved.

Baldacci's major legislative priority was the Dirigo Health plan, a pioneering initiative to use federal and state dollars to expand access to health care. It was approved with bipartisan support. Dirigo was designed by Trish Riley, a DHS bureau director in the Brennan administration, and director of the National Academy for Health Care Policy; she joined the Governor's office. Dirigo offered a new insurance plan for individuals and small businesses, but Baldacci decided not to charter a new nonprofit company, along the lines of MEMIC, but instead ask private insurers to do it. Anthem, which had taken over the nonprofit Maine Blue Cross during the King administration, with few objections, was a for-profit that's now among the largest and most profitable health insurers in the nation. After purchasing Maine Blue Cross, it raised rates steeply to acquire substantial reserves—the lack of which was one reason the

Blue Cross affiliate was sold. When the request for Dirigo proposals went out, Anthem was the only bidder.

The second component of increased access was expanded Medicaid eligibility, which required convincing the Bush administration to grant a waiver allowing federal funds to be used to subsidize more people. The waiver was crucial to Dirigo's insurance coverage, and the basis for Riley's projection it would cover more than 100,000 Mainers within three years. The administration didn't respond, and Baldacci never pressed the point, either in Augusta or in Washington, despite his congressional experience. Two years later, the waiver was rejected, and Dirigo never came close to enrollment goals announced at the outset.

The state-funded insurance program did proceed, financed through a levy on all health insurers, and representing savings produced by the cost-containment features of the legislation—chiefly a voluntary cap on hospital costs. While the insurance commissioner didn't agree to the full "savings offset" the administration calculated, the amount certified was loudly protested by insurers, and Anthem filed suit against the state at the same time it was the sole provider of Dirigo insurance. Although Anthem lost every court motion, the resulting uncertainty undermined public confidence, and conservative groups eagerly denounced Dirigo as a "failure," even before the insurance plan took effect.

Baldacci never effectively defended his chief legislative creation. In addition to a passive approach to the federal waiver, he didn't explain how Dirigo could be made to work. His staff could only convince him to visit businesses that had purchased Dirigo policies, appearances that failed to shore up sagging public support. Yet Dirigo was a model for the plan Massachusetts adopted in 2006, often dubbed "Romneycare," after Mitt Romney, the Republican governor who implemented it. There were differences, including the Massachusetts mandate for individuals to buy subsidized insurance, a feature not included in Dirigo because of concerns that some Mainers, with lower incomes, couldn't afford even subsidized plans. And Massachusetts, in turn, became the model for the Affordable Care Act after it created nearly universal access to health care for one state.

Baldacci's other major policy proposal in 2003 was repeal of the personal property tax on business equipment, a key source of municipal revenue from large manufacturing plants. In his first budget, Angus King had devised BETR—Business Equipment Tax Reimbursement—where the state repaid businesses for any tax due because of new investments. BETR helped convince two computer chip manufacturers in South Portland and an auto parts maker in Bangor to expand, and initial costs to the state were modest. Many "rust belt" states had abolished business equipment taxes in the 1970s and '80s, hoping to keep plants open, but by the time Maine tried it, manufacturing employment was dropping nationwide.

Eight years later, BETR had become a major budget line, peaking at $65 million annually. Late in the King administration, lawmakers reduced BETR reimbursements from 100 percent to 90 percent, creating discontent among businesses. Baldacci had a decision to make, and, urged by chambers of commerce, pushed to repeal the tax altogether. Legislative Democrats were dismayed. They welcomed Dirigo, but repealing a business tax wasn't on their agenda, and the House caucus under Speaker Pat Colwell revolted. It wasn't until 2006, under Speaker John Richardson, that repeal succeeded, and it was a singularly complicated solution.

BETR remained in place for the twelve years that businesses had been eligible. After that, new equipment was exempt, and the state reimbursed municipalities 50 percent, as required by the state Constitution when the state reduces a local tax. Towns thus receive only half the proceeds from new assessments under the Business Equipment Tax Exemption program (BETE). The state maintains assessments on three equipment classes: taxable before 1995, reimbursed under BETR for the ensuing twelve years, and exempt under BETE after 2006. The programs cost the state more than $100 million a year, and OPEGA, the legislative evaluation agency, has twice studied the program and found no measurable statewide economic benefits.

TAXPAYER RIGHTS

If the MMA referendum posed a direct challenge to his leadership, and his ability to raise money for schools, Baldacci was soon beset on the opposite side of the fiscal coin by referendums to cut taxes statewide. Anti-tax crusader Carol Palesky qualified a 2004 ballot measure, modeled on California's Proposition 13, to cap property taxes at 1 percent of assessments. Since Maine's statewide average was 1.8 percent, it would have imposed crippling cuts on county, municipal and school budgets, and was decisively rejected, with 63 percent voting no.

A more sophisticated effort followed two years later, with the Maine Heritage Policy Center basing its effort on Colorado's spending cap system known as TABOR, for Taxpayer Bill of Rights. It seemed more reasonable, because it allowed for population increases and inflation—but it made no allowance for economic growth, and the only way to override budget limits would be another referendum. A year earlier, Baldacci had convinced the Legislature to enact the LD 1 system of budget caps at all levels, ones less restrictive than TABOR. Despite the preventive effort, the 2006 referendum was closer than in 2004, with 54 percent saying no; another effort seemed possible, though it didn't occur. Two more tax limitation questions, one to cut motor vehicle excise taxes, the other to require referendum approval for all local budgets, were decisively defeated in 2009.

The many referendum campaigns may have failed, but for Baldacci they reinforced an aversion to new programs or spending, even though the Legislature retained Democratic majorities, though smaller than in John Martin's heyday. Progressive Democrats were always skeptical of Baldacci, and after the setbacks of Dirigo Health, and the lack of new initiatives such as those offered by Ken Curtis and Joe Brennan, disappointment set in.

Even the relatively straightforward task of implementing Medicaid expansion under MaineCare became a disaster. The administration hired a computer consultant who'd never previously designed a state Medicaid billing system. The results weren't tested while the existing system continued, and when the new system went online its failure rivaled the Longley administration's snafus, when unpaid bills piled up in DHS office hallways. Because the program was now larger, and health care costs had climbed relentlessly, the problem was even more daunting. Despite attempted fixes, the new system billed so chaotically that the now-DHHS made "prospective payments" to hospitals based on historic averages, not current claims. The MaineCare program acquired such significant debt it wasn't until after Baldacci left office that his successor as governor, Paul LePage, used a revenue bond on future liquor sales to finish paying hospitals. Baldacci approached his 2006 re-election campaign with flagging approval numbers.

'INDEPENDENT' CHALLENGE

As candidates began announcing, Baldacci got an unpleasant surprise. Barbara Merrill, wife of Phil Merrill, had been elected to the House from Appleton in 2002 as a Democrat from a largely Republican district, and re-elected in 2004. It was evident she planned to run for governor, but didn't enter the Democratic primary. Instead, she ran as an independent, using Clean Election funding. To do so, she had to leave the Democratic caucus just two days before announcing. The caucus numbered only seventy-six, and without Merrill, Democrats no longer had a majority. Leaders had to plead with Joanne Twomey, a disaffected Democrat from Biddeford who'd switched to independent, to switch back so Speaker John Richardson could continue to preside.

Merrill published a campaign book called "Setting the Maine Course: We *Can* Get There From Here," which is considerably quirkier than its Curtis or King predecessors; it concludes with three bean-dish recipes. While there are occasional proposals—Merrill endorses a water extraction tax referendum for which organizers were then, unsuccessfully, gathering signatures—most of the text is a folksy paean to the delights of rural community and town government, and bromides in place of policy initiatives, such as "Let's make Maine the free enterprise state" and, on schooling, "No parents left behind."

While campaigning, Merrill criticized Baldacci at every opportunity, but it's difficult to find consistent arguments. She faulted the governor for poor fiscal management, citing the tax anticipation note caused by inadequate revenues, then advocated further tax cuts, including abolishing the corporate income tax. Still, Baldacci's unpopularity benefited Merrill, as voters sought a plausible alternative.

They almost had one. Peter Mills, after serving five Senate terms and one in the House, ran for governor as a Republican. With a family legislative history dating back nearly a century, he never considered an independent bid despite his maverick tendencies; he had many supporters outside the Republican Party and some skeptics within it. Any doubts about his administrative abilities were answered when he later headed the Maine Turnpike Authority and put a troubled agency back on course. But 2006 was not his year. In a scant primary turnout, he fell 2,500 votes short to Chandler Woodcock, a lightly regarded fellow state senator from Farmington who was the first avowed GOP conservative nominated in decades—a sign of things to come.

The four-way November ballot, with the Green Party's Pat LaMarche joining Baldacci, Woodcock and Merrill, fractured the electorate. Baldacci won, but only with 38 percent, followed by Woodcock with 30 percent, Merrill with 22 percent, and LaMarche with 10 percent, the highest total ever for a Green, but also the party's last hurrah. After the election, the Maine Governmental Ethics and Election Commission looked into Merrill's Clean Election financing, which included paying Phil Merrill more than $100,000 to produce media and broadcast material. The spending was found to be legal, but the Legislature later defined restrictions to family use of Clean Election funds, and increased the hurdles for future candidates.

SECOND TERM BLUES

John Baldacci began his second term from a precarious perch. He blistered his Cabinet at its first meeting, upset that reaching school funding goals he'd agreed to earlier would cost far more than he expected. He demanded a way to pare back the increase, and Deputy Education Commissioner Jim Rier said it was reasonable to reduce state support for local administration, since Maine had 290 school districts and half that many superintendents. Thus was born the most consequential and contentious initiative of Baldacci's second term: school consolidation.

In his budget address, Baldacci outlined a plan to shrink the number of districts to twenty-six, based on the regional Career and Technical

Education centers serving high school vocational students. This was plausible—CTE students were bused daily from wide geographical areas—but would face resistance from the deeply embedded "local control" mindset. Having proposed the plan, Baldacci had little more to say.

Instead, the Education Committee was given until March to devise a plan that could pass the Legislature. Republicans had Peter Mills, who'd returned to the Senate, with Libby Mitchell, now majority leader, heading the Democrats, who ranked the titular Senate chair, Peter Bowman. These two veteran legislators were charged by their caucuses with fulfilling the goal outlined by Baldacci. Day after day, Mills and Mitchell sat on opposite sides of Bowman and debated, until Mills finally realized Democrats had no intention of offering any consolidation plan. All they were willing to do was spend $3 million to hire facilitators who would travel the state, visiting school districts possibly interested in merging. The final straw for Mills was when Mitchell insisted that school unions—several towns with their own school boards, sharing only a superintendent—were just as "consolidated" as school administrative districts, the SADs authorized by the 1957 Sinclair Act, with a single regional school board and integrated school management, purchasing, and transportation. On March 6, what Mills called "the high water mark of my disgust for the Education Committee," he surprised even himself by walking out and writing a minority report.

Mills's plan followed the Sinclair Act outline, and would have required each municipality with fewer than 2,500 students to join with neighboring communities; no more than eighty districts would remain. To get there, it recommended incentives modeled on Sinclair—enhanced subsidies for merging districts, preferences for school construction funding, and grants for consolidation planning and implementation. The minority and majority plans went to the Appropriations Committee, which appointed a four-member subcommittee to review them.

The subcommittee was chaired by Democratic Representative Emily Cain, but dominated by Republican Senator Karl Turner, a financial consultant in his fourth term. Turner adopted the 2,500-student and eighty-district goals, but rejected incentives to ease the transition. Asked why, he said, "The towns have had 20 years to consolidate, and they haven't done anything." That they hadn't actually been asked before didn't faze him. If towns refused to consolidate, Appropriations decided, they'd be assessed a 2 percent penalty, deducted from their annual state allotments.

The Appropriations Committee consolidation plan was included in the 2007 biennial budget, rousing considerable opposition and little support; the penalties were widely resented. Some large new regional districts were formed—as Regional School Units, not SADs—but many later disbanded, after penalties were removed in 2011. Opponents united behind a referendum to repeal the consolidation law, but in 2009, voters rejected it 2-1. As Mills pointed out, the state was already dividing school districts, as various towns withdrew from SADs to gain short-term financial advantage. Measured by its original goal, school consolidation failed. There are still 242 school districts, and school unions survived, reclassified as "Alternative Organizational Structures."

One reason consolidation failed was that Baldacci rarely spoke of any educational advantages from regional districts, for students and teaching staffs, emphasizing only budget savings. The state "booked" $36.5 million in decreased subsidies for local administration, though what was saved at the local level was never determined.

Baldacci's second cost-saving initiative was to abolish the county jail system and turn over administration to the state, as Ken Curtis had proposed back in 1966. The Department of Corrections reported that costs were rising faster in jails than state prisons—like rural schools, jails are often small and inefficient. The proposal also made sense because Maine has had, since the 1970s, a unified prosecutorial and judicial system, which sentences all inmates housed in both county and state institutions. District Courts replaced part-time municipal judges, and eight District Attorneys coordinate prosecutions with the Attorney General's office.

The jail merger was no more successful than school consolidation, and Baldacci never pushed the point. The only result was a Board of Corrections charged with coordinating jails statewide. It depended on county sheriffs relinquishing budget surpluses to a common fund, something many were reluctant to do. The Legislature balked at authorizing spending to fund a property tax cap, and the system collapsed when the next governor, Paul LePage, refused to appoint new members to the Board of Corrections.

Taxation was a third policy area where, except for the business equipment tax repeal, Baldacci was unwilling to get involved. Despite entering office with sinking revenues, and leaving amidst the biggest financial downturn since the Great Depression, he never requested a general tax increase, unlike every other Democratic governor in the Northeast. The only exception was a $1 per pack increase in cigarette taxes, which he accepted because of the intention to reduce youth smoking. In his final budget, Baldacci began cutting revenue sharing and school funding, a trend his successor was only too happy to continue.

Legislative Democrats, meanwhile, set their sights on tax reform. After five years, they developed a revenue-neutral plan to lower the top income tax rate by substantially expanding goods and services subject to sales tax. A Taxation Committee plan initially had bipartisan support, but when it went to the floor, only Democrats supported it. An earlier version had included sales tax on personal services, derided as "the haircut tax," while in the enacted bill, the sales tax covered labor charges on automobile repairs—another flash point. The bill decreased the top income tax rate from 8.5 percent to 6.75 percent, but the sales tax expansion drew Republican ire. Baldacci, who'd remained aloof, finally weighed in and, as a result, the sales tax expansion for ski lift tickets and a real estate transfer tax increase were eliminated. Republican senators launched a people's veto petition, and tax reform was repealed in June 2010, with 60 percent opposing the law.

ALL THE WAY DOWN

The 2010 campaign began early among Democrats. Attorney General Steve Rowe attempted what Joe Brennan had done successfully, but where others fell short—to use his legislatively selected office as a springboard to the Blaine House. He announced early, and began touring the state to drum up support. A native of Oklahoma, Rowe was elected to the House in 1992 from Portland, chaired the Business and Economic Development and Natural Resources committees, and won respect for his courtesy and even-handedness. He challenged Libby Mitchell for the speakership in 1996, and was Democrats' consensus choice two years later for his final term.

Rowe then ran for attorney general. The three-term incumbent, Andrew Ketterer, withdrew rather than face Rowe. As attorney general, Rowe had served the four-term maximum before launching his gubernatorial bid more than a year before the primary. For a while, his was the only name in the news.

Libby Mitchell entered the race in August. Her term as speaker ended in 1998, and she won the seat held by Senate President Beverly Daggett, who was term-limited, in 2004. At the post-election caucus, John Martin, who'd also shifted to the Senate, in 2000, ran against Beth Edmonds, a children's librarian from Freeport, for Senate president—a contest that encapsulated the struggle between the old and new Democratic Party. Edmonds won by a single vote. Mitchell was then selected majority leader without dissent; she served two terms with Edmonds. In 2006, Martin began his final Senate term, taking the consolation prize of assistant leader and forming an uneasy triumvirate with Edmonds and Mitchell. Mitchell became Senate president in 2008, the first woman to preside over both House and Senate. She could have served two terms, but instead tried to become Maine's first female governor, amid a year of political turmoil, nationally and in Maine.

When Mitchell announced, she immediately took the lead. She was better known than Rowe, and her legislative history went back almost as far as Martin's, to 1974, when she won a rural House seat from Vassalboro as Democrats took the majority. Mitchell grew up in Gaffney, South Carolina, and witnessed the first stirrings of the civil rights movement when Furman University, where she enrolled, decided to integrate. With her husband, Jim Mitchell—they're not related to the Waterville Mitchells—she moved to Maine in 1971. Jim Mitchell was among the Yale Law graduates, along with Peter Bradford and Kermit Lipez, recruited to work for Ken Curtis. Libby Mitchell wanted to be a teacher, but with two young children, she worked part-time.

Jim Mitchell intended to move back to his native Arkansas, but after working for Curtis he caught the political bug, running in the 1st District Congressional race in 1976, and hoping to oppose David Emery in his first re-election bid. He finished second in the primary to Rick Barton, however, and with his wife in the Legislature, she became the focus of the family's political aims. Jim Mitchell served thirty-seven years as Kennebec County probate judge. Libby Mitchell succeeded him after he died in 2016.

Libby Mitchell brought all of the assets of a long legislative career, along with liabilities. She never lost a legislative race, or a leadership contest, but stumbled when running for major offices. She lost to Bill Cohen for U.S. Senate in 1984, taking just 26 percent. In 1990, seeking the 1st District Congressional seat vacated by Joe Brennan, she ran a distant third behind Tom Andrews and Jim Tierney. Her rise as the sole woman, much of the time, in Democrats' legislative leadership, and the first to reach the top, was a lonely journey. Yet by the time she became Senate president, she was the third woman to serve there. And by inauguration day, she would be 70 years old.

Mitchell won the June primary easily. She took 34 percent, and 42,000 votes, with the remainder split almost equally between Steve Rowe; Pat McGowan, who'd served as John Baldacci's Conservation commissioner since his congressional runs; and political novice Rosa Scarcelli, who recruited Dennis Bailey as campaign manager, and was the youngest candidate.

The seven-way Republican primary was less predictable. Peter Mills ran again, as did the future congressman Bruce Poliquin of Georgetown. Steve Abbott, Susan Collins' chief of staff, bid for moderates. Matt Jacobson, a railroad executive and head of Maine & Co., touted his business background. Waterville Mayor Paul LePage announced, as did his mentor, Bill Beardsley, president of Husson University. The frontrunner was Les Otten, a brash and acerbic ski area entrepreneur who'd built Sunday River into a major resort, merged it with Sugarloaf, but then led the American Skiing Co. into bankruptcy. Otten had the most money, and dominated the airwaves. Yet his campaign hit a pothole when he unveiled a campaign design that viewers immediately saw resembled Barack Obama's 2008 logo; it was redesigned.

The previous year, LePage had taken to rural Maine as perhaps no candidate had since Ed Muskie. He spoke at countless churches, clubs, fairs and suppers, and on primary day pulled off an upset. He won Republican votes by as dominating a margin as Libby Mitchell had among Democrats. He polled 49,000 votes and won every county except Hancock and Oxford, taking 37 percent. Otten finished a distant second;

Mills was third. For the first time in decades, there were more Republican votes—10,000 more—than in the Democratic primary.

As had happened regularly since Jim Longley in 1974, a former Democrat joined the race as an independent. Eliot Cutler had been an intern in Ed Muskie's Washington office as a Harvard student, then was deputy press secretary for the 1968 vice presidential campaign; Don Nicoll hired him as a legislative assistant. George Mitchell tapped Cutler as scheduler for the 1972 presidential campaign, and he excelled at these early political jobs. Cutler then joined Walter Mondale's 1976 vice presidential campaign, and was appointed by President Carter as deputy director of the Office of Management and Budget. In Muskie's office, he had worked on the Clean Air Act of 1970 and the Clean Water Act of 1972, sometimes claiming authorship.

After leaving the Carter administration, he co-founded Cutler & Stanfield, an environmental law firm. Its sale in 2000 made him a wealthy man who, like Angus King sixteen years earlier, could self-fund a gubernatorial bid. Cutler had numerous national and international connections; he lived in China, and there acquired furniture and antiques for his Maine oceanfront home on Shore Road in Cape Elizabeth, which in 2017 he listed for sale at $11 million.

When Cutler returned to Maine to campaign, he went to visit George Mitchell at his ridgetop house in Seal Harbor, on Mount Desert Island. Years earlier, when Cutler was serving at OMB, Mitchell had delivered a rare chastisement by letter, satirizing Cutler's headline-grabbing self-promotion, and concluding, "You have finally achieved that for which you have striven these many years: you are now more important than Senator Muskie."

Since Muskie's death in 1996, Mitchell had been the most eminent and respected Democrat in Maine. When Cutler sought his blessing, Mitchell asked whether he'd run as a Democrat. When Cutler said he wouldn't, Mitchell said, "Eliot, you're a lifelong Democrat. If you run as a Democrat, I'll support you. Otherwise, you know I can't."

Cutler's estrangement from the Democratic Party continued. When he decided to run again four years later, he claimed that, in a meeting with Ben Grant, state party chairman, Grant told him he'd "clear the field" in 2014, guaranteeing that Cutler would be unopposed in a primary. Grant said he never made such a promise.

In the fall of 2010, Libby Mitchell had a knotty problem. Her two opponents charged she would govern just like the unpopular John Baldacci, with whom she'd served in leadership for six years, and daring her to say where she differed. Her available choices were to ally herself closely with the departing governor, or set herself apart. There were opportunities to do so. Mitchell, in a position of influence on the Education Committee, had opposed Baldacci's school consolidation ideas, preferring the school union arrangement she said had worked well for Vassalboro. She also headed the legislative oversight committee for OPEGA, which issued its report finding no significant benefits from Baldacci's repeal of the business equipment tax. She chose neither alternative: to cut ties with, or declare her support for Baldacci's policies, and remained on the defensive. In debates, Cutler took shots at both Mitchell and LePage, but his barbs went mostly at Mitchell, as they did with the Democratic nominee four years later, Mike Michaud.

Despite surrounding turbulence, polling in the 2010 governor's race remained remarkably consistent. LePage and Mitchell ran neck and neck, with Cutler trailing far behind. Yet no poll ever showed Mitchell in the lead, and in the final weeks, many Democrats and sympathetic independents concluded Mitchell couldn't win. Thousands began moving to Cutler; he may have doubled his vote count in the last two weeks. The effort to deny LePage the election failed. Cutler led early, but as the rural towns came in—LePage's base from his countless appearance there—Cutler's lead shrank, then disappeared, just as George Mitchell's had thirty-six years earlier. LePage polled 36.7 percent, defeating Cutler by 10,000 votes, who had 35.9 percent—percentages almost identical to the Longley-Mitchell race. Cutler carried Cumberland County decisively, but won only three small counties, Hancock, Knox and Sagadahoc. LePage took the other twelve. Libby Mitchell polled 18.8 percent, the lowest proportion for a Democratic nominee in a century.

Democratic losses continued down the ticket. The legislative races were a debacle. Democrats had held the House for thirty-six years, but they lost it, surrendering twenty-three of their ninety-five seats and ending up in the minority, 78-72. In the Senate, they lost six of their twenty seats, relegated to the minority by 18-16. The losses exceeded even those they'd suffered in the Gingrich sweep of 1994, when they lost fourteen House and four Senate seats. The Republicans now controlled the Blaine House, and both legislative chambers.

The downfall of the Maine Democratic Party, which had dominated state politics for more than three decades, does not have a single cause, nor did it come about through a single event. Failures in leadership, unwise decisions by candidates, parochial recruitment efforts, shriveling of the party's organization, and a failure to coordinate campaigns and messages all played a part. By 2010, the party had nowhere to go but up—or remain in the minority.

RENEWAL

SEVEN

Recovery

"We must think anew, and act anew. We must disenthrall ourselves."
— Abraham Lincoln, Annual Message to Congress, 1862

Nationally, the Democratic Party had its greatest success in the New Deal era and the years following World War II. Franklin Roosevelt transformed American politics by employing the federal government in a leading role toward recovery from a catastrophic economic downturn that left one-third of the nation unemployed, as the shadows of another European war lengthened. The New Deal's achievements were preceded and made possible by another movement twenty years earlier, the Progressive era, which ushered in direct election of U.S. senators, votes for women, and a progressive federal income tax, all of which increased democratic representation and citizen equality. Roosevelt's wartime leadership put an end to the isolationism that had dominated American foreign policy between the two world wars, and greatly expanded the role of the Executive Branch. He was also the most successful Democrat in history, leading to twenty years of White House control, the longest such stretch since the Republican Party's post-Civil War dominance.

The burst of post-war prosperity and growth at first seemed to solidify the New Deal approach to American public life. Government played an increasing role in providing the basics of education, health care, housing and transportation. Economic equality increased, as nearly everyone benefitted from the growth, not only of the economy, but of American leadership in the world. Federal and state spending rose, as did voter satisfaction, and Republicans and Democrats regularly worked together to strengthen this consensus.

In Maine, Ed Muskie was able to channel these forces of optimism and growth into his groundbreaking campaign for governor in 1954. With his partner, Frank Coffin, as chairman of the state Democratic Party, he laid the building blocks for a thiry-year run of growth comparable to the earlier Democratic successes nationally. State parties were aided by the U.S. Supreme Court's decisions establishing the then-revolutionary principle of "one person, one vote," whose effects were far-reaching, though less celebrated than contemporary decisions broadening civil and legal rights. America had become an urbanized country, but representation in state legislatures, until the 1960s, was still based on town and county lines, with huge disparities in the number of voters per district. Then, as now, voters in cities tend to support Democrats, while Republicans are more successful in small towns and rural areas. For a time, individual voters became more important than special interest blocs.

In 1963, the nation was stunned by the assassination of John Kennedy, a seemingly unthinkable event, and though Lyndon Johnson led a brief and consequential revival of New Deal policies, Vietnam soon created a morass for the president, and for his party. The shift in partisan strength toward Republicans began with the election of Ronald Reagan in 1980, who ousted Jimmy Carter, the first "outsider" candidate to win election as president. Carter, with no experience in Washington, was unsuited to his role as national Democratic Party leader, and the fractures in a famously "big tent" political party began to widen.

Reagan also succeeded in reorienting the political debate toward rejecting a robust government role, and explicitly favoring the interests of private business concerns. His derisory line about "I'm from the government and I'm here to help" was sufficiently vague to deter rebuttal, but all the more effective because many Democrats themselves wondered if the New Deal was becoming a historical artifact.

The underpinnings of Reagan's economic policies are laid out in the Powell memo of 1971, written for the U.S. Chamber of Commerce by soon-to-be Supreme Court Justice Lewis Powell, appointed by Richard Nixon the same year. It prescribed a much more aggressive defense of business interests against government encroachment. While the Powell memo itself didn't advocate the dismantling of government programs and removal of effective regulation that Newt Gingrich brought to Congress after the 1994 election, it has helped define the path taken by the Republican Party ever since.

Another tectonic shift was the race-based "Southern strategy" begun by Richard Nixon and continued by Reagan, who launched his 1980 presidential campaign outside Philadelphia, Mississippi, where three civil rights workers had been murdered sixteen years earlier. A generation later, Republicans have dislodged Democrats from their dominant position in southern states. There, Democrats' blue-collar economic policies had long co-existed—increasingly uneasily, after the civil rights movement—with segregationist impulses. The Republicans who now control southern politics may have similar positions on race as the old segregationists, but they consistently side with business, not labor, in congressional votes.

After the reverses of the 1994 congressional election, President Bill Clinton led the Democratic Party into an undefined "center," winning re-election two years later after telling the nation that "the era of big government is over," even as the political dominance of business interests was growing in both major parties. Barack Obama, though elected in 2008 amid the sharpest economic downturn since the Great Depression, declined to change course. Despite the Affordable Care Act's other achievements, it increased the range and scope of private interests within the nation's health care system. In nearly all its traditional domestic policy roles, the federal government plays a lesser part than it did before Reagan, and the decline has gone nearly unchallenged.

For a time, Maine Democrats avoided the infighting that marked national conventions beginning in 1968—although they had some of their own at that year's state convention—and continued to build coalitions and win new adherents. But since the end of the Brennan administration, those elected as Democratic leaders have increasingly given ground to advocates of tax cuts, privatization of government functions, and reduced public investment. The burgeoning economic inequality that was accelerated by the Reagan tax cuts has now "trickled down" to shape state budgets, including Maine's.

The choice between "big government" and "big business" was always a false one, yet it continues to shape attitudes at the State House. This theory holds that Maine's state government became too big, taxed too much, and over-regulated business. Yet the implementation of downsizing, tax cuts and relaxed regulation has left the state, and its economy, worse off than before. The robust economic and population growth of the 1970s and 1980s has been replaced by stagnation and fears of further decline, at least everywhere north of Portland. The "small government" approach has been tried, and has failed. And, in one key respect, it was based on a false premise.

The anti-tax fervor that began during the King years, and became incessant during the Baldacci administration, held that Maine was "the highest taxed state," based on the "tax burden" rankings of the Tax Foundation in Washington. Maine, always near the top, ascended to first or second on the list, all based on a faulty interpretation of the data. The Tax Foundation counted all taxes paid within a state, including property tax, as a "burden" on its residents, and Maine has a higher proportion of property taxes paid by non-residents than any other state. The Tax Foundation later revised its formulas to consider only taxes paid by residents, and Maine's ranking immediately dropped to 15th.

It's been many years since either political party focused on making government more effective, while providing the necessary financial resources to accomplish its aims. Nationally, Republicans have been faulted as "the party of the 1 percent." Democrats cannot succeed in regaining their traditional constituency of working people, across the boundaries of race, class and religion, however, if they persist in trying to represent the 10 percent.

A PARTY'S PROBLEMS

The Maine Democratic Party's decline stems in part from a drift away from those who once supported it most strongly. Like the national party, it has often emphasized social issues at the expense of economic issues. Yet its institutional failures are also notable, and recovery cannot begin until they are addressed. Not every state's Democratic Party has suffered the same fate.

The first problem is the most obvious: After the first generational shift from Ed Muskie and Frank Coffin to younger leaders, the party has been dominated by the same cohort for nearly forty years. Ken Curtis was the youngest governor elected anywhere in the nation when Mainers chose him in 1966, but the generation he brought into politics has been unwilling to cede power long past the point when "baby boomers" began to retire from other professions.

Joe Brennan's fifth bid for governor was at least one too many, and his U.S. Senate campaign in 1996 was ill-conceived. Brennan's 1964 legislative classmate John Martin long overstayed his welcome, using the House Speaker's chair in ways that strained the boundaries of a citizen legislature. Even today, Martin continues to serve in the House, and will soon complete fifty years in the Legislature. He is still afforded a prime position on the Appropriations Committee, much as Louis Jalbert was many years earlier. Martin's leadership record led to a Legislature saddled with term limits for *every* legislator, regularly cutting short careers that might have developed the leaders any political party so sorely needs. Because Maine, uniquely, has no statewide elective office other than governor to which lawmakers might aspire, legislative term limits are a burden on Maine's entire political system, one that shows no sign of diminishing.

Nor are Brennan and Martin the only examples. The party's recent nominees for governor have been less successful than those of the 1960s and 1970s in large part because they present no energizing ideas, have little appeal to new voters, and seem motivated more by a sense of entitlement, or obligation, than a real passion for public service.

At the Legislature, where Democrats are still in the majority much of the time, they have proven unable to innovate, to concentrate on issues that might lead to enactment of important legislation if pursued concertedly over several years. It's at the committee level that bipartisan initiatives and regional alliances are often conceived, but there, too, Democrats have been content to sit back more often than take the lead.

Maine's joint legislative committee system is shared by few other states, but, over the years, has proven its worth. Periodically, though, such structures need adjustments and realignment. It's telling, however, that the only two revisions taken in decades were initiated by Republican Senate presidents, Jeffrey Butland in 1995 and Kevin Raye in 2011. Obvious problems concerning session lengths, budget procedures, and proliferation of bills go unaddressed.

DIVISIONS AND DIVERSIONS

Erosion of the party's structure and organizing abilities may be less obvious, but it's an even more serious problem for Democrats. Humorist Will Rogers' most famous line from the 1920s, often rendered, "I don't belong to any organized party, I'm a Democrat," retains a grain of truth. Throughout its history, the Democratic Party has been a broader, more diverse coalition than the other major parties it faced, and thus more vulnerable to the forces of division.

In Maine, it's most evident in the number of former Democrats who choose to cast themselves as independents to run for governor, beginning with Jim Longley in 1974 and continuing through Angus King in 1994, Barbara Merrill in 2006, and Eliot Cutler in 2010 and 2014. It's in the nature of electoral politics to seek advantage wherever it can be found, but if a party's nomination is not a major political prize, its future is in doubt.

A new challenge arose in the 1980s with the founding of the Green Party, the first durable third party in at least a century. The Green Party has been generally unsuccessful in electing candidates, and has only one-tenth as many members as the Democrats. It has elected one two-term legislator, and a handful of municipal seats in non-partisan elections. It hasn't had candidates for Congress or governor since 2006. Yet it has, at times, represented a significant source of progressive energy that was once channeled largely through the Democratic Party.

Another diversion of energy has been the advocacy and proliferation of referendum questions as an alternative to legislative action. After the initiative system was adopted by constitutional amendment in 1911, then employed the same year to replace party caucuses with primary elections, it was rarely used. Only seven campaigns occurred over the next six decades, and only one of them—dedicating gas taxes to the Highway Fund in 1935—was successful. The attempted income tax repeal in 1971 ushered in a new era of direct democracy. Six questions were considered in the 1970s, thirteen in the 1980s, sixteen in the 1990s, and twenty-seven more since 2000. While the referendum's appeal cannot be denied, its frequent use—especially for basic issues such as wages and taxes—could supersede the legislative process, as it has in other states. Despite the Legislature's flaws, only laws created through give and take, amendment and compromise, can reflect the necessary complexity of public solutions—as ballot questions, sometimes crafted by a single group or individual, cannot. And in the end, legislators have the last word.

At one time, State House lobbying was mostly the province of business interests and regulated utilities, but has increasingly been employed by advocacy groups of all kinds. While organized groups should be as free as individual citizens to petition their representatives, it's startling to realize that, in staff and contributions, a long list of organizations outpaces the Maine Democratic Party itself. Lobbying has unquestionably increased as legislators' experience has declined, leaving the Legislature less likely to find creative compromises rather than heed one coalition or another.

Major candidates haven't had to depend on parties since the rise of television as the dominant campaign mode, but organizing remains essential for the Legislature, county offices, and officially non-partisan municipal posts. And parties remain the only way of coordinating campaigns into what was once called "the ticket." It has been highly effective for Maine Democrats, from the first attempt in 1954 to major victories in 1966 and 1982.

Most candidates, including those at the top of the ticket, campaign in isolation, lacking the kind of cross-fertilization that occurs when people actually listen to each other's speeches and informal talk, and learn how to improve their presentation and sharpen their focus. More active party organizations, from local to state, would provide the backbone for public events that can at least balance the flattening, and sometimes deadening, depictions on-screen and online. The media strategies that dominate today's campaigns alienate voters more than persuade them, and are a poor substitute for outreach and neighbor-to-neighbor discussion.

It isn't possible to replicate the political world of earlier times, but candidate recruitment is another vital and neglected tool that state parties can use to prevent their major races from being dominated by out-of-state money. Legislative recruitment has left the Democratic Party office and ended up at the State House, creating a parochial atmosphere where House and Senate campaign offices compete with each other for candidates without any reference to the vital lower rungs of the political system. The Leadership PACs routinely used by legislative leaders to fund rank-and-file legislative campaigns create further myopia, since they are wielded by lawmakers who will soon be gone themselves. As Allen Pease once observed, "It might help them win leadership positions, but it doesn't necessarily work to the overall benefit of the party."

A rebuilt system would include a much more comprehensive array of effective municipal, county and state committees, leading up to the key roles once provided by the state chair and members of the national committee. No party can police its own nominees, nor should it try to, but no party can succeed without having some influence over who runs for office.

There have been some encouraging signs. The state party has begun hiring organizers and expanding its staff. But the citizen remains the essential element of party-building, each of whom can persuade others to engage in the unglamorous work of politics. Municipal committees that are mere e-mail lists, or a state committee that lists more than 120 members, are unlikely to create an effective nucleus capable of persuading people that politics is more than endless fundraising appeals, or online petitions, but entails face-to-face contact with those who remain on the sidelines. Sensing a political emergency, more people are getting involved. Many more are needed.

GLASS CEILING

No discussion of the weaknesses of Maine's Democratic Party would be complete without considering the role of women, and how the party and this clear majority of its supporters have somehow failed to be on the same page. Compared with the records of state parties in New Hampshire and Vermont, successful female candidates and office-holders have been rare in Maine. The state has yet to elect a woman as governor, and while three Republican women have represented Maine in the U.S. Senate, there's been no comparable Democratic breakthrough; it wasn't until 2008 that Chellie Pingree became the first Democratic woman to win a U.S. House seat.

The New Hampshire contrast is particularly stark. Following the 2016 election, the state became the first in the nation to have four women as its congressional delegation, and all are Democrats. The electoral achievements of the two senators, Jeanne Shaheen and Maggie Hassan, both former governors, are especially impressive. Neither was an innovative governor, and were constrained, as Ed Muskie and Ken Curtis sometimes were, because they served with Republican legislatures. Shaheen dismayed progressives when she vetoed a state income tax passed by lawmakers in response to a state Supreme Court order on education funding, killing the measure. But she ousted Senator John Sununu, Jr. in 2008 on her second try, after losing to him in 2002. Hassan defeated another first-term Republican incumbent, Kelly Ayotte, in 2016, who had taken 60 percent of the vote when she won the seat in 2010.

Vermont has elected only one woman as governor, but she was a pioneer in many respects. Democrat Madeleine Kumin became lieutenant governor in 1980, and though she lost her first bid for governor in 1982, came back to win in 1984. Her family were Jewish refugees from Europe, and she faced many challenges while working her way up in the Legislature. Only New Hampshire and Vermont still elect their governors for two-year terms, and Kumin was the first woman from any state to be elected governor three times; Jeanne Shaheen was the second. Neither Kumin nor Shaheen sought a fourth term.

Kumin was later U.S. deputy secretary of Education and ambassador to Switzerland, where she had been born in 1933. Vermont has only one U.S. House seat, and the state has yet to elect a woman to Congress. No one doubts that Vermont women can be competitive, however. Barbara Snelling, widow of a former Republican governor, but a lieutenant governor and a political force in her own right, was widely seen as the frontrunner against incumbent Democratic Governor Howard Dean before she suffered a stroke during the 1996 campaign, and withdrew from the race.

The pioneer among Democratic women in Maine was Lucia Cormier, born in Rumford in 1909, a little over four years before Ed Muskie. A Franco, she headed the modern languages department at Stephens High School and earned an MA in education from Columbia University. First elected to the Maine House of Representatives as a Democrat in 1946, she served six terms until she stepped down to run for the U.S. Senate against Margaret Chase Smith in 1960—the first time two women had contended for a Senate seat; the race was featured on the cover of *Time* magazine. Like Elmer Violette six years later, her Franco heritage was highlighted in the race, but after her defeat it was many years before another Democratic woman became prominent in Maine politics.

There have been successes among presiding officers at the Legislature. Three women served consecutively as Senate president from 2002 to 2010—Beverly Daggett, Beth Edmonds and Libby Mitchell—and two women have served as House speaker, Mitchell from 1996-98 and Sara Gideon, selected in 2016. None recorded any significant legislative achievements, however, and Mitchell, the only one who sought higher office, was repeatedly unsuccessful.

The causes of these disappointing results are arguable. Are Democratic women in Maine simply suffering from bad luck, or are there more fundamental factors at work? Women who have been elected elsewhere have, in candid moments, talked about their difficulties with male colleagues in the often hyper-competitive world of electoral politics, and are unanimous that breakthrough elections are important in paving the way for successors. While few voters, and fewer candidates, expect voting to follow gender lines, Maine Democrats need to explore more deeply than they have before why women still appear limited by a "glass ceiling" in a party that aims to be inclusive and diverse.

THE POWER OF IDEAS

Sustaining its early successes is something the Maine Democratic Party has been unable to achieve, and the institutional decline has been especially steep. The Lewiston convention of 1954 put Democrats on the state's political map. Today, conventions barely get noticed by the press, or the voters. An occasional convention speech will make news, but the sustained attention to party platforms and the issues surrounding them has disappeared, and needs to be brought back.

At one time, the best minds the party could muster conferred with rank-and-file delegates and produced documents that were memorable, and the basis for legislative action. Simply looking for the kind of consensus a party must seek to communicate effectively to voters can achieve its own momentum. Giving candidates a voter list and asking them to knock on doors—the standard prescription today for House and even Senate candidates—puts them in an uncomfortable, uninformed position where they're less likely to be effective even with voters who happen to be home, and are willing to give them a hearing.

An initial experiment would be a series of statewide issues conferences, giving party members meaningful work to do. The brainstorming we now associate primarily with business development should be returned to the public sector, and political parties are still the logical places to start. With a platform worthy of the name, voters would be able to test how candidates they elect to office perform their assigned roles. Not everything in a platform results in meaningful legislation, but attempting to translate ideas into policy is what separates an effective Legislature or local government from one that merely presides.

Though it's not the current conventional wisdom, ideas are what drive politics, not personalities. Good candidates can't be created by formulas or focus groups; even in the unlikely event they win, they won't be able to accomplish much. In 1948, the *Lisbon Enterprise* lamented the "issueless" campaigns Mainers were then subjected to: "Nobody is allowed to say anything that has the least to do with government or the office being sought. Those running comment how noble it is to dig clams, grow blueberries, teach school, and wait on tables." Suitably updated, those days have returned.

By 1962, Ed Muskie was able to conclude an issues conference in Augusta by reviewing eight years of accomplishment, and saying, "Let us continue to be the party of ideas, to dare support ideas we believe to be sound even though public support may be uncertain, and to assert leadership in the task of mobilizing public opinion behind what we believe to be right." For a time, Maine's elections were about more than the personalities and egos of the candidates, and could be again. There might even be another campaign book by a Democrat.

Commitments of time, money and leadership are essential if party organizations are to regain their role in recruiting candidates, and in convincing the candidates who do step forward that their fellow Mainers are better political guides than national groups or fundraisers. Party committees need recruits, too, and are an ideal place to create and explore the opportunity, diversity and inclusion that Democrats believe in. The party can then support and test candidates while they hone their skills, provide reasons to vote that transcend sound bites and advertisements, and get out the vote.

Party unity will always be elusive and imperfect, but if the organization can regain its substance, the benefits of staying inside the tent, and not freelancing, will increase markedly. As Don Nicoll recently put it, "There are moral imperatives that need to be articulated, but more people need to engage in the practical business of politics." The attractions of single-issue voting, and the temptation to demonize one's opponents, diminish markedly when one is part of a community.

LOCAL OPTIONS

Efforts to rebuild the party's structure, from top to bottom, must run in parallel with reconsideration of the relations between Maine governments at all levels, something rarely attempted and never fully achieved. The lack of statewide offices creates a gulf impeding further advancement for those who have served well in the Legislature, and are looking for a new challenge. Political opportunities in towns, cities and counties are even harder to find. While the Maine Democratic Party's efforts to rebuild local committees show signs of promise, such political work will not have its appropriate rewards until municipal and county governments are again attractive places to begin a political career.

Maine's local government began with the creation of towns, and long predates statehood. Despite the incorporation of twenty-three cities, all but a handful during the nineteenth century, municipal organization has never progressed much further. County government, the basis for school organization, taxation and public safety in most of the country, is weak or absent in New England, whose roots extend two centuries earlier and whose early forms, including the town meeting, are surprisingly persistent.

The tax arguments that recurred in the 1990s weren't baseless; Maine does have relatively high costs for local government, particularly schools. A former State Planning Office director, Evan Richert, aptly summed things up by calling municipalities "frugal, but inefficient." Though two other New England states, Connecticut and Massachusetts, effectively abolished county government, that's not a likely step for Maine—with a land area equal to the rest of New England, scattered settlement and a population density similar to the Midwestern states.

The last comprehensive study of the relations of state, county and municipal government occurred in 1982, as the Brennan administration readied for what proved to be a more expansive and successful second term. The Cabinet Committee, chaired by Transportation Commissioner George Campbell, worked for a year and produced a relatively modest blueprint for change. At the time, the Legislature still approved all county budgets, a tedious and contentious task. Then, as now, counties depended on property taxes for most of the services they do provide.

Some of the committee's recommendations, such as a four-year term for sheriffs, were ultimately adopted, but most were not, including a proposal that state revenue sharing be extended to counties as well as municipalities. Reform legislation that included provisions for aligning various regional agencies with counties failed, after House Speaker John Martin sided with those who favored abolishing county government altogether. Today, budget committees composed of municipal officials control spending for a majority of county governments, leaving little leeway for the commissioners charged with oversight. Maine remains without any effective form of regional government, and it needs one.

One tradeoff, simpler but more radical than a full-scale reorganization, would quickly improve services while reducing costs. John Baldacci's proposal to incorporate county jails into the state system failed, but the problem persists. Not all county jails need to remain open; some could be closed and converted to other public uses. County sheriffs rarely exert a direct role over jails, except for their budgets, and jail administrators could as easily work for the state as the county.

Law enforcement remains why most sheriffs seek the post, and where the public can most legitimately expect direct services. After schools, police departments are the most expensive municipal service, and many town departments are too small to be effective. Federal guidelines for police agencies from the 1970s recommended at least ten fulltime officers to properly investigate and solve crimes and offer twenty-four-hour patrols; with the increased sophistication of investigative techniques, minimum staffing would be higher today. Yet the majority of municipal police departments are far smaller than this, have high expenses, and struggle to retain officers. Establishing counties as primary law enforcement agencies, except for larger cities such as Portland, Lewiston and Bangor, would offer many benefits. It would also provide enhanced authority for elected sheriffs, with clear job descriptions that they now lack.

Mandating such an outcome would likely fail in a state with strong "local control" traditions, but incentives for consolidation similar to the Sinclair Act for schools would work. Counties could offer satellite police stations, strategically located, while maintaining a unified force of well-trained officers, detectives and criminologists. Municipalities accepting county policing would enjoy lower costs, and towns that have no regular police protection would gain it. The state would support the arrangement financially with revenue sharing and transition grants. Government would become more effective by ending the overlapping and sometimes confusing jurisdictions of state, county and local police forces.

School organization remains a larger and seemingly intractable problem, yet we already know what works and what doesn't. The Sinclair Act of 1957 created more than sixty integrated regional school districts in a state that had never had any, reducing the number of districts by nearly half. The School Consolidation Act of 2007 produced only eleven new regional arrangements, ten conversions from other regional formats, and one district created by a private and special law. Withdrawals began almost immediately, several of the new districts disbanded, and many smaller towns remain outside any formal regional structure. Short of the Legislature creating new districts by fiat, something many Mainers would find unthinkable, the incentive approach used in 1957 is vastly superior to the penalty-based law that failed to accomplish much in 2007.

The problem of excessively decentralized public education remains urgent. Per pupil costs remain higher than average, yet Maine ranks thirty-second among the states in teacher salaries, and by far the lowest in New England. A former Education commissioner surveying the vast sweep of rural Maine found "empty classrooms," where teachers are hard-pressed to cover the basic curriculum.

There are already examples of what could be done. In 1961, eight towns in rural Oxford County formed the Oxford Hills School District, jointly creating one of the state's largest high schools. In 1998, the state funded an expanded "comprehensive high school" there that fully integrated academic and vocational programs, eliminating the traditional separation between them. While the new school has thrived, it hasn't yet been replicated anywhere else in Maine. In Limestone, the Maine School of Mathematics and Science was created in 1995 as a statewide magnet school after the closing of nearby Loring Air Force Base removed most of the students from the area, and is regularly ranked among the top public schools in the nation. Yet the magnet school, too, remains unique.

Better organized schools and counties would create opportunities for better governance as well. Few young people now see serving in local office, except perhaps the largest city councils, as an opportunity for advancement—and rarely as a reason for getting involved in local party committees. There have been notable exceptions in the past. Bennett Katz served in the state Senate, and was twice majority leader. He helped enact the income tax and create the University of Maine at Augusta. His first elected office was on the Board of Alderman, when the capital still had bicameral government, and his motivation for running was to improve trash collection in his neighborhood. Jon Lund, publisher of *The Maine Sportsman* and noted conservationist, was elected to the House as a

Republican and later became attorney general. The issue that elevated his profile was cleaning up the junk cars that then crowded the banks of the Kennebec River, and which he found could be ordered removed by existing nuisance laws. If coordination between Maine governments can be improved, there will be many more such stories.

CUTTING TO THE BOTTOM

When Angus King called Maine's budget process "a disaster," he had a point, though perhaps not the one he thought he was making. Through his "Productivity Realization Task Force," King hoped to provide spending discipline and efficiency. For a time, state budgets had "accountability" goals that sought "measurable outcomes." Before the 1991 budget disaster engulfed them, John Martin and Charles Pray launched a Restructuring Commission that reported the following year; a few recommendations were ultimately adopted by future administrations, including King's, but by the time its major findings would have been implemented, Pray was already out of office. The two efforts were similar in their stress on business solutions—the 1992 commission suggested Total Quality Management, a manufacturing sector regimen—as a model for the state budget.

King also emphasized business practices as a guide to government decision-making, not recognizing that government's core functions are fundamentally different than those involved in creating products and services, finding customers, and earning a profit. Public services are precisely those the private sector cannot reliably provide through a business model.

Large transportation networks can only be built and maintained through public resources, and the same has proved true for health care, education and the legal system. Providing them at acceptable costs is largely a political, not a managerial process. We should remember that private companies created the pollution, unsafe food, hazardous workplaces, and other ills through pursuit of competitive advantage, with government then stepping in to regulate in the public interest. The expectation that government can function well by replicating business practices is doomed to failure.

Maine's budget-making is flawed not because it isn't "businesslike," but because it has become entirely revenue-based. One Restructuring Commission recommendation that was implemented, the Economic Forecasting and Revenue Forecasting committees, have gone well beyond the original intent of proponents, which was, after the failures of McKernan administration budgeting, to provide accurate and reliable numbers. They are now used, by both parties, as the effective arbiters of how much the state will spend. While Executive Branch agencies still compile budget requests based on perceived needs, the budget itself is fixed in advance, and the Legislature's job becomes merely dividing up the pie according to available revenue.

During the later King administration, revenues grew faster—in part due to improved federal fiscal policies from the 1990 and 1993 budget agreements—than during the previous two decades, and it could be argued that the state overspent for a few years as a result. Since then, however, revenues have lagged, and shortfalls have been exacerbated by repeated agreements to cut taxes, first under the Baldacci administration, which focused on reducing business taxes, and accelerating during the LePage years, where the governor targeted business and personal income taxes with singular intensity.

After the voters' rejection of their tax reform initiative, legislative Democrats accepted tax cuts each biennium until 2017, even as reductions began cutting into state programs across the board. Municipal revenue sharing was the hardest hit, with a 60 percent reduction since 2010, but many state budget lines show cuts of one-third or more. The spending gap has grown; historically, Maine General Fund spending amounted to just over 6 percent of its gross state product, but now it is far below that level. The gap today amounts to more than $500 million per biennium. Since Maine's constitution forbids deficit spending, these deficiencies threaten to become permanent. State government doesn't have enough revenue to carry out its basic responsibilities.

Nor have cuts in state spending produced prosperity. Maine's per capita personal income continues to be the lowest in New England, and the gap with several other states has widened since the Great Recession.

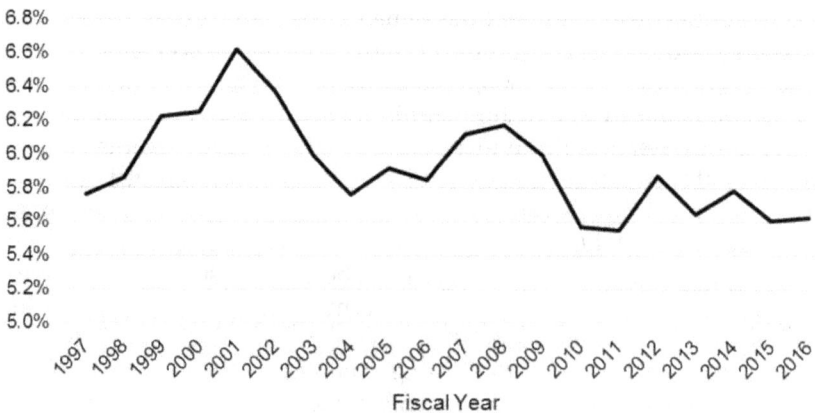

Maine General Fund Spending as a Percentage of State GDP, 1997-2016. *Source*: Maine Center for Economic Policy analysis of data from the Maine Office of Fiscal and Program Review and NAICS GDP data from U.S. Bureau of Economic Analysis

We suffer the ills of low economic growth and population stagnation, as well as bearing the burden of reduced public services.

Breaking this vicious cycle will require a new approach to the state budget. Rather than seeing projected revenues as definitive, no matter how many times they have been ratcheted down, we need to assess public needs first. Ironically, the smallest units of Maine government, towns and cities, still use this traditional approach to budgeting. The selectmen or council compile budget requests, examine their likely effect on the tax rate, then decide what to present to the public. Municipal tax rates rise or fall annually based on a political process where expenditures and revenues are weighed in the same balance. Ideological perspectives on taxes are not the driving force.

Similar assessments in state government were the rule in the post-World War II period. Lawmakers established benchmarks for current services, then prepared a supplemental budget for new programs. During their administrations, Ed Muskie and Ken Curtis used the supplemental budget more vigorously than some of their predecessors, but Republican legislators were willing, and sometimes enthusiastic, participants. All that changed with the election of Ronald Reagan. Cutting taxes has become the primary goal of one party, with acquiescence from the other, and even the hollowing out of public education and other vital programs hasn't been an effective deterrent. It's been many years since the supplemental budget was a meaningful exercise.

Since tax-cutting has failed to produce the predicted benefits, legislators must reconsider their role in crafting a budget. Income inequality, which has risen in Maine as it has throughout the nation, means that public investment must increase if we are to have any hope of maintaining a middle class standard of living. While campaigning, Democrats continue to say they support government as a means to provide economic and educational opportunity, but their actions in office often do not support their words. The decline in the party's electoral fortunes may owe more to this inconsistency than to any other single cause.

Reversing declining support for higher education, rebuilding our crumbling roads and bridges, investing in economic growth sectors, and supporting community development cannot be done with slogans, but requires specific, tangible pledges that voters can take seriously. Programs like these were the foundation for Democratic successes in the past, and their neglect has had dismaying consequences, for the party and for the people of Maine. The state budget will be the key to setting things right.

IMAGINING CHANGE

The Maine Democratic Party's recovery may resemble its 1954 inception in outline, but the details will be different. One of the hardest parts of renewing and revitalizing any institution is seeing how the future can be different from the present. The problem is more acute for Maine, which often sees itself as at the end of the line, in a far corner of the nation. Economically, the picture is flawed—ties of history, culture and trade bind us closer to Canadian provinces than we care to admit—but politically, it's a reasonable description.

State government is unusually dominant in Maine, whose sheer geographical size would seem to call for some kind of regional government. Yet the state neglects its counties, maintains highly decentralized and numerous local governments, and suffers from unnecessary gaps between what's practiced in Augusta and its effect on communities small and large. Cooperation is frequently difficult, or absent, and the citizen legislature has become ineffective in addressing and mediating the interests of those it represents.

Maine needs more than a change of officeholders to adapt to a new century and take advantage of opportunities most states would envy. People all over the world want to come to Maine, but our systems are ill-adapted to respond to those desires. State and local governments are only one piece of what needs to change, but here change can be more rapid and effective than elsewhere if we understand and can articulate what needs to be done. The final chapters will consider another state government that both resembles and differs from Maine, and then sketch key ideas and proposals for what additional reforms are most pressing, and where we can increase and redirect our public resources to accomplish the most good for all of us who live in Maine and have aspirations for our state.

EIGHT
A Different State

"The American people will always vote for someone who is strong and wrong before they will vote for someone who is weak and right. We appear to be weak and right because we will say whatever it takes to win. And once you are willing to say whatever it takes to win, you lose."
— Howard Dean, speech to DNC Women's Leadership Forum, 2003

When Maine is compared to other states, it's usually the only other state it borders—New Hampshire—that comes to mind. Politically, though, a comparison to Vermont, the third state in the sub-region we call Northern New England, is much more apropos. The two states share early histories as territories claimed by other colonies—for Maine, Massachusetts; for Vermont, New York, and later New Hampshire. Vermont made its break first, becoming the first state added to the original thirteen colonies in 1791. Maine had to wait until the Compromise of 1820 to become the twenty-third state, with its admission as a free state balanced by Missouri as a slave state.

The two states share fiercely independent attitudes and an idealization of rural values. They were solidly Republican longer than almost any others, bonded to the hard-won Union through devotion to the abolitionist cause. Vermont's pre-statehood constitution of 1777 abolished slavery and eliminated property restrictions for voting; its motto is "Freedom and Unity." Maine contributed proportionally more soldiers for the Union than any other state, including the scholar, Civil War hero, and Republican governor, Joshua Chamberlain.

These persistent loyalties were aptly illustrated when James Farley, Franklin Roosevelt's postmaster and political fixer, deconstructed the famous slogan, "As Maine Goes, So Goes the Nation," referring to its unique September election. After Roosevelt's 1936 Electoral College sweep, taking all but two states, Farley quipped, "As Maine Goes, So Goes Vermont."

Vermont and Maine, unlike the state between them, both had vigorous government reform movements following World War II. New Hampshire retains its four hundred-member House of Representatives and twenty-four-member Senate, as well as its Colonial-era Executive Council to limit the governor's authority. But Vermont's reforms, unlike Maine's, started within the dominant Republican Party, and the states have traveled parallel but strikingly different paths in years since.

Beginning with the election of Governor Redfield Proctor, founder of the Vermont Marble Co., in 1878, business and utility interests dominated Republican and state politics for generations. The "Proctor dynasty," as it became known, elected four Proctors as governor through 1944; those serving between Proctors were equally allied to railroads, industrialists and private power companies.

The first break in Proctor dominance came with the election of George Aiken as governor in 1936. Though a Republican, Aiken celebrated the common man, and the Vermont farmer, and began his political work in the Legislature. A horticulturalist, he was assigned to chair the House Conservation Committee, and discovered it had jurisdiction over rivers and streams. Aiken defeated the House speaker's bill to construct eighty new dams. As he saw it, "The utility boys were trying to take over the state." Two years later, he became House speaker himself, then lieutenant governor, as voters warmed to his message.

Though Vermont never had large-scale public power projects comparable to the Dickey-Lincoln dams Ed Muskie wanted for Maine, as governor, Aiken organized rural electric coops that remain the backbone of electricity distribution. He later recalled that a discouraged farmer "received renewed hope, faith and income after he received electricity." He was instrumental in launching maple sugaring as a statewide "brand," and in promoting dairy cooperatives.

In 1940, after flirting with a presidential bid, Aiken won a U.S. Senate seat, and stayed thirty-four years before retiring to his orchards in Vermont's Northeast Kingdom. He was an unconventional Republican. He once startled a Lincoln Day dinner broadcast nationally by saying, "The greatest praise I can give Lincoln, on this, his anniversary, is that he would be ashamed of his party's leadership today." Aiken authored the federal food stamp program, gained U.S. participation in the St. Lawrence Seaway, and zealously promoted the agricultural interests of Vermont and the nation.

The next reformer was Ernest Gibson, an Aiken protégé, who won the 1946 Republican primary for governor over incumbent Mortimer Proctor, the last of the Proctor line. As one observer put it, "Like all dinosaurs, the Proctor dynasty was dead before the body knew it." Gibson, "a liberal, energetic hero of the Pacific campaign" was part of the same wave of returning World War II veterans as Ed Muskie. Unlike Muskie, he was a Republican in a Republican state, and put his ideas to work immediately. Gibson expanded the state's commitments to public education, health and welfare programs, and raised the revenues necessary to finance them, including converting the 2 percent flat-rate income tax to a progressive levy. Gibson defeated his party's "regulars" so decisively they despaired of recovery, but in 1950 he resigned to accept a federal judgeship from President Truman, and Republicans returned to their previous patterns for another decade.

RISE OF THE DEMOCRATS

As in Maine, registering as a Democrat roused suspicion. William Moran, an author and producer for CBS News and Vermont Public Television, wrote of the early days, "It was not easy to be a Democrat in Vermont. Any man who told his neighbors he was a Democrat was regarded as contrary and a little queer. Unruly children were frightened by parents who warned that the Democrat down the road had a black tongue and would come after them if they did not behave."

And for Democrats, there was no result quite comparable to Muskie coming out of nowhere to win in 1954, but through the 1950s they made incremental gains at the Legislature. In 1958, they elected William Meyer as the state's sole congressman, but he lasted just one term.

Then, in 1962, the first Democrat elected governor in more than a century, Philip Hoff, narrowly defeated incumbent Republican Ray Keyser, and declared to cheering supporters, "One hundred years of bondage—broken." Significantly, Hoff didn't gain as many votes on the Democratic ballot line as Keyser on the Republican line. Keyser tallied 60,035 Republican votes, and Hoff 56,196 as a Democrat. But because Hoff also received 5,000 votes on the lines of two small, short-lived parties, he ended up winning by 1,200 votes—an early example of "fusion politics" that Vermont has since perfected, but has never been practiced in Maine.

Hoff, an outspoken liberal, served three terms, through 1968, in an administration thoroughly in sync with Lyndon Johnson's Great Society programs. He told an interviewer, "We were proceeding on the basis that really there was nothing we couldn't do, that we could get rid of poverty . . . that we could provide a prosperous and enjoyable life for every citizen. It was a very positive time." His program expansions and willingness to flout Vermont's still conservative social conventions—he was an early backer of Eugene McCarthy's 1968 presidential bid, and endorsed a summer exchange program bringing several hundred black children from Harlem to rural Vermont—contributed to his decision not to seek re-election. His 1970 U.S. Senate bid against Republican incumbent Winston Prouty fell far short; Vermonters had never elected a Democratic senator.

Hoff wasn't through with politics. He chaired the state Democratic Party, and in the 1980s served in the state Senate. He was a frequent critic of another Democratic governor, Madeleine Kumin, thinking her too timid in advocating the party's traditional agenda.

Hoff's last term as governor was the most significant. Like Ken Curtis in Maine, he believed a progressive income tax was the fairest way to finance the expansion of government services then underway in almost every state. He proposed, as Curtis had done, making the state income tax a percentage of federal income tax liability, and Republicans in the Legislature—unlike in Maine—accepted the idea. While Vermont's current top rate is 8.95 percent on income above $400,000, the effective rate can vary from year to year as the Legislature adjusts the required proportion, providing revenue flexibility that Maine's income tax now lacks. As a University of Vermont historical summary explains, "The income tax has in a sense served as Vermont's 'rainy day fund,' as state government has increased the tax rate in poor economic times to help balance the state's books and then reduced the rate as the economy has improved." During its first three decades, the adjustable tax varied from a low of 23 percent of federal tax liability to a high of 28.75 percent.

Another key reform occurred earlier during Hoff's tenure. Vermont then had a unique system of allowing each incorporated town or city one representative in the House—and only one. As the state grew, the results were peculiar. Burlington, with 35,000 people, had the same representation as towns of two hundred residents. The system was faulted by an electoral commission as early as 1849, but nothing was done until the U.S. Supreme Court's "one person, one vote" decisions forced reapportionment of state legislatures. Vermont's 246-member House was reduced to 150 members, with a thirty-member Senate. Traditionalists despaired. The reapportionment committee's chairman, Emory Hebard, who lost the argument, said years later, "I feel it is one of the worst things we did to the state of Vermont." But Richard Mallary, the Republican chosen speaker, said, "The dominance of the old-timers, small-towners was gone. We had lots of people who . . . were going to come in and change the world. There was a sense anything was possible."

The new, more streamlined House, apportioned by population, led to greater competition, but also great comity between the two parties. The first Democrat to become House speaker, Timothy O'Connor, led the 1975 session even though Republicans still held a 78-70 majority.

Hoff's successor as governor, Deane Davis, surprised many, including his own Republican Party. Davis was sixty-seven, and had been a lawyer, prosecutor, state judge and then president of the National Life Insurance Co., Vermont's largest. Unlike most of his predecessors, who worked their way up the political ladder, Davis had never sought election before.

He ran, he said, to "restore order" after the tumult of the Hoff administration, but his solution was not to scuttle the expanded programs Ernest
Gibson and Hoff had championed, but to install a state sales tax at 3
percent; Vermont was then one of the few states without one. Many
Republicans opposed the sales tax, but enough sided with Democrats to
win a majority; unlike Maine, Vermont has no provisions for "emergency" legislation by two-thirds.

Some Republicans were even more surprised by Davis's advocacy of
Act 250, which passed in 1970 and required regional review of major
housing and commercial development. It arose from a commission Davis
had appointed to scrutinize the second home development spawned by
the state's successful promotion of skiing and rural life, much of it on thin
mountain soils or around sensitive lakeshores. Ironically, the first big
project rejected under Act 250 was a regional shopping center outside
Burlington many feared would drain vitality from the city's downtown.
Maine has no comparable controls; the Site of Location law enacted
under Ken Curtis is targeted primarily at industrial development, of
which there has been relatively little in recent decades. Davis also introduced Cabinet-style government to Vermont about the same time Curtis
did in Maine.

Another decision related to skiing had profound effects on both Vermont's economy and its politics. Thomas Watson was CEO of then-bur-
geoning IBM, and liked his winter vacations in Vermont as a retreat from
New York City. An economic development committee in Burlington had
built a 32,000 square foot industrial building on spec in the late 1950s,
and Watson decided IBM should take the entire space for mainframe
computer manufacturing. IBM's commitment began a high-tech manufacturing cluster that transformed Burlington from a declining mill town,
whose factories were polluting Lake Champlain, to a center of prosperity
and population growth, displacing the traditional centers of southern
Vermont and Rutland County, and playing a role similar to Portland's
revival in Maine.

REPEAL OF THE 'MOUNTAIN RULE'

The alternation from the first Democratic governor back to a Republican
inaugurated a new pattern in Vermont politics, replacing the "Mountain
Rule" observed under the previous century of Republican dominance.
Vermont is divided, north to south, by the Green Mountains, a continu-
ous chain from the Berkshires in Massachusetts well into Canada.
Governors alternated between the west and east sides, spawning complaints that the governor's chair was being decided by State House politicians a decade in advance. The elections of Hoff and Davis broke the
pattern, and ushered in alternation between the parties. Since then, a

Democrat has succeeded a Republican, and vice versa, each time an incumbent has retired—Vermont has no term limits—right up to the present. Though the Legislature is now dominated by Democrats and Progressives, Phil Scott is the new Republican governor—a former lieutenant governor and NASCAR driver.

Vermont's two-year term for governor provides flexibility Maine has lacked since Muskie's four-year term constitutional amendment passed in 1957; the only time Vermonters considered such an amendment, in 1974, they turned it down. Except for Deane Davis, Vermont's recent governors have all served in the Legislature or a statewide office, often both. The lieutenant governor, who presides over the Senate, is the most frequent route, but the leap has been made by those elected attorney general, treasurer, secretary of state, and even auditor. Maine's tradition of Senate presidents becoming governor ended with the four-year term, with the last instance the succession of John Reed after the death of Clinton Clauson in 1959.

Vermont's innovation continued under Democrat Tom Salmon, who succeeded Davis after the 1972 election. Salmon, a committed environmentalist, decided the road-building that marked the Interstate highway era, and had done much to open Vermont to newcomers and visitors, had reached its goals; henceforth, the state would maintain existing road networks and look for alternatives to construction. Salmon convinced lawmakers to enact a tax on land speculation, fiercely resisted by realtors but popular in most rural communities; the only comparable Maine statute is the Baldacci-era limitation on "liquidation harvesting," stripping timber from a woodlot and re-selling as house lots. Salmon, ruggedly handsome, had a considerable out-of-state profile with conservationists, but was less adept at the larger political scene. He lost a bid for U.S. Senate in 1976, and was then appointed University of Vermont president.

There were fruitful exchanges between governors in those days. When Ken Curtis was finishing his second term and Salmon was beginning his first, Curtis visited Vermont for a round of talks and campaigning. Afterward, Salmon wrote to Curtis on November 20, 1973, saying "Your appearance here in Vermont was uplifting to the spirit of those of us who believe that honesty, integrity and straight talk are important words in the English language."

SENIOR SENATOR

Besides Deane Davis, the other exception to "climbing the ladder" is Patrick Leahy, the first Democrat elected U.S. senator, in 1974. Leahy was thirty-four, only four years over the minimum age, when he launched his Senate bid against Richard Mallary, by then the state's Republican congressman, in the race to succeed the now-legendary George Aiken. Many had expected Tom Salmon to make the race, but he stayed put for the moment. Phil Hoff had appointed Leahy, then just twenty-six, as Chittenden County prosecutor, which encompasses Burlington. Originally a part-time job, Leahy made it full time, taking cases the state usually handled, and winning thirty-two convictions in his first thirty-five jury trials.

Leahy pioneered new campaign techniques, such as then-novel biographical ads, and won backing from rural constituencies. In the post-Watergate election, he benefited from anti-incumbent sentiment in a way George Mitchell, trying to succeed Ken Curtis in Maine the same year, did not. The election produced only a narrow victory for Leahy, as did re-election contests in 1980, the Reagan landslide year, and even in 1986, when George Mitchell, now in the Senate, helped orchestrate a Democratic sweep that made Leahy chairman of the Agriculture Committee; he later chaired Judiciary.

A low point for Leahy was when he leaked confidential files from the Iran-Contra committee to a reporter, disrupting the Senate-House inquiry, then tried to minimize his resulting resignation. But he engaged whole-heartedly with causes that interested few other senators, such as landmines. Leahy's bill created a federal fund to compensate victims, which now bears his name, and he promoted the international treaty that banned these explosives.

Leahy, like his predecessor, George Aiken, believes in seniority, and surpassed Aiken's Vermont record of thirty-four years in 2008. He hasn't observed the retirement tradition of Maine senators, such as Muskie, Mitchell, Bill Cohen and Olympia Snowe, and was re-elected in 2016 to an eighth term that will span forty-eight years in the Senate—longer than any other senator except Robert Byrd, who died in office, and equaling one hundred-year-old Strom Thurmond. Vermont's other U.S. senator, Bernie Sanders, is a newcomer by comparison.

The most dynamic Republican governor of this period was Richard Snelling, brash and outspoken and often unpredictable. He followed Tom Salmon by promoting his business expertise, and served four terms. As House Republican leader, he almost single-handedly defeated Governor Salmon's special session bill for a sales tax increase, and insisted state government should tighten its belt. But he was also critical of the Vermont Yankee nuclear power plant's management; vetoed a bailout for a failing racetrack; and opposed a "no growth" state budget his fellow Republicans put together, saying "a government which panders to the immediate demands of the public for superficial solutions can only continue to erode the confidence on which it rests."

Though far more savvy about politics than Maine's Jim Longley, he also fired off lengthy letters to reporters and editors he thought had "got it wrong." Unlike Longley, he engaged in dialogue, and conceded that, based on their reporting, "for most of us in public life, we are what you say." Despite his imperious demeanor, he had a healthy skepticism about his own importance, once telling a reporter, "If you want to get into the history books, you take a molehill. You call it a mountain and move it. Making government productive, making it work, that's not the stuff of which heroes are made."

"BROADS FOR MADELEINE"

The boisterous Snelling, though not quite done, was succeeded in 1984 by Madeleine May Kumin, not only Vermont's, but one of the nation's first women elected governor. She was far too cautious for many fellow Democrats in the Legislature, and less cooperative than the press expected; she had come to Vermont to write for the *Burlington Free Press*, and her brother, Edgar May, was a Pulitzer Prize-winning reporter. Kumin started in the House, serving three terms and chairing Appropriations, and sparred frequently with Snelling in that role.

In 1978, she ran for lieutenant governor, expecting to face the incumbent, who was, however, defeated in the September primary by Peter Smith, an ambitious young Republican who expected to ride Snelling's coattails. Late in the campaign, Smith said condescendingly of his opponent, "Oh, all the broads will vote for Madeleine." The response was immediate. "Broads for Madeleine" T-shirts appeared at rallies, and Kumin won the race, and re-election in 1980.

Kumin decided to run for governor in 1982 after Snelling announced his retirement, but he changed his mind after a *Free Press* editorial called on him to seek another term. Kumin, who'd been the frontrunner, was now an underdog, but campaigned hard. Based on the enthusiasm of crowds, she thought she could win, but fell short and minced no words. In a diary entry, she said, "I truly believed I would win. I have made a fool of myself."

Vermont's two-year term, and the way its politicians move between the Legislature, statewide office, and Congress, make defeats less conclusive, and Kumin tried again, after Snelling finally retired in 1984. Her Republican opponent was John Easton, state attorney general, a consumer advocate with an appealing campaign tactic—working a day every week at a blue-collar job, calling it "Working with Vermonters." Ahead in the polls, he, like Peter Smith before him, underestimated his opponent. He told a reporter that, considering Vermont's fiscal problems, the next governor would "be a caretaker." Kumin pounced, saying, "Being a caretaker is not my job description . . . The new governor should offer ideas and new initiatives. You have to approach the job with a sense of excitement and a sense that change is possible." She won by 3,600 votes.

Kumin received a frosty reception from Peter Welch, the first Democrat to become the Senate's president pro tem, who handles day-to-day business. Things were more congenial with House Speaker Ralph

Wright, a Democrat selected, like Timothy O'Connor, despite a Republican majority of 78-72. Wright's reputation matched John Martin's in Maine, and he was often compared to Boston politicians like Tip O'Neill. He was tough—and to his opponents, ruthless—but also stepped down after ten years in the post. He and Kumin had complementary techniques, useful in pushing through her signature initiatives, including a school finance reform bill and Act 200, a growth management law that mandated statewide and regional planning. Unlike Maine's weaker and less comprehensive statute, Act 200 remains in force.

The former governor, Richard Snelling, restless in retirement, decided Vermont needed him again, and launched another bid for 1990. Kumin, who'd already been re-elected twice, bowed out. She said she could win, but added, "I don't have to run to prove a point. I have proven I can do the job."

THE "ACCIDENTAL" GOVERNOR

Richard Snelling won the 1990 election easily over Democrat Peter Welch, who'd left his Senate president pro tem post, but his fifth administration was short. In August, the day before Vermont celebrated its two hundredth anniversary of statehood, Snelling died at home of an apparent heart attack while his wife, Barbara, was traveling on business. It was the first time in decades a lieutenant governor had succeeded after the death of a governor, and the first time it involved a partisan change. A Burlington physician, Democrat Howard Dean, was the new governor.

From this inauspicious beginning, Dean became not only Vermont's longest-serving governor, but also its most consequential. He served eleven years, was elected five times consecutively, and got closer to the presidency than any Vermonter had since Calvin Coolidge—though Bernie Sanders came even closer in 2016. Coolidge, governor of Massachusetts before becoming vice president, was also an "accidental" chief executive, succeeding to the presidency after the death of Warren Harding in 1923.

At first, few thought Dean would even stand for election in 1992. His wife was also a physician, they worked in the same practice, and Dean intensely guarded his family's privacy. This became a hindrance when, a decade later, Dean ran for president and, to his aides' consternation, said he expected his wife to maintain a practice in Washington even if they occupied the White House.

Dean kept Snelling's Cabinet in place, which already had bipartisan elements. Amid the steep 1991 recession that was to exact such a huge political price in Maine, Dean could be grateful Snelling and House Speaker Ralph Wright had already agreed to a $90 million tax increase package described as "the largest in history." Unlike John Martin, who waited until John McKernan presented a $300 million tax increase on his own, then accepted it, Wright and Snelling, though from opposite parties, worked collaboratively. On the 1991 legislative session's opening day, Wright found Snelling waiting outside his office. The governor wanted to discuss his budget plan; Wright already had his own. The tax package was larger, and increased income taxes more, than Snelling preferred, but he largely agreed, knowing the speaker could bring other Democrats on board.

Dean continued to defer to his predecessor's agenda, even into his first elected term. Those who knew him only from his presidential run could be surprised by his stances on Vermont issues, and those he saw as adversaries, confounding supporters and opponents alike. Liberals in his own party were "arrogant." Right-wing Republicans were "crackpots." Nor did he spare judges, saying, "People don't get enough time and they get off on technicalities." He once accused the state Supreme Court of releasing "five murderers in the space of 12 months," when, acting on appeals, they had ordered one release and four new trials.

Vermonters liked their new governor, though. They approved his arranging his schedule so he could attend his children's soccer games. Dean was the first outdoors enthusiast among modern Vermont governors, reflecting a statewide passion, and could often be found hiking the Long Trail, running the length of the state, or canoeing on the Connecticut River.

He got his first taste of regional campaigning when he toured New England to promote the Clinton health care plan in 1993. Ironically, Dean's own health care plan suffered the same fate in the Legislature as Bill Clinton's did in Congress. When it came time to pull the plug, after nearly two years of debate, Dean didn't hesitate, much to the dismay of Speaker Wright.

When Clinton later succeeded in winning approval for the Children's Health Insurance Program, Dean used it enthusiastically, and Vermont became the first state to cover nearly every child.

Dean's mettle, and his ability to lead, was tested not once, but twice, by decisions from the Vermont Supreme Court he'd tangled with earlier. The rulings forced lawmakers to confront unpopular issues at a high personal cost. The first came in 1997, when the court declared Vermont's financing of education unconstitutional. Such decisions were common as, faced with declining support for funding public schools, advocates pressed their case in more than 30 states, and were successful in most of them. New Hampshire's high court made a similar ruling, though it's instructive how different the political responses were. Ironically, Maine's constitutional wording was deemed insufficient to merit a court challenge, but even without any judicial prod Maine has provided, since the Curtis administration, more state funding for education than either Vermont or New Hampshire.

In New Hampshire, the Legislature approved an income tax in a state with no broad-based tax, but Democratic Governor Jeanne Shaheen vetoed it. Subsequently, legislators adopted a statewide property tax, redistributing a relatively small pool of money from "property rich" municipalities, or "donor" communities, to a somewhat larger number of "property poor," or "receiver" districts. Without a substantial source of state funding, tax relief remains modest.

In Vermont, the court said, "To keep a democracy competitive and thriving, students must be afforded equal access to all that our educational system has to offer," and Dean and the Legislature listened. Their proposal, Act 60, roused fervent objections from legislators representing wealthier communities. A lobbyist for the "gold towns" around Burlington, home to many lawyers and IBM executives, said, "This is civil war." Novelist John Irving, who lived in Dorset, denounced it as "Marxism." An Act 60 architect, Democratic state senator and future governor Peter Shumlin bluntly responded, "You had a great deal, and it's coming to an end."

In Maine, the Uniform Property Tax, similar in some respects to Vermont's Act 60, was repealed in a 1977 referendum, but Vermont's version stuck, though the burden on wealthier communities was eased in 1998. It was a much more comprehensive response than New Hampshire's because Vermont already had sales and income tax revenues to draw on.

Dean supported the deal, and signed Act 60. The Republican Party shed its moderate stance and declared war on supporters, which included many incumbent Republicans. Dean's 1998 Republican opponent, Ruth Dwyer, made the new law the focus of her campaign. Although a handful of incumbent lawmakers were defeated, Dean's support didn't waver. Although his winning margin over the previous election dipped, he still won 55 percent. Two years later, Dwyer was back, with a different issue.

No one was expecting what came to be called the "civil unions" decision when the Supreme Court handed it down on Monday, December 20, 1999. Major decisions usually came later in the week, but Christmas was looming. It shocked just about everyone. For the first time, an American court found an existing marriage statute unconstitutional. The case, *Baker v. Vermont*, had been argued a year earlier, to packed galleries. A trial judge had denied claims by three same-sex couples for marriage licenses, ruling the state was justified in preserving "a link between procreation and child rearing."

The Supreme Court decided otherwise, but its ruling was hard to decipher, and there were a variety of opinions from different judges. One of the five justices preferred full recognition of same-sex marriage. Another, speaking for the majority, quoted a law review article that said, "When a democracy is in moral flux, courts may not have the best or final answers." The judge may have been recalling the response to the U.S.

Supreme Court's *Roe v. Wade* ruling in 1973, which struck down abortion laws nationwide even though just one state, New York, had a statute resembling the court's requirements.

It was clear that same-sex couples must be granted the legal benefits of marriage, but the court stayed its ruling to allow passage of a law meeting its requirements. It could take the form of marriage, or recognition of domestic partnerships. The term "civil union" emerged, somewhat mysteriously, during legislative debate.

Initially, responses were muted. Mary Bonauto, representing the plaintiffs, called the ruling "a legal and cultural milestone," but Vermont's Catholic bishop, Kenneth Angell, focused on the domestic partnership option, calling it "a decisive victory for traditional marriage." By the time lawmakers convened, however, the bishop had shifted his position, saying partnerships were "step one toward full acceptance of same-sex marriage," and he questioned the court's authority.

There had never been legislative hearings like these. Some 1,500 people showed up, on both sides of the issue, during a snowstorm. A week later, 2,000 attended a hearing, with another 1,500 assembled outside.

Just hours after the ruling, Governor Dean made his position known. He expressed an immediate preference for domestic partnerships, rather than "gay marriage." When he gave his state of the state address a few weeks later, he was statesmanlike, saying, "This is the year that we will make every effort to comply with the new Supreme Court ruling, which confirms that all Vermonters—including gay and lesbian Vermonters—are to have equal benefits under the law. We were the first state to outlaw slavery in 1777. We will remain in the forefront of the struggle for equal justice under the law."

Yet at a press conference, asked about his feelings, Dean said, "It makes me uncomfortable, the same as anyone else." In a book he wrote following his presidential bid, he describes the atmosphere he grew up in, where he "picked up a lot of things about gay people that weren't nice or true." Yet, "having grown up under the civil rights movement, I also believed that equal rights under the law could not be abridged no matter what I thought about gay marriage." Dean's honesty helped provide cover for lawmakers in a similar bind.

In the end, the civil unions law, Act 91, passed both House and Senate decisively, and Dean signed it. This time, the backlash was much stronger than two years earlier over Act 60. Ruth Dwyer declared the law "would tear the state apart," and vowed to repeal it while launching another bid for governor. A state senator said, "We have many bewildered people out there." In the Legislature, support for the bill was bipartisan, but during the campaign the Republican Party made opposition a rallying cry. Dean made a point of praising Republicans who'd voted for the bill, startling many at the Democratic Party convention where he spoke. It was not enough. Some seven senators and twenty-nine representatives who'd voted yes either retired or were defeated. Richard Mallary, who returned to the state Senate after his loss to Patrick Leahy for U.S. Senate, was among those ousted.

Vermonters hadn't lost confidence in Dean, however. He retained a wide margin over Ruth Dwyer, as he had in 1998, though the Progressive Party candidate, Anthony Pollina, polled 10 percent, helping establish progressives as a "third force." The third-party bid almost upset another part of Vermont's constitutional balance, however. As with the Electoral College's selection of presidents, Vermont's governors must receive a majority of the vote to be seated, or the decision goes to the House of Representatives. In 2000, Republicans had just taken a House majority, in large part due to the backlash against Act 91. Dean got 50.4 percent, sparing the state further turmoil in what was already a highly unsettled time.

Through the National Governors Association, Dean spoke to large and enthusiastic audiences, leading him to consider a run for president in 2000. When news leaked out—originating in what Dean thought, perhaps naively, was a courtesy call to Al Gore—it became clear his Vermont constituents didn't want their governor running while still in office. When Dean decided to enter the 2004 race, he didn't seek re-election in 2002.

U.S. Senator John Kerry and House Minority Leader Dick Gephardt were considered the frontrunners against George W. Bush, the Republican president seeking re-election, but Kerry stumbled badly, and Dean—in unlikely fashion, given his reputation back home—electrified audiences with a simple message. At the DNC's winter meeting on February 21, 2003, he began by saying, "What I want to know is why in the world the Democratic Party leadership is supporting the president's unilateral attack on Iraq! What I want to know is why are Democratic Party leaders supporting tax cuts! The question is not how big the tax cut should be. The question should be, 'Can we afford a tax cut at all?'" Kerry and Gephardt both voted for the Iraq war resolution Bush proposed, as did Hillary Clinton, and Dean said he couldn't understand why. "I'm here to represent the Democratic wing of the Democratic Party," he said, and that became the mantra for the rest of his meteoric campaign.

Dean, unlike Bernie Sanders, wasn't identified with the party's liberal wing, and his campaign's appeal was more basic: Why can't the Democratic Party stand up for its own traditional principles, and why did it support a Republican president's rush to war?

Candidates from small states often struggle to raise money. Ed Muskie's 1972 campaign for president was crippled by meager fundraising, but Dean became the first presidential candidate to use the Internet effectively to raise large sums from small donors. The McCain-Feingold Act, just taking effect, briefly limited big donors, and Dean had plenty of money to take his message to voters nationwide.

What Dean didn't have, coming from a very small state, was a sizeable staff and sophisticated political organization, and it proved his undoing. He allowed his success to be judged on his showing in Iowa—a state where he hadn't even planned to compete—and when he lost to Kerry there, his campaign was essentially over. But the two big questions he asked about his party leadership had still not been answered.

Nevertheless, Dean did something defeated candidates almost never do—he campaigned energetically for the ticket all summer and fall. And after Kerry's defeat in November, Dean volunteered for an often thankless task, Democratic National Committee chair. He deployed his fundraising prowess, and proclaimed a "50 state strategy" to help all state parties, not just those where national staff thought Democrats could win congressional seats. By all accounts, Dean's success as DNC chair helped lay the groundwork for Barack Obama's success four years later. In office, however, Obama did what most presidents do: treat the DNC as a vehicle for his own re-election. The "50 State strategy" withered, and Democratic losses mounted in both legislative and congressional contests.

THE "SOCIALIST" INDEPENDENT

At first, Bernie Sanders was no more credible as a statewide candidate than he was to national audiences when, twelve years after Howard Dean, he announced his 2016 campaign for president. After bringing his life-long Brooklyn accent to Vermont, he made several statewide runs as the nominee of the Liberty Union Party, an early left-wing coalition; his best showing was in the 1976 governor's race won by Richard Snelling, where he got 6 percent. But a supporter pointed out he'd done much better in Burlington, and was especially popular in the blue collar wards that felt neglected by the Democrats who'd dominated city politics for years.

Sanders abandoned his long-shot statewide bids to run as an independent for Burlington mayor in 1981. The five-term Democratic incumbent, Gordon Paquette, supported a property tax increase, and a developer's plan to build upscale condominiums on the Lake Champlain waterfront. Sanders opposed the tax increase, and said the city should develop its waterfront as public space. The Republicans had no candidate, and Sanders shocked everyone when he beat Paquette by ten votes. As in every race until 2016, Sanders was an independent, but national reporters focused on his self-description as a "socialist," reinforced by their references to "The People's Republic of Burlington."

Sanders took political organizing more seriously than Howard Dean had, and, as mayor, developed a pragmatic reputation that earned re-election three times. By 1986, he ventured statewide again, but his bid for governor was resented by Democrats, as Madeleine Kumin sought her third and final term against Republican Lt. Governor Peter Smith, who won that office subsequent to his 1978 defeat by Kumin. Sanders got just 14 percent, but when he tried for the open congressional seat in 1988, his pledge to make corporations and the wealthy pay their fair share of taxes struck a chord. Sanders led the polls for weeks, and the Democratic candidate, House Leader Paul Poirier, never made a strong impression. Peter Smith, despite his second defeat by Kumin ten years earlier, won the seat, but Sanders immediately prepared for a rematch in 1990. Democrats, noting his populist appeal, fielded only a token nominee, and Sanders easily won a two-way race, the first of his eight terms in the House.

The Progressive Party was beginning its rise, but Sanders never accepted its nomination. Illustrating the symbiotic relationship he forged with Democrats, Sanders took the precaution of seeking the Democratic nomination while running for the U.S. Senate in 2006, a seat left open by retiring Republican-turned-independent Jim Jeffords. Sanders won the Democratic primary, then ran as an independent. He attempted the same feat in 2016, though there's no doubt that, if he'd won, he would have accepted the Democratic nomination for president.

VERMONT VS. MAINE

How is it that the nation's second smallest state produced two serious contenders for the presidency more than a generation after Maine's day in the sun with Ed Muskie? As always with politics, cause and effect are elusive, but it's striking what Vermont has kept, and what Maine has lost, over the ensuing years.

The first, and perhaps most important factor, is that Vermont has retained the competitive two-party system that Frank Coffin first envisioned, and helped achieve, but which has declined steeply in Maine in recent years. "Competitive" doesn't mean simply having two candidates on the November ballot. It means that a diversity of views within each party can be accommodated and even encouraged; legislative party-line voting is kept to a minimum; and voters have a real choice of views among candidates in primary elections, rather than the "litmus test" checklists that now often prevail. Vermont's Republican and Democratic parties used the talents of such idiosyncratic and powerful personalities as Governor Richard Snelling and House Speaker Ralph Wright without any hint of a constitutional crisis, and made transitions to other leadership styles smoothly and without major disruptions.

The only recent time either party made frankly ideological, single-issue appeals was when Ruth Dwyer ran for governor in 1998 and 2000 as an opponent of property tax reform, then same-sex civil unions, and convinced the Republican Party to follow her lead. Both times Howard

Dean won re-election, as voters credited his steady and even-handed leadership even though they might have differed with him on particular issues. The 2000 election also marked a sharp decline in the ability of Republicans to win legislative races, from which they haven't yet recovered. On election night, Dwyer said, "The people of Vermont clearly don't believe what we believe."

Yet Jim Douglas, who became a four-term Republican governor, won his first term in 2002, succeeding Dean. A former House majority leader, treasurer, and secretary of state, Douglas campaigned as a moderate and emphasized fiscal, rather than social issues. And he took office despite winning only 45 percent of the vote. His Democratic opponent, Lt. Governor Doug Racine, honored a previous agreement the candidates had made to withdraw in favor of the plurality winner, a pledge then ratified by the House of Representatives.

How does a competitive system work? It starts with a vigorous and credible party committee, with strong chairs, which can mediate the inevitable differences between candidates who all believe they deserve the party's support. Vermont has maintained its party infrastructure, while the Maine Democratic Party's abilities have declined. Where candidates feel free to seek advantage by leaving the party to file as independents, it's a sign that all is not well.

Since 2000, there's been a significant third party in Vermont, the Progressives, who now have nine House members, the only official caucus, aside from Republicans and Democrats, in any state legislature. In the Senate, with only thirty members, there's no formal caucus, but there are two "Progressive Democratic" senators, and three "Democratic Progressive" senators—along with only seven Republicans. In Vermont, Democrats have worked fruitfully with Progressives, despite some uneasy moments—a striking contrast with Maine, where Democrats and the Green Party have feuded for years. As an electoral force, Maine's Green Party is almost non-existent, running few legislative candidates and electing none, but the resentments persist.

The fusion politics of Vermont are facilitated by its non-partisan voter registration system, which may be unique. While it has "open primaries," there are still separate party ballots, unlike the South and, now, in California. Voters must choose one party's ballot, and can influence the choice in whatever contests are most important to them. Since 1977, candidates no longer appear on the November ballot simultaneously on more than one party line, as Phil Hoff did in 1962. They can, however, and often are, nominated by more than one party. In such instances, candidates choose which nomination to accept, but generally retain the loyalty of voters who favored them in the other primary—hence the dual designations for five current senators, who ran as Progressives or Democrats.

Independents have had little success in winning major offices in Vermont. The one exception, Bernie Sanders, has a unique political history and, thus far, no successors. And even Sanders was willing to run in a Democratic primary when it suited him. There are usually several independents in the Legislature, though they are now fewer than the Progressives.

At least as important as Vermont's election law is its wide variety of state elective offices, an even sharper contrast with Maine. Mainers can elect only their governor, and vote for two legislators. In Vermont, voters also choose the lieutenant governor, attorney general, secretary of state, treasurer and auditor—and governors rarely win the top job without having served in another state office first.

Vermont's system has the obvious advantage of allowing more choices, as well as the ability of voters to test the mettle of candidates before deciding to trust them with greater authority. Those elected to head the four state agencies also take a more expansive view of their authority, sponsoring special commissions, study panels and public outreach efforts, differing from their counterparts in Maine, who often put a premium on keeping peace with the legislators who chose them, and are at a disadvantage in dealing with the Executive Branch and the governor.

There are more subtle effects, too. One is the easy interchange not only between state positions, but between state and federal offices. It's not uncommon for candidates to try out for one office, only to succeed in another. There are six ways, not one, to make an impression on voters statewide. It's also not unheard of for a successful officeholder to later return to the Legislature, or to chair the party.

Finally, Vermont has been able to avoid the malaise of poor representation that has increasingly afflicted Maine politics. When Maine's binary electoral process produces no clear results, gridlock has often ensued. Attempts to substitute independent candidacies, legislation by referendum, term limits and, most recently, ranked choice voting as a way of breaking the impasse have produced meager, and sometimes counterproductive, results.

Vermont has no term limits for any office, independents rarely matter, and there's no initiative and referendum provision in the state constitution. Maine has term limits for governor, for "constitutional officers" selected by the Legislature, and for every legislative seat; and there have been dozens of referendums in recent decades substituting a single ballot vote for the legislative process. Mainers now seem far less satisfied with their state government than Vermonters do with theirs.

It's not possible, nor would it be desirable, to adopt Vermont's system wholesale as a substitute for the one Maine has developed over nearly two hundred years of statehood. Some elements, though, seem ripe for consideration, as will be described in the final chapter.

NINE

The Future

"What is government itself but the greatest of all reflections on human nature?"

—James Madison, Federalist Papers, No. 51

Government plays an essential role in our lives. In the twentieth century, the great waves of reform came at the start, with the Progressive Era, and then, amid the crisis of the Great Depression, the coming of the New Deal, and its echo three decades later in the Great Society. We are overdue for another reform effort nationally, but perhaps the work can begin in the states, even one as small as Maine.

Efforts to shrink, downsize or otherwise contain government and shift its functions to the private sector have proceeded apace over the past forty years, and almost no one seems satisfied with the results. Examining the structure of government, and reconsidering not only what it does, but how it does it, was an integral part of all three reform movements of the last century. It is still the right place to start.

Not all reforms are created equal. When the Maine Democratic Party began assembling its agenda in 1954, abolition of the Governor's Council rose to the top. The council, like those then surviving in New Hampshire and Massachusetts, reflected suspicion of the royal governors the British monarchy had imposed on the colonies before the Revolution. In Maine, its election by sectional groups of legislators guaranteed that lines of authority were blurred, and governors had no independent authority over state contracts or even some of their own appointees, many of whom had their own fixed terms. It's remarkable Ed Muskie and Ken Curtis were able to accomplish as much as they did while constrained by Republican councils.

It took twenty years to assemble the two-thirds legislative majority needed to pass the constitutional amendment abolishing the council, and

185

the breakthrough came at a time when Democrats would have been able to dominate the council themselves, and act as a check on governors, as Republicans once had. They didn't hesitate, however, and governors ever since have had full executive authority, as well as, thanks to the Cabinet-style government approved under Curtis, control of all important appointments. In all the years since, there's been no longing to re-create the Governor's Council. It vanished almost without a trace, unneeded even before it was disbanded.

Maine Democrats never found an effective answer, however, for the other positions chosen by the Legislature that perform executive and administrative functions—the so-called "constitutional officers," including the attorney general, secretary of state and treasurer; a fourth post, auditor, was added by statute.

The reformers were divided. Some favored creating a popularly elected lieutenant governor, as forty-three states do, either separately or on a ticket with the governor. The idea never caught on. The 1964 party platform, at a time when the Governor's Council existed and the Cabinet did not, advocated having the governor appoint the attorney general and secretary of state, and abolishing the treasurer position. The same document wanted the commissioner of Agriculture appointed by the governor—another post the Legislature then controlled. By the end of the Curtis administration, reform energy had waned, and state government has seen remarkably few changes in the ensuing forty years, though the problems persist.

There was no effective response to the crisis of 1991 in state government. The major attempted changes to perceived ills since then, legislative term limits and ranked-choice voting, both enacted by referendum, are clearly insufficient, and, in the case of term limits, have made things worse. The early reformers did not complete their work. Much remains to be done.

The suggestions that follow do not represent a comprehensive program of reform, which must be the work of many minds over several years. They are an attempt to start a conversation, and focus on structural reforms that can make Maine government, through its elections, political parties, and the Legislature, more representative, and hence more democratic. While either party could initiate them, it's more likely that the Democratic Party, as it has in the past, will take the lead.

VOTING REFORM

Maine has fewer elective positions than any other state. All but seven states have lieutenant governors, and all but seven elect their attorney general. Thirty-seven states elect treasurers, and thirty-five elect their secretary of state. Maine is the only state that entrusts this responsibility to the Legislature, and its selections have no accountability to the voters, and no parallel in any other state. The only comparable example of indirect election was when state legislatures selected U.S. senators, and that practice was abolished by a Progressive era constitutional amendment more than a century ago.

Indirect democracy, whether it comes from the Electoral College or Maine lawmakers selecting key state officials, goes against the American grain, which has seen a steady progression toward greater inclusion in the electorate, and direct elections for the executive and legislative branches; Maine has been wise, however, not to permit election of judges conducting or reviewing criminal trials. Direct election provides not only greater accountability to the voters; it ensures the kind of independent authority that Maine's attorney general did not have during the "Ballot-gate" crisis of 1993, when corruption at the Legislature had to be investigated by officials accountable primarily to the Legislature.

Wholesale change can be difficult, and the two most important posts suitable for direct election are attorney general and secretary of state. The first oversees all legal matters concerning the state; the second, the orderly and even-handed administration of elections, an increasingly pressing concern. Electing officials to these posts would help right the balance of authority, with the Legislature constrained by term limits, that has shifted markedly to the governor's office.

Countless bills to require election of one or the other of these posts have been considered and rejected, and it's doubtful legislators will ever move to limit their own authority; it will take a more concerted effort. The arguments against election, however, are flimsy.

An objection to "more campaigns" is the most frequent and least logical caveat. The idea that this would "politicize" important state jobs is equally faulty. There is plenty of politics involved already, mostly in the form of who now runs for the constitutional offices. With few exceptions, they are former legislators, usually from the House, since those members provide most of the votes in the joint convention. Since the attorney general has always been a lawyer, that limits the talent pool to a handful of former legislators who belong to the majority party. A post that should be open to the best legal minds in Maine is instead the province of a few.

Elections would take some getting used to. Fortunately, Maine has the Clean Election Act that provides public financing, and it could easily be extended to cover two more offices. In fact, it would be wise to require that candidates use public money. While courts haven't upheld mandatory public financing to date, the precedents are relatively recent, and no state has made this kind of electoral change in decades. These provisions could be made severable in implementing legislation, to ensure that an adverse court ruling doesn't invalidate the authorizing constitutional amendment.

The case for election of the state treasurer is weaker than for the other two posts, and its responsibilities could be included in the executive branch. The state auditor position has had disappointing results; it might be more effective in tandem with the legislative oversight agency, OPE-GA, or with a new charge focused more on the state budget.

Independent authority and a better balance within state government are the direct benefits of an elected attorney general and secretary of state. An indirect but equally important benefit would be to establish a new electoral path to the governor's office. The traditional succession, from Senate president to governor, disappeared when the governor's office was transformed by a four-year term, abolition of the Governor's Council, and Cabinet government.

The two existing routes are a return from the U.S. House of Representatives, and a career in private business. Neither has produced well-rounded candidates. Congressional service in a two-member House delegation bears scant relation to the administrative and consensus-building skills needed by a successful governor, and the natural progression in elective office is from state to federal government, not the reverse. Business backgrounds are perhaps even less helpful. They provide only a small part of the job description, and a governor must employ persuasion and leadership-by-example to work effectively with the Legislature and the bureaucracy, not coercion.

Vermont is only one of numerous states where other statewide offices are the proving ground for prospective governors. Success in other elective positions is a much more reliable indicator of ability and political skill than the ones Maine is now using.

It's now difficult to see legislative service as more than an incidental part of a governor's training. That owes something to the negative examples of past legislative leaders, but much more to the imposition of term limits on what is still a part-time job. Citizen legislatures that serve their voters well almost always have key members who've served a decade or more, something impossible under Maine's eight-year limit. Legislative committees have a new House or Senate chair almost every session, and often both. Assistant House leaders are tracked into their posts in their second term, making it impossible for them to perform and understand the important role of committees.

While it's difficult to find anyone making a convincing argument for the benefits of term limits, there is an unfortunate sense they've become permanent—unfortunate because since they are inherently undemocratic. Term limits take choices away from voters, who might well want to continue with their representative or senator, or replace them sooner, than in eight years—the limit has become a de facto ticket to re-election for third and fourth terms, since challengers often await the "automatic" appearance of an open seat. More crucially, term limits have sapped the ability of lawmakers to provide strong and effective leadership within the House and Senate. The revolving door in leadership posts virtually guarantees a governor will win most of the debates, and many House speakers and Senate presidents have visibly struggled in their first, crucial year.

The overwhelming evidence that term limits have not accomplished what the voters expected when they were enacted in 1993 might justify a repeal effort, which could succeed by majority vote in the Senate and House, but would also require an effort to inform and educate voters about what has gone wrong. The damage of term limits is incremental and cumulative, without the clarity and drama of a scandal that galvanizes reform. But the damage has been extensive. The inexperience that makes committee chairs and floor leaders largely ineffective has also diminished the ability to compromise and write effective laws. This inevitably leads to increased party-line voting, and the stalemate that ensues whenever one party doesn't control both the governor's office and the Legislature. It doesn't necessarily produce good laws even when there is one-party control.

The twin problems of the constitutional officers and legislative term limits are really two sides of the same coin. In both instances, voters end up with fewer choices than in other states, and they sense that those they do elect are not serving them well—at least in part because of these structural defects. The rise in the number and complexity of questions referred to the ballot through initiative and referendum is one predictable response.

Yet the results of referendum questions have, overall, been disappointing. The people's veto can be seen as a simple, effective response to overreaching by lawmakers. Crafting good policy by referendum, however, is much more difficult. Attempts to rein in taxes during the Baldacci administration and to expand them during the LePage administration all came to nothing. Forest conservation and timber management were unlikely to improve by referendum, had that 1996 question passed. Eight questions on legalized gambling have created a hit-or-miss patchwork that serves no one well except perhaps casino operators. It has uniquely disadvantaged Maine's Indian tribes, compared with other states. For some questions—three unsuccessful attempts to close Maine Yankee, or three successful attempts to legalize marijuana—referendums may be the only avenue, but the process cannot, not should it, replace the Legislature.

There's been one successful attempt at electoral reform through referendum—the Clean Election Act of 1996, though even that measure had to be repaired by a new referendum in 2015 after an adverse U.S. Supreme Court decision and legislative underfunding. Public financing has democratized the ability of citizens to run for the Legislature, and remains a potential benefit for all candidates, and the state as a whole.

The referendum imposing legislative term limits has not been a success. Repealing that law, and electing the constitutional officers through constitutional amendment, should be considered together—a grand bargain between governors, the Legislature and the voters. Legislators will be reluctant to give up choosing the attorney general and secretary of state, but virtually all understand how term limits undermine their own effectiveness, and their ability to choose qualified leaders.

The only legislative term limit that should remain is the one on presiding officers—the House speaker and Senate president. Leaders who don't understand what the federal Constitutional Convention called "rotation in office"—that in a democracy no one is irreplaceable—have been a problem in other states as well. There's now a limit in legislative rules of six years, which should be retained.

It's been a long time since voters were presented a bargain that would benefit their own interests as well as those of the state. Electing more officials statewide, and reopening the path to legislative experience and expertise by repealing term limits, would go a long way toward improving representation, and discourage still more attempts to create legislation by ballot.

A final, and urgent, voting reform has both state and national implications, and added significance for the Democratic Party. In 2016, for the fifth time, the candidate with the most votes—three million more votes—was not elected president. All five times, dating back to 1824, a Democratic nominee was denied the presidency even while outpolling his or her opponent. Since it's happened twice in the past four presidential elections, we can no longer ignore this deficiency at the heart of our national electoral system.

The Electoral College was created as part of a compromise that preserved slavery, and gave the slave states additional representation in Congress to reflect their black male slaves. It has no legitimacy in democratic terms. Since it's part of the Constitution, however, it remains until amended or abolished, and no such attempt has succeeded. In recent years, an alternative legal route that uses existing constitutional provisions has gained ground, adopted by states representing 165 electoral votes.

The National Popular Vote Compact will take effect when states representing 270 electoral votes, a majority, enact identical statutes that direct all their electors to vote for the candidate winning the popular vote. States already instruct their electors; Maine is one of two states that divides its vote by congressional district, so the variation from existing practice isn't a great leap.

Proposals to join the compact have been considered several times, but rejected. Two opposing arguments were advanced at the bill's latest legislative hearing in 2017. The first was that, as a small state, Maine benefits because its electoral votes are greater than its proportion of the national population. The objection is irrelevant; the "small state" constitutional compromise involves U.S. Senate representation, not president elections, in which all votes should count equally, but do not.

The second argument is that Maine might cast its electoral votes for a candidate not favored by its own voters. This objection is also irrelevant. No one thinks the candidate favored by their town or county should be seated as governor rather than the one favored statewide. Presidents should be elected by the national electorate, not the states. Maine will have one more opportunity, in 2019, to join the compact before another presidential election takes place. It can help the nation advance another step toward Abraham Lincoln's "more perfect union."

PARTY REFORM

Maine now has four political parties, the most in a century, yet this development has yet to create better party organization or campaigns. Still, the advent of the Libertarian Party, along with the Democratic, Republican and Green parties, invites consideration of how the party system could be revived and improved.

Party platforms, and especially the debates surrounding them, are still the key to defining what a party stands for, and even members who may not agree with a plank can shape its wording, and make it thoughtful and inclusive, rather than blunt or formless. Although there's plenty of party-line voting in Congress, and it's increasing in state legislatures like Maine's, it's also surprising how few bills truly represent any defined party principle. Instead, positions are often dictated by the special interests sponsoring them, which precludes the creative thinking among legislators that produces good compromises. The public interest isn't well represented when campaign contributions or lobbying prowess prevail. Ill-defined and unread platforms have not served the Maine Democratic Party well. It's time to return to a traditional exercise that once drove the party's growth and acceptance by widening circles of Mainers.

It's equally important to understand how well-intended election reforms may hinder party-building rather than help. The attempt to impose ranked choice voting is incompatible with the system of partisan general elections, and should not have had the Maine Democratic Party's endorsement, as it did in 2016. Ranked choice may be suitable for non-partisan elections or primary elections, but has different implications in November contests normally decided by nominations. It fell to Justice Joseph Jabar of the Maine Supreme Judicial Court, during oral arguments on the constitutionality of ranked choice voting, to point out that it would "fundamentally change" the nature of how we vote in traditionally partisan elections.

Supporters have presented ranked choice as an insurance policy against undesirable outcomes, yet it also fragments consideration of which candidate each voter believes should hold the office. A single choice is inherently different than a multiple choice exercise, and the variable participation of voters in the additional "rounds" only adds to the uncertainty.

Burlington, Vermont, was one of the first cities to adopt a ranked choice system, for mayor, the position where Bernie Sanders first made his mark in 1981. In 2005, ranked choice voting was used for the first time, but was repealed in 2010 after voters were dissatisfied with the first outcome where the plurality winner wasn't elected. It turns out that deciding an election by second, third and fourth place votes isn't necessarily an improvement; in this case, an unpopular incumbent stayed in office in large part because he was better known than his main challenger.

There's another way to achieve the favorable outcomes sought by ranked choice voting supporters, which include "civility." Maine has an unusually large proportion of voters not registered with any party, who are "unenrolled," or "independent." They participate in only part of the electoral process, and the four parties ought to do a better job of attracting members. American elections have rarely featured more than two "major parties" at a time, but it's possible to accommodate additional parties without resorting to a multiple choice ballot.

New York is the only state that allows candidates to be listed on multiple parties' ballot lines in the general election. Vermont, which once did, is a more relevant example for Maine. While its non-partisan registration system would be a major change, the simpler step of allowing more than one party to nominate the same candidate could be easily accomplished. Historically, and in contemporary politics, the role of "third parties" has been to influence the larger electoral debate, not necessarily to elect large number of candidates.

If a candidate were nominated by both Green and Democratic voters, for instance, and chose to run as a Green, there would be no chance of "splitting the vote," the main purpose of the more elaborate, and constitutionally flawed, ranked choice voting measure passed in 2016. Conversely, a candidate nominated by both Republicans and Libertarians, could run as a Libertarian with the same outcome. In each case, new caucuses could be formed at the Legislature, and the major parties would have to adapt to competing views and political philosophies.

The party system isn't going to change overnight, but the possibility of multiple nominations could leaven a party system that now leaves out far too many voters. If they saw a purpose for joining a party, and the prospect of influencing elections, many would. For the governor's race, and potentially for other statewide offices, a candidate with a dual nomination would have an additional endorsement far more valuable that those bestowed by interest groups.

The Clean Election Act can also be helpful in promoting multi-party competition, because it provides the means for conducting campaigns without the necessity to raise money before doing anything else. Several studies have shown that Maine's Legislature has become more diverse, with working-age people more common, than in other states with citizen legislatures. The ability to join a party and campaign on its program should attract more young people, as well as bringing new ideas into politics.

LEGISLATIVE REFORM

The thorough overhaul of the Executive Branch that Governor Ken Curtis and a Republican Legislature carried out hasn't been accomplished for the Legislature itself. During his first decade as House speaker, John Martin did promote significant improvements in how legislation was researched and drafted, and in the pay and conditions under which law-makers do their jobs. Non-partisan fiscal and policy offices allowed the Legislature to respond, and propose alternatives, to the governor's agenda. Committees acquired analysts and clerks, and the majority and minority offices offered limited shared staff to legislators as well.

In his last years, however, Martin seemed bent more on enhancing and preserving his own power than improving the institution he dominated for so long. A few senior aides became highly paid extensions of the presiding officers' authority, while rank-and-file House members shared one junior staffer among ten members. And there have been no significant changes since Martin departed as speaker in 1993.

The Curtis-era reforms that did involve the Legislature were never fully implemented. Though longer annual sessions were scheduled, the annual budgets supposed to follow them never did. The logjam created in the first year of each legislature, as the four House and Senate caucuses maneuver around passing a budget by two-thirds, is counterproductive, and prevents new ideas from being properly considered, since any bill requiring an appropriation is put off to the last minute, usually with inadequate funding available. If spending isn't proposed by the governor, it's rarely approved.

The last-minute crush in adopting a supermajority budget has led not only to two shutdowns of state government, but to routine mismanagement of the state's business, as the power of individual leaders, whether in the minority or majority, is inappropriately enhanced. Even the Appropriations Committee, which retained an important role in crafting the budget in John Martin's day, has been repeatedly bypassed, with leaders directly negotiating the final product, a task for which they are ill-suited.

We can get the Legislature functioning again with a few relatively simple changes. Along with the repeal of term limits, almost everything needed for legislative reform can be performed by rule or statutory changes.

As soon as possible, the Legislature should adopt the annual budgets that were supposed to be part of annual sessions. Recognizing its status as a citizen legislature, each session should be set at four months, with adjournment in April. The Clean Election Act has encouraged working-aged people to run for the Legislature; keeping the job part-time would allow many more talented people, especially those self-employed, to serve.

If these changes are adopted, Maine could return to budgets by majority, as in other state legislatures and Congress. Our system cannot function effectively without majority rule, and Maine's current budget procedures virtually guarantee the majority cannot carry out its program. This is a subtle, demoralizing factor in why even the most capable legislators cannot produce the results their constituents expect. Maine has inadvertently sapped its ability to innovate.

An earlier budget will also be a godsend to counties, municipalities, and—especially—school districts, many of which get the majority of their funding from the state. Local boards are dependent on revenue figures from Augusta, and recent stalemates have made it impossible to adopt local budgets on time. Unpredictable budgets take a toll on local officials; serving in local office should not present these kind of trials, and fewer qualified people will run as long as finances remain outside local control.

April adjournment would still leave lawmakers within the ninety days now required for ordinary legislation to take effect; that's where the two-thirds "emergency" budgets came from. The problem requires a constitutional amendment, which could shorten the interval to forty-five days, to remove the temptation for extending sessions. Most states don't require such long delays for legislation to take effect. The amendment should also eliminate the distinction between the first and second year sessions.

Maine legislators debate and vote on too many bills—usually more than 2,000 every two years. Numerous bills are near-duplicates, and many are filed session after session, though they've been rejected time and again. Sunday hunting, and attempts to modify the automobile excise tax, are among the hardy perennials. They've been debated literally hundreds of times, and never succeeded.

To replace the "open filing" that now prevails, a Committee on Legislation would screen proposals at each session's outset. The Legislative Council, consisting of the ten leaders, could continue to hear appeals. The new committee would select bills for drafting, and propose committee references, which take up an inordinate amount of each chamber's time. By no longer considering repetitious or poorly conceived bills, lawmakers could devote their time to the budget, and major bills that now rarely receive the scrutiny they deserve. The Committee on Legislation would need guidelines, including assurances each caucus is treated fairly, and that each legislator could choose to file bills.

Finally, lawmakers need to re-examine the joint committee structure. Previous revisions have created such awkward hybrids as the Legal and Veterans Affairs Committee, a merger of the Legal Affairs, and the Aging, Retirement and Veterans committees. Merging the Labor Committee with the Business and Economic Development Committee has created another odd duck.

The Criminal Justice and Public Safety Committee operates without much public involvement, an increasing concern now that capital funding for courts and corrections now longer requires voter-approved bond issues. Finally, the State and Local Government Committee isn't an effective mediator among the interests of state, county, and municipal government. This is unacceptable, given that the state provides direct aid of more than $1 billion a year to towns, cities and school districts—a third of the General Fund budget.

To date, reducing the number of committees has been the only impetus for change. The Legislature may still have too many committees, or too few. Only a thorough analysis of the flow of legislation, and the effect restoration of a majority budget would have on each committee's work, can answer those questions.

BUDGET REFORM

When an annual budget, enacted by majority, becomes the rule, there will be a liberating effect throughout the State House. One of the few significant recent changes in budget preparation has been inclusion of committees of jurisdiction for departments and agencies they oversee. These committees meet with Appropriations to make recommendations, but the process is often fruitless. The size of the budget has been determined by the economic and revenue forecasting committees before the Legislature convenes, and delaying the budget until June mean new initiatives are rarely properly considered.

Majority budgets would give each lawmaker a meaningful role, as well as reviving the distinction between current services and supplemental budgeting. "Current services" doesn't mean the state continues everything it's already doing. Budget requests should entail detailed interchanges between lawmakers and the administration, finding savings while also considering requests for personnel and other improvements.

For this to happen, budget presentation needs to be radically simplified. Maine's template, almost unchanged for sixty-five years, is so confusing and often obscure that only a handful of legislators truly understand it—in 2017, it weighed in at 832 pages. Accounting for federal funding is poor, and each budget contains errors attributable in part to its complexity. A plain-language summary for legislators, and the public, ought to be available before any final votes are taken. The next governor can take the initiative, in presenting the budget, to incorporate some of these changes. The Legislature can improve its own process, but leadership from the Executive Branch will be needed to ensure a cooperative and creative budget blueprint.

Each legislative session identifies new spending priorities, and much work goes into them—in recent years, workforce development, and the opioid addiction crisis. Yet identified needs get minimal funding because the budget process, as now practiced, doesn't allow the focused consideration a supplemental budget invites. Revenues as well as spending should be included; the straitjacket of revenue forecasts can be broken. Then participation by committees and individual legislators will be meaningful, not symbolic.

Courage will be required. We didn't become a tax-averse culture overnight. The ideological campaign against taxes, and its parallel effort to dismantle public programs, have been lamentably successful, but the public is beginning to realize that an economy based on lower taxes and lower wages has left the average person, and average family, worse off than before. Government has the means, and the opportunity, to pursue a different direction.

The final section of this chapter outlines a program of public investment intended to buttress Maine's economy, and create the future tax revenues needed to support the whole range of programs a humane and responsive state government needs to offer. It is not comprehensive; numerous issues, from renewable energy and broadband communication to housing and health care, are not covered. Instead, opportunities that are neglected or rarely discussed will be the focus.

HIGHER EDUCATION

Thinking back, Ken Curtis said recently that the University of Maine System was his most important achievement as governor. Or, as he characteristically put it, "If I'm remembered for anything, it would be that."

The seven institutions that now comprise the system consisted, at its founding in 1968, one Land Grant university campus in Orono, five teacher's colleges, or "normal schools," in Farmington, Machias, Fort Kent, Presque Isle and Gorham, a junior college in Portland, the University of Maine Law School, and the brand-new University of Maine at Augusta, chartered three years earlier as a continuing education center. It wasn't easy to bring such geographically dispersed and culturally diverse campuses together, but most indicators suggest a fair degree of success. Under Curtis, funding increased markedly and enrollments grew rapidly. Today, the system enrolls nearly 40,000 students and offers programs and courses that involve countless Mainers each year.

The system has had numerous ups and downs, however. Its most difficult period came under Curtis's successor as governor, James Longley, who was a fierce critic and repeatedly cut the system's budget during his four years as governor. Although funding levels were partially restored during Joe Brennan's second term, they fell again during the 1990s recession, and every economic downturn since then. Each time state revenues have fallen, higher education funding has been seen as discretionary, and reduced accordingly, under the theory that higher tuition can make up the difference. The shortfalls, however, are never made up. Over the last three decades, the proportion of state funding vs. tuition has fallen from 70 percent of the budget to less than 45 percent. While some of the shift represents a nationwide rise in college costs, the results—with a majority of the costs paid by students—are unfortunate for a state with below-average incomes, and whose economic future depends on knowledge, research and a well-trained workforce.

As recently as the 1980s, a consensus held that higher education should be a focus throughout Maine state government and the private sector. That consensus has eroded. The Great Recession that began in 2008 has been especially damaging, with "flat funding," and effective reductions for six consecutive years. Some nine hundred jobs were lost, including more than three hundred faculty members, with reductions especially steep at the University of Southern Maine, until then the fastest-growing campus, and at the Muskie School of Public Service, which offers the state's only graduate courses in public administration. The continuing shift away from state funding and toward tuition has left University of Maine System graduates with larger debts than those with degrees from Bowdoin, Bates and Colby. Low-income students are the worst off. The educational opportunity that once existed for Mainers of modest means has been sharply constricted.

Another way of looking at the university system's declining state support is to track a state budget line that also disproportionately involves the young—those who commit crimes and are incarcerated. In 1986, Maine spent $78 million for university system support, and $33 million for the Department of Corrections, less than half as much. By 2016, university support totaled $200 million, but Corrections spending had risen far faster, to $178 million. When the expenses of county jails, about $90 million, are added, Maine taxpayers are paying far more for incarceration than they are for higher education, even when the community college are added. Looking at the annual rates of increase for universities vs. corrections (See chart on next page), it's obvious the state's priorities are askew. Confining Mainers behind bars—including many whose major problem is mental illness—has been funded far more generously than providing

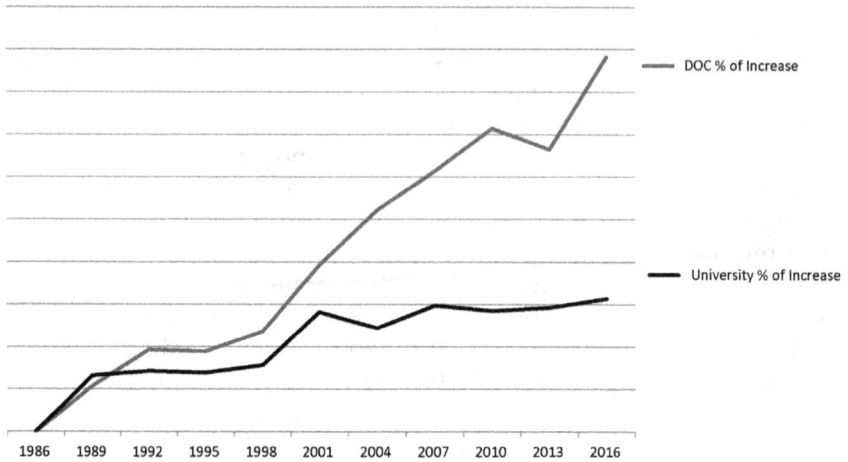

University vs. Corrections Spending

the education that is the best way to encourage early success in life, and deter the criminal activity that often results from early failure.

Investments in infrastructure, including research facilities, are similarly out of whack. University and community college campuses struggle to maintain their buildings, while lawmakers allocated $140 million in 2016 to overhaul and expand the Maine Correctional Center in Windham, without significant public involvement.

The University of Maine conducts research on a world scale, using federal grants to develop prototypes for offshore wind turbines that could be used globally. Unfortunately, state government's priorities have been elsewhere, with the current administration stubbornly invested in energy sources with declining prospects, such as natural gas, and shutting off opportunity for both land and sea-based renewable sources, including solar. Aligning state policy with sound research priorities should be imperative for the next administration.

Funding the university system is ultimately an act of faith for the Legislature. In a budget document of more than eight hundred pages, the university budget is a single line; its allocation is made by the board of trustees and the chancellor. The next governor should take a different approach to the all-important chancellor position, traditionally a career educator. A prominent Mainer versed in the arts of persuasion and outreach, as well as educational ability, is essential to fulfill higher education's considerable potential.

Experimentation should be encouraged. Several campuses have expanded out-of-state enrollment by matching tuition rates from the student's home state, though this is still a small fraction of overall enrollment. House Speaker Libby Mitchell once proposed a year of free tuition at all campuses, which, given tuition increases, would be more difficult now than it was in the 1990s. Free or reduced tuition at the community colleges, where costs are lower, could be a worthy trial of the concept, which is designed for families and students understandably reluctant to take on the present financial risks.

In sheer economic terms, there's probably no better use of state dollars than investing in education. Underinvestment in higher education has reduced Maine's prospects, and campuses have retrenched as budgets are downsized. Restoring the university as the high priority it was at its beginnings would accomplish more than almost anything else the next administration could do.

Another focus for state investment should be its natural resource economy, a traditional source of strength that's been declining for a half century. The greater Portland area has income levels and economic growth comparable to the rest of New England; counties elsewhere have been in deep recession for years, a slump that's worsened since 2008. Rural Maine cannot prosper again unless its resources, in the broadest sense of the term, are again put to use.

FORESTS

Immense forests are the most vivid impression for first-time visitors to Maine, and it's understandable. Trees occupy a greater proportion of its land area than any other state. The coast was settled first, is more picturesque and more visited, but the value of fisheries are but a small fraction of what woodlands have generated. Even today, after significant declines in employment, forest products produce 6 percent of the gross state product. Meanwhile, opportunities for recreation and tourism in the North Woods are much greater now than when Baxter State Park and the Allagash Wilderness Waterway were created and, despite oft-expressed fears to the contrary, are compatible with continued timber harvesting, since trees—unlike minerals and fossil fuels—are a completely renewable resource.

The key to sustaining harvesting while increasing visitation will be adding value to the forest itself, and well as its products. The paper industry that controlled use of the forest for a century is much smaller and requires less of the resource; there are no paper mills remaining in the entire Penobscot River watershed—the heart of the Maine woods. While paper was a high-value product in the early twentieth century, prices have been falling, in real terms, for decades. The greatest value for Maine's forests—on the boundary between the hardwood forests of the eastern United States and the boreal, conifer forests of Canada—lies in growing larger trees over long rotations, owned by companies investing for the long term.

There are examples of this kind of forest management. The Baskahegan Company dates back nearly a century, when Milliken & Co., the nation's largest privately owned textile manufacturer, acquired 100,000 acres of mostly cutover spruce and fir acreage in Washington County, which it managed haphazardly, much like other out-of-state landowners. In the 1980s, Roger Milliken moved to Maine and employed then-novel techniques of sustainable, high-yield forestry that since have turned the company's holdings into a model of long-term management, conserving the natural assets of streams, lakes and ponds while growing trees of multiple species and ages.

The resulting forest is healthier, resistant to pests like the spruce budworm, and uses Maine's remarkable natural regeneration capabilities to re-create forests more like those that existed before logging began in the nineteenth century—attractive both to visitors and woodland managers alike. It yields much larger, more valuable trees, and is managed more like a small ownership than the industrial techniques familiar from paper mill days. Contemporary harvesting techniques, where GPS supplements "timber cruising," can use all elements of trees above the ground, but much depends on whether "patient forestry" becomes the standard for landowners on a larger scale.

Despite synthetic alternatives, wood has kept its share of construction markets, both for residential and commercial uses, better than one might expect. New applications such as laminated "mass timber" are helping redefine what sawmills and wood manufacturing plants produce. "Whole tree" operations that utilize all available wood fiber are needed to increase competitiveness, with low-grade wood used to power manufacturing, as well as new biomass electricity plants to replace those built a generation ago that are now obsolete. State finance agencies should focus on these investments in new plants.

Commercial forestry is in transition, not lasting decline, and Maine's access to markets remains a major advantage. The University of Maine's School of Forest Resources is experiencing a revival of student interest, and the Advanced Structures and Composites Center there does nationally significant research on new wood-based products.

Recreation offers even greater growth potential, as tourism becomes better established as Maine's largest single economic sector. The Appalachian Trail corridor and adjacent trail systems are being transformed from lonely footpaths traversed mainly by through-hikers to year-round hut systems offering overnight accommodations, almost entirely through private and non-profit investment.

The Katahdin Woods and Waters National Monument, established in 2016, is already winning converts from those who originally saw it as a threat to traditional uses. Accessible to the Northeastern and Mid-Atlantic states, the Maine Woods' potential is vast and largely untapped. There's room for a larger national park someday, and the Moosehead

Lake region, along with Katahdin and the Penobscot River watershed, would be suitable for controlled growth; there will still be plenty of room for wilderness preserves, for those who prize them.

The state can contribute to growth in the north woods, bringing new residents as well as visitors to the area. Its Land for Maine's Future program is a national model for state-led land conservation. It needs two changes, however, to become more effective. As now structured, the Land for Maine's Future Board solicits grant proposals, then chooses from those that rank highest, with categories for public recreation, forests, working waterfront, farmland and wildlife habitat. The program needs its own strategic plan, which should be coordinated with state economic development agencies, including tourism, to identify purchases the state should pursue. The program also needs a continuing source of funding besides the bond issues which only periodically allow it to purchase land and conservation easements. A general fund appropriation and designated revenue source are essential to future stability.

Understanding the potential for renewed growth in the forest sector, ensuring various state efforts are coordinated and properly supported, and tapping available federal resources, could go a long way to revive prospects for the forested northern three-quarters of Maine's vast landscape.

AGRICULTURE

Maine began as a farming state, but farming was declining as a livelihood even before the Civil War. Ken Curtis said of growing up during the Great Depression in the hamlet of Curtis Corner, in Leeds, "That was the end of the family farm. I saw my father killing himself, doing things the way he was taught, and I couldn't fall into that same trap."

Bulk agriculture—potatoes and milk, chiefly—no longer has the role in Maine's economy and farm acreage it once did, yet the densely populated Northeast is still there. Maine has more available farmland, with proven growing potential, than all of the other New England states combined. Reorganizing its farming practices and objectives, identifying new crops and marketing opportunities, encouraging entrepreneurship and creating economies of scale are all parts of the puzzle. The labor-intensive nature of farming, and its far-reaching benefits to local communities, however, are a strong incentive to put public resources behind an age-old way of life that could bring new hope to Maine's rural areas.

The first wave of young newcomers to old farming towns came with the "back to the land" generation, spurred by the upheavals of the 1960s. They came for many reasons, and the "native vs. newcomer" dynamic created conflict, but also lasting community benefits. As farmers, however, the newcomers were mostly untaught, and their farming techniques left much to be desired. Since then, however, small-scale farming has become increasingly sophisticated, aided by such leaders as Stewart Smith, who returned from the U.S. Department of Agriculture to become Maine commissioner during the Brennan administration, and Eliot Coleman, who pioneered organic techniques that measurably extend the growing season. Both Smith and Coleman still farm in Maine, mentors to new generations.

The Maine Organic Farmers and Gardeners Association, or MOFGA, is best known for the Common Ground Fair in Unity each September, but it nourishes young farmers through apprentice programs and education, in a role once played by the Grange and 4-H. Recent expansion of farmers markets, Community Supported Agriculture, and farm-to-table programs with restaurants in Maine's growing urban districts have all encouraged small-scale but full-time enterprises—and helped Maine to become that rare state where the average farmer is younger than two decades ago, not older.

The craft brewing industry is an example of a largely spontaneous expansion of agriculture based on urban innovation. Maine brewing has grown from a handful of pioneers in downtown Portland in the 1990s to a statewide array of more than seventy commercial beer-makers; there are brew pubs even in such out-of-the-way places as Lubec and The Forks. Original ingredients were imported, but as the industry matures, Maine farmers are starting to grow the hops and barley that goes into recipes, on land where potatoes or corn were harvested. Grass-fed beef, artisanal cheeses, and heirloom potato varieties show that, at least on a small scale, agriculture has an inviting future in Maine. Getting beyond local markets and small-scale successes, however, will require much greater investment.

The Maine Farmland Trust has tried to take on the larger question of how farming, a highly capital-intensive business, can attract those with ideas and knowledge but little cash, and connect them to farming careers. Through conservation easements on existing farms that likely would have been sold for development, it's ensuring that the land base isn't further fragmented or converted to other uses. The trust is experimenting with "food hubs" that support community agriculture, but also play the vital role of collection and distribution that's now more typical of grocery store chains than farm coops.

This is where state government should come in. To date, it has been mostly a bystander to these fruitful changes. The Department of Agriculture, Conservation and Forestry, a 2011 merger of Conservation and Agriculture, has unfulfilled potential in encouraging and organizing new-wave farming. The food hub is an important focus, but if it is only local in scope, it will not put Maine farming back on the map. A program comparable to the Land for Maine's Future, focusing solely on farms, and a bond issue similar to those allocated to the Maine Technology Institute would be effective ways to launch a new public effort to reinforce and extend recent efforts by non-profits.

Innovation has not been a hallmark of Maine's state government in recent years. Charting a new course in agriculture, and finding a new generation's Stewart Smith and Eliot Coleman, will be a major test, working toward the goal of restoring throughout rural Maine one of our most traditional and satisfying ways of life.

TRANSPORTATION

What's now the Department of Transportation was once the largest and most important of all state agencies. Highway building began long before the Interstate Highway Act of 1956 that made the federal government a major player. Maine's fuel taxes have been dedicated to the Highway Fund since 1935, and before the rise of the Department of Health and Human Services, DOT had by far the largest budget and number of employees. Support for transportation, now including ports, rail and pedestrian modes, has always been bipartisan and statewide; back when there were a variety of biennial bond issues on the ballot, transportation was always among the most popular.

How DOT has fallen since then. When its commissioner has presented the budget to the Legislature's Transportation Committee in recent years, he points out that, without any significant improvements or reconstruction, there's still a $75 million annual shortfall between what fuel taxes and vehicle registrations bring in and the maintenance needs of the state highway system. He then asks for a $100 million bond issue, paid by the General Fund, that still leaves the state $25 million a year short. Without contributions from the Maine Turnpike, it's doubtful that even the two recent shared capital projects Maine has undertaken, the Memorial and Sarah Long bridge replacements between Kittery and Portsmouth, N.H., could have gone ahead.

The Transportation Committee's response has been to outline a program of gas tax, vehicle registration and driver's license fee increases to fill the gap, but that gets the cart before the horse. The way to interest the Legislature, and the public, in rebuilding vital infrastructure is to map how it would affect every legislative district, and every municipality in Maine, as Committee Chairman Peter Danton and Commissioner George Campbell did back in 1983. And today, we have a lot more sophisticated means of presenting information than index cards.

The Brennan administration's road building spurt was the last time Maine made much of a dent in the often dismal condition of its rural roads, and in removing urban bottlenecks. The federal funding Senator George Mitchell brought to Maine in the 1990s fueled major highway projects, including three bridges—by far the system's most expensive links—and the Downeaster rail service to Portland, but did not provide the system upgrades that would at least allow Maine to match its northern New England neighbors, New Hampshire and Vermont. Higher road standards have been written into statute, but the state has no hope of reaching them without significant increases in funding. Mainers have grown used to living on and commuting over substandard roads, with punishing frost heaves in winter and potholes every spring. But it need not be so.

The transportation picture is broader, too, than in was in 1983. Since the 1990s, some 15 percent of federal fuel taxes have been allocated to transit and rail, and about 1 percent to trail and pedestrian projects. Despite these relatively small proportions, results have been dramatic. The Downeaster began pulling into Portland in 2001, and stimulus funding from the Obama administration allowed the extension of service to Brunswick in 2012; tracks suitable for passenger trains run from there to Rockland.

Statewide passenger rail service seemed feasible after the "Big Dig" in Boston was designed to include a rail connection between North and South stations, but the line wasn't built. Had it been, the Canadian provinces of New Brunswick and Nova Scotia envisioned subsidizing service, through Maine, connecting with the Eastern U.S. corridor's high-speed service to New York and Washington. Those who doubt the Canadian commitment to public transportation should consider Nova Scotia's payments to restore ferry service from Yarmouth to Portland: tens of millions of dollars from Canada, with no contribution from Maine.

There is another route, though. Amtrak has now completed or is constructing high speed lines through Connecticut and Massachusetts, via Springfield and Worcester, that, bypassing Boston, could bring passenger trains through Maine. One more link, to Lowell, would be required, but given existing investments it makes excellent sense. A major regional effort, including New England's governors and congressional delegations, would be necessary to produce cooperation from all partners, but it's a more likely avenue than local efforts in Auburn-Lewiston and Bangor to restore service. Bringing service to interior Maine, including Augusta and Waterville, needs far great passenger numbers than Maine alone can provide. This could be Maine's "east-west highway" of the future, changing the nature of how people move around the state.

Maine's Office of Tourism promotes "carless" vacations in places like Acadia National Park and some coastal peninsulas, but train service could allow Maine's seasonal visitors, still predominately from the Northeast, to vacation much as visitors to Europe do. The obstacles are considerable, but the vision is compelling.

The Appalachian Trail is a Maine landmark, with 281 miles, more than any other state except Virginia and Tennessee—and no other state has Katahdin as the goal. Though hiking trails have grown markedly, for daily use the "rail trails" reclaimed from unused rail corridors attract many more thousands. Projects in Augusta-Gardiner, Portland, Lewiston-Auburn and elsewhere have attracted new residents and changed the image of Maine's downtown centers. For more strenuous trips, the eighty-seven-mile Downeast-Sunrise Trail, running from Ellsworth through Machias to the Bold Coast, is a model for what could be done throughout the state. Driving was the mid-twentieth century's near-universal form of transportation. It's not likely to be nearly as true in the twenty-first.

FUNDING

No business remains solvent without figuring out an investment plan aimed at remaining competitive. For thirty-five years, however, the federal government and many states have pretended they could function effectively without a financial plan, and without carefully weighing the tradeoffs between taxes and spending. Instead, the mantras of lower taxes and less government have been invoked as if they could answer all questions, and resolve all dilemmas. They can't.

It's sobering to realize how serious Maine's public under-investment has become, in the General Fund just as much as the Highway Fund. Always a conservative borrower, using ten-year bonds instead of the typical twenty years, Maine has become downright stingy, and its capital investment has fallen sharply. In constant dollars, the state's general obligation bond debt has fallen by half since 1993, from more than $900

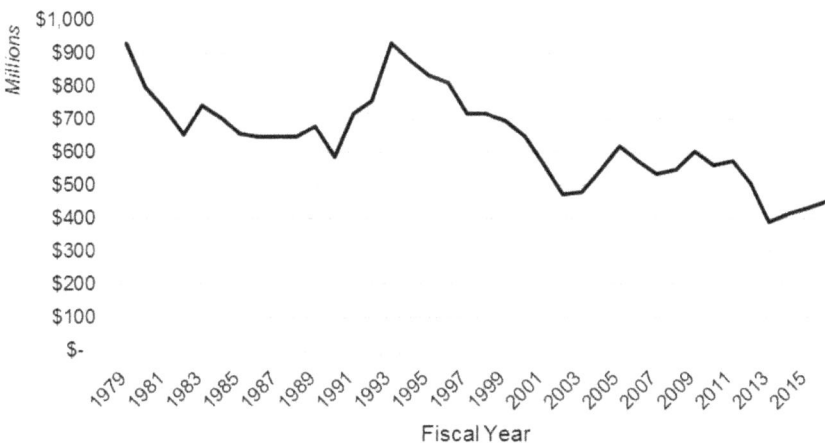

Maine General Obligation Bonds, 1979-2016. *Source*: **Maine Center for Economic Policy analysis of data from the Maine Office of Fiscal and Program Review, inflation adjusted to fiscal year 2017 dollars.**

million to about $450 million, and will continue to decline. In recent years, voters have rarely been asked to approve more than $200 million in borrowing, yet a package twice that amount could still be seen as thrifty. The deferred maintenance in state buildings and traditional local aid programs for community water and sewer systems continues to grow as fast, or faster, than our crumbling roads and bridges, yet it's rare to hear a legislator even mention the subject.

Though the investment priorities sketched earlier in this chapter do not come with a specific price tag, if we want Maine to grow again, we cannot do it without substantial new public investment. In that spirit, the following revenue sources may constitute what a veteran legislator once called, perhaps naively, "low hanging fruit."

The simplest place to start is transportation funding, because the relationship between the funding sources and spending is so clear. Maine, like other states, has for nearly a century relied on gasoline and diesel fuel taxes to build and maintain roads; since 1935, all revenues raised from fuel taxes have been dedicated to Maine's Highway Fund. Dedicated fuel taxes provide the bulk, but vehicle registrations, license and title fees are other significant revenue sources. Town and cities are allocated the proceeds from vehicle excise taxes, a "personal property" tax on cars that continues as long as the vehicle remains on the road. Though not required, most municipalities allocate these revenues to their road budgets.

The main problem with fuel taxes as the means to fund transportation is that their value declines over time. It's possible to argue that income or sales tax rates should remain stable, since their proportion to the overall economy remains relatively constant. It isn't possible to make this argument about fuel taxes, whose value erodes annually at the rate of inflation. Since the "no tax" pledges became operative, the nation's, and Maine's, under-investment in transportation has mushroomed. The federal gas tax of 18.4 cents per gallon was last increased in 1993; in constant dollars, that now represents 9.5 cents. Maine's gas tax is now thirty cents a gallon, after a period of inflation indexing during the Baldacci administration; indexing was repealed in 2011. The tax's value peaked in the Brennan administration, at fourteen cents a gallon. Today, it would have to be forty-nine cents to provide similar revenue.

The inertia against raising the gas tax is curious, given that drivers understand the relationship between what they pay at the pump and the condition of the roads they drive on. Restoring Maine's road system to maintenance levels, and then considering improvements, will take time, but it begins with an effort to inform the public of the alternatives, and providing a choice. As long as voters understand what they're being asked to pay for, reasonable increases aren't the electoral black hole they've long been assumed to be.

Maine should also consider a feature of federal law not employed here—using a portion of fuel taxes for rail, port and pedestrian projects. Most Mainers are well aware of the looming consequences of global warming. Along with the state's aging population, and the opportunity to attract new visitors, we need much greater emphasis on expanding public transportation, which is far more fuel-efficient than individual vehicles. The Land for Maine's Future program has shown that even modest amounts of state funding can attract considerably greater amounts of federal and private grants, and transportation could offer similar opportunities.

Maine's personal income tax was contested when it was first enacted in 1969, with a top rate of 6 percent, but the dramatic support it received from voters in a 1971 referendum attempt to repeal it, with 3-1 support for the tax, seemed to settle the question. The top rate was raised to 10 percent in 1976, lowered to 8.5 percent in 1989, in response to federal tax reform, and was then subject of a years-long attempt by Democratic legislators during the Baldacci administration to lower the top rate again by expanding sales taxes; the Democrats' plan was enacted on party-line votes in 2009, then repealed by voters the following year.

The LePage administration made no secret of its disdain for the income tax, and convinced lawmakers to twice lower the top rate, which now stands at 7.15 percent. Voters approved a 2016 referendum to raise the effective top rate to 10.15 percent for higher income taxpayers, but it was repealed by lawmakers in 2017. Given this vexed history, it would be wise to leave the income tax question aside, for now.

Given the startling levels of economic inequality in Maine and the nation, there's little doubt higher income taxpayers should be required to pay more, but Maine's tax has other internal problems. The simple, smoothly progressive design of the original income tax, with six brackets from 1 percent to 6 percent, has been distorted over the years; the top rate is imposed at income levels well below those of other states, or the federal tax code. It remains the largest single source of state revenue, but until Maine is presented a comprehensive plan for taxes, and spending, attempting a quick fix for the top rate is unlikely to succeed. Ultimately, restoring a progressive structure similar to the original 1969 law, suitably updated with new brackets for higher incomes, is the best solution.

More revenue could be available from business taxes, however, with less difficulty, simply by adjusting current tax programs and seeking one additional source of "low hanging fruit." Beginning with the King administration, and continuing through the Baldacci administration, the state has made a veritable mess of the personal property tax on business equipment.

Forgiving taxes on business purchases of new equipment became fashionable in the "rust belt" states that were shedding manufacturing jobs during the 1980s, but did little to stem the tide. Maine came late to the game; in 1995, Governor Angus King, proposed, and the Legislature enacted, a state reimbursement for taxes paid on new purchases, dubbing it the Business Equipment Tax Reimbursement, or BETR. Towns and cities continued to get the revenue they'd always collected. There were a few initial expansions of manufacturing operation, but no requirements in the legislation to create or maintain jobs. For the two decades since, the tax break has continued for almost every business in Maine, though OPE-GA, the Legislature's accountability agency, has issued two reports failing to identify any overall economic benefits.

In 2003, Governor John Baldacci, confronted with the program's growing costs, decided not to reduce them, but to make new equipment tax-exempt altogether. It took three years to convince fellow Democrats at the Legislature to go along with BETE, or the Business Equipment Tax Exemption. Starting in 2007, businesses paid nothing to towns or cities, and municipalities were reimbursed just 50 percent by the state, the minimum required by the state constitution. All business equipment continues to be assessed. Taxes are paid for one category, reimbursements are offered for another, and exemptions apply to yet a third time period. This confusing tax regimen makes it difficult to identify the full costs, but the state is investing least $50 million per biennium in BETR, with a greater, and growing, sum split between the state and municipalities for BETE — well over $100 million per biennium. Given the lack of identifiable benefits, and the continued assessment on individuals of other personal property taxes, such as motor vehicles, BETR and BETE should be phased out and these substantial revenues returned to the state and municipalities.

Amid the bevy of anti-tax referendums of the twenty-first century's first decade, there was one campaign that would have created a new tax, but fell a few hundred signatures short of qualifying for the ballot in 2006. Dubbed a "water extraction tax," it would have imposed a twenty cent per gallon tax on water bottlers producing more than 500,000 gallons a year. Then, as now, the primary effect would be on one company, Nestle Spring Waters, a subsidiary of the major international company that purchased the Poland Spring resort and since has expanded to half a dozen other Maine sites. Poland Spring is now the leading brand in much of the country, and Maine is critical to its appeal.

Ten years ago, those concerned about taxing Nestle speculated the company would leave Maine if a tax were applied; those worries now seem implausible. The state has invested millions of dollars in land conservation, water resource protection and responsible forestry that in essence created the product Nestle now sells. Though each division's financials aren't broken out, the parent company had estimated sales of $90.8 billion and profits of $8.66 billion in 2016. Its pays only property taxes in Maine, and regular utility rates to municipal systems supplying water.

Extraction taxes are employed worldwide on commodities such as fossil fuels, minerals, gems and other profitable resources. Alaska does without an income or sales tax, and has the nation's lowest gas tax, because of its extraction taxes on gas and petroleum. Such taxes seem unfamiliar in Maine, yet the capital timber tax on all trees cut commercially is directly comparable. Forest land is taxed at "current use" rates, reflecting the lack of demand on public services for undeveloped land. When timber is harvested, the state collects revenue based on the value of the products being sold.

Both forests and groundwater represent renewable resources that Maine supplies in abundance in part because of enlightened public policy, and public investment in resource protection. A water extraction tax is an idea whose time has come.

CODA

The achievements of the Progressive Era, the New Deal, and the Great Society have been durable—more so than is commonly appreciated. The sagas of presidencies and war, the framework around which much of our history has been written, distract us from the reality that daily life has been shaped, and improved, as much from the patient work of legislatures and Congress, as from directions given at the top.

These twentieth-century legacies have not been lost, but they have been eclipsed. The appetite of voters for truly new answers to the dilemmas we face is unknown, but the arrival at the State House in recent years of legislators with intelligence, integrity and a firm commitment to representing their constituents is encouraging. When Maine elects another governor with a plan, it is likely that there will be others ready to use their own expertise to refine, revise, and carry it out.

Afterword

We argue about politics more than we converse and discuss. From my earliest days as a journalist, I heard people—people of good will, often those of high standing in the community—talk about how they didn't want to get involved in the "dirty business" of politics. There was too much "mudslinging" in campaigns, nor did they enjoy the "sausage-making" that attends the passage of legislation, even sound and far-sighted legislation.

These habits of mind have cost us dearly. If good people don't get involved, it is inevitable that, even in the world's longest functioning democracy, many of those who run for high office feature arrogance, power-seeking and narcissism as prominent traits.

It was not always this way. In Maine's Democratic party, the careers and examples of Frank Coffin and Ed Muskie, and some of their successors—including Ken Curtis, George Mitchell, and Joe Brennan—made the case that politics, in the service of good government, was worth the time, effort and aggravation it took.

Those times are not too distant for many Mainers alive today to remember—and for young people, who have lacked similar examples, to learn about. Belief in the possibilities of Frank Coffin's "positive government" may have ebbed, but we forget that many of the most successful reforms of earlier eras also looked hopeless at the start.

Joe Brennan said that "an imperfect plan, boldly articulated and vigorously implemented, will succeed." Government, when it works well, represents a process of amendment and adjustment, not gains that will never have to be reconsidered or revisited. As Allen Pease also reminds us, "Power unused may be power abused." Voters rightly expect that those they elect do more than position themselves to be elected again, however much celebrity-style coverage of politics may lead us to forget such truths.

As an optimist by temperament, I choose to believe that the campaigns ahead, and the elections that follow, can begin to right the balance between private and public, individual and community, tradition and change. If we are to restore public life to what it ought to be, it will be by an act of collective will, but it starts with the individual efforts all of us can make.

Sources

BOOKS

Barringer, Richard (Editor), *Changing Maine*, Portland, Maine: Edmund S. Muskie Institute of Public Affairs, 1990.

Barringer, Richard (Editor), *Changing Maine: 1960-2010*, Gardiner, Maine: Tilbury House, Publishers, 2004.

Barringer, Richard (Editor) *Toward a Sustainable Maine*, Portland, Maine: Edmund S. Muskie Institute of Public Affairs, 1993.

Berthelot, Helen Washburn, *Win Some Lose Some: G. Mennen Williams and the New Democrats*, Detroit: Wayne State University Press, 1995.

Bradford, Peter Amory, *Fragile Structures: A Story of Oil Refineries, National Security, and the Coast of Maine*, New York: Harper's Magazine Press, 1975.

Brunelle, Jim, *Maine Almanac*, Augusta, Maine: Guy Gannett Publishing Company, 1978.

Coffin, Frank M., *Life and Times in the Three Branches* (unpublished memoir), Vol. 1: Early Years; Vol. 2: Law, Politics, Congress, AID; Vol. 3: The Judicial Years, 2004.

Coffin, Frank M., *On Appeal: Courts, Lawyering, and Judging*, New York: W.W. Norton, 1994

Coffin, Frank M., *The Ways of a Judge: Reflections from the Federal Appellate Bench*, Boston: Houghton Mifflin Company, 1980.

Cutler, Eliot, *A State of Opportunity*, Portland, Maine, 2013.

Graff, Chris, *Dateline Vermont*, North Pomfret, Vermont: Thistle Hill Publications, 2006.

Hofstadter, Richard, *The Age of Reform: From Bryan to F.D.R.*, New York: Alfred A. Knopf, 1989.

Johnson, Willis, *The Year of the Longley*, Stonington, Maine: Penobscot Bay Press, 1978.

King, Angus, *Independent for Governor: Making a Difference*, Brunswick, Maine, 1994.

Lipez, Kermit, *Kenneth Curtis of Maine: Profile of a Governor*, Brunswick, Maine: Harpswell Press, 1974.

Lippman, Theo, Jr. and Donald C. Hansen, *Muskie*, New York: W.W. Norton & Company, 1971.

Lockard, Duane, *New England Politics*, Princeton, N.J.: Princeton University Press, 1959.

Merrill, Barbara, *Setting the Maine Course: We Can Get There From Here*. Appleton, Maine: Setting the Maine Course, 2005.

Mitchell, George, *The Negotiator: A Memoir*, New York: Simon & Schuster, 2015.

Nevin, David, *Muskie of Maine*, New York: Random House, 1972.

Palmer, Kenneth T. (Principal author), *Maine Politics and Government, Second Edition*, University of Nebraska Press, 2009.

Peirce, Neal R., *The New England States: People, Politics and Power*, New York: W.W. Norton, 1976.

Potholm, Christian P., *This Splendid Game: Maine Campaigns and Elections, 1940-2002*, Lanham, Maryland: Lexington Books, 2003.

Rooks, Douglas, *Statesman: George Mitchell and the Art of the Possible*, Camden, Maine: Down East Books, 2016.

Witherell, James L., *Ed Muskie: Made in Maine, 1914-1960*, Thomaston, Maine: Tilbury House, Publishers, 2014.

Woodard, Colin, *The Lobster Coast: Rebels, Rusticators, and the Struggle for a Forgotten Frontier*, New York: Penguin Books, 2004.

INTERVIEWS

Interviews by the Author

Dick Anderson, Falmouth, Maine, April 21, 2016
Phil Bartlett, Augusta, Maine, February 17, 2017
Severin Beliveau, Augusta, Maine, October 13, 2016
Shenna Bellows, Augusta, Maine, March 17, 2017
Larry Benoit, Cape Elizabeth, Maine, October 8, 2014
Seth Berry, Richmond, Maine, March 31, 2016
Leon Billings, Portland, Maine, November 15, 2014
Peter Bradford, Augusta, Maine, August 17, 2017
Ed Bonney, Freeport, Maine, January 20, 2017
Joe Brennan, Portland, Maine, October 29, 2016
Tony Buxton, Augusta, Maine, November 13, 2014
Bill Bridgeo, Augusta, Maine, October 19, 2016
Mike Carpenter, Augusta, Maine, February 15 and July 18, 2016
Brownie Carson, Brunswick, Maine, November 1, 2016
Jim Case, June 6, 2016
Nancy and Bruce Chandler, Kennebunk, Maine, October 24, 2014
Dana Connors, Augusta, Maine, July 25, 2016
Ken Curtis, December 19, 2014; South Portland, Maine, September 8, 2017
Wayne Davis, Portland, Maine, October 18, 2016
Sara Gideon, Augusta, Maine, January 19, 2017
Gay Grant, South Gardiner, Maine, August 3, 2017
Jared Golden, Augusta, Maine, May 15, 2017
Chris Hall, Portland, Maine, June 22, 2016
Sam Hemingway, August 8, 2017
Bob Howe, Augusta, Maine, October 31, 2016
Troy Jackson, Augusta, Maine, January 27, 2017
Willis Johnson, Gardiner, Maine, March 30, 2016
Theo Kalikow, Portland Maine, December 5, 2016
Roger Katz, Augusta, Maine, February 29, 2016
Angus King, Brunswick, Maine, November 4, 2014
Nate Libby, Augusta, Maine, March 20, 2017
Kermit Lipez, Portland, Maine, April 12, 2017
Jon Lund, Hallowell, Maine, April 28, 2016
John Marsh, West Gardiner, Maine, January 23, 2017
John Melrose, Vassalboro, Maine, February 28, 2017
Roger Milliken, Portland, Maine, November 22, 2016
Peter Mills, Portland, Maine, March 16, 2016
George Mitchell, Seal Harbor, Maine, August 26, 2014 and South Portland, Maine, April 18, 2017
Don Nicoll, Portland, Maine, April 21, June 1, October 18, 2016; January 13, March 8, April 18, 2017
Chris Pearson, August 24, 2017
John Piotti, Belfast, Maine, September 12, 2016
Katie May Simpson, Augusta, Maine, January 19, 2017
Alison Smith, August 18, 2017
Rick Stauffer, Portland, Maine, May 18, 2016
Tae Chong, Portland, Maine, June 28, 2016
Jim Tierney, Brunswick, Maine, January 20, 2017

David Vail, August 25, 2017
Charlotte Warren, Augusta, Maine, January 17, 2017

Governor Joseph E. Brennan Archives, Oral History

Richard Barringer, December 12, 2014 *
Joseph E. Brennan
George Campell, October 19, 2014 *
Kevin Concannon
David Flanagan, July 20, 2015 *
Frank McGinty, October 18, 2014 *
Michael Petit, December 12, 2014 *
Gordon Weil, October 19, 2014 *
* Interviewed by Dick Davies

George J. Mitchell Oral History Project

Bowdoin College Library, Special Collections, Brunswick, Maine
John E. Baldacci, interview by Andrea L'Hommedieu, February 24, 2010
Joe and Connie Brennan, Interview by Andrea L'Hommedieu, October 24, 2009
Bob Tyrer, Interview by Brien Williams, March 12, 2009
Gordon L. Weil, Interview by Andrea L'Hommedieu, August 17, 2009

Edmund S. Muskie Oral History Collection

Bates College Archives and Special Collections, Lewiston Maine
John Baldacci, interviewed by Andrea L'Hommedieu, August 1, 2007
Richard Barringer, interviewed by Andrea L'Hommedieu, March 25, 2002
Denis Blais, interviewed by Don Nicoll, Stuart O'Brien, and Rob Chavira, June 22, 1998
Coffin, Frank Morey, interviewed by Don Nicoll, Stuart O'Brien and Rob Chavira, July 21, 1998
Peter Cox, interviewed by Mike Richard, August 23, 1999
Ken Curtis, interviewed by Don Nicoll, Stuart O'Brien, and Rob Chavira, July 21, 1998
Caroline Glassman, interviewed by Greg Beam, August 17, 2000
Dan Gwadosky, interviewed by Andrea L'Hommedieu, January 18, 2002
Bennett Katz, interviewed by Jeremy Robitaille, July 13, 2001
Peter Kyros, Sr., interviewed by Don Nicoll, December 6, 2000
Joe Mayo, interviewed by Greg Beam, August 16, 2000
Martin, John, interviewed by Don Nicoll, October 10, 1998
Pat McTeague, interviewed by Jeremy Robitaille, June 13, 2001
Phil Merrill, interviewed by Andrea L'Hommedieu, June 27, 2000
Peter Mills, interviewed by Andrea L'Hommedieu, May 30, 2000
Libby Mitchell, interviewed by Nicholas Christie, August 3, 2001
Ed Muskie, Shep Lee, Don Nicoll and Frank Coffin, interviewed by Chris Beam, August 6, 1991
Don Nicoll and Frank Coffin, interviewed by Erin Griffiths and Chris Beam, November 20, 1996
Allen and Violet Pease, interviewed by Andrea L'Hommedieu, January 31, 2001
Allen and Violet Pease, interviewed by Nicholas Christie, July 11, 2001
Ed Pert, interviewed by Stuart O'Brien and Rob Chavira, July 24, 1998
Jerry Plante, interviewed by Mike Richard, July 8, 1999
Carlton "Bud" Reed, interviewed by Marisa Burnham-Bestor, February 7, 2000
John Reed, interviewed by Don Nicoll, January 27, 2003
Harrison Richardson, interviewed by Greg Beam, July 17, 2000
Neil Rolde, interviewed by Robert Ruttmann, July 6, 2000
Ed Schlick, interviewed by Stuart O'Brien and Rob Chavira, July 13, 1998

Jim Tierney, interviewed by Marisa Burnham-Bestor, January 21, 2000
Stan Tupper, interviewed by Don Nicoll, Stuart O'Brien, and Rob Chavira, July 20, 1998
Elmer Violette, interviewed by Don Nicoll, October 11 and 31, 1998
Gordon Weil, interviewed by Greg Beam, July 20, 2000

ARCHIVES AND COLLECTIONS

Frank Morey Coffin Papers, Special Collections, University of Southern Maine Library, Portland, Maine
Kenneth M. Curtis Papers, Special Collections, University of Southern Maine Library, Portland, Maine
Maine State Law and Legislative Reference Library
Maine State Library
George J. Mitchell Papers, Bowdoin College Library, Brunswick, Maine
Edmund S. Muskie Papers, Bates College Library, Lewiston, Maine
Vermont State Archives and Record Administration

ARTICLES AND REPORTS

Ballot Tampering in Two Election Recounts for the Maine House of Representatives, Report of the Attorney General of Maine and the United States Attorney for the District of Maine, 1993
Corrections Alternatives Advisory Committee, Final Report (Maine), 2006
Establishment of the Katahdin Woods and Waters National Monument, The White House, August 24, 2016
"If I Can't Do It, It Can't Be Done," The Life of Louis Jalbert, Steven Stycos (senior thesis), 1976
Maine Action Plan, Secretary of State Kenneth M. Curtis, October-November, 1966
Maine Political Handbook, 1964, Maine Democratic Party, Lewiston, Maine
Maine Political Handbook, 1966, Maine Democratic Party, Lewiston, Maine
Maine Political Handbook, 1968, Maine Democratic Party, Lewiston Maine
Maine Turnpike Authority, A Chronology of Milestones, 2015
Ed Muskie Testimonial Dinner program, 1964
Report of the Visiting Committee to the University of Maine, January 1986
Special Commission on Governmental Restructuring [Maine], Final Report, 1991
State & Local Relations: The Challenges of the Eighties, Report to the Governor of the [Maine] Cabinet Committee on State and Local Relations, 1982
Vermont State Government Since 1965, Michael Sherman (Editor), University of Vermont, Burlington

NEWSPAPERS

Bangor Daily News, Bangor, Maine
Kennebec Journal, Augusta, Maine
Maine Sunday Telegram, Portland, Maine
Maine Times, Topsham, Maine
Portland Press Herald, Portland Maine

Index

www.ingramcontent.com/pod-product-compliance
Lightning Source LLC
Chambersburg PA
CBHW070407270326
41926CB00014B/2743